IN CHRIST

THE
GRACE
CONNECTION

Wrap Your Heart Around God's
Grace And Be Forever Changed

STEVE GOSS

Published by Freedom In Christ Ministries International
4 Beacontree Plaza, Gillette Way, Reading RG2 0BS, UK.
www.freedominchrist.org

ISBN: 978-1-913082-91-8

For

Willow, Isabella, and Eliza

CONTENTS

FOREWORD

I have just discovered that, over the last couple of years, no fewer than six lottery prizes of £1,000,000 (a little over $1,250,000) have been won by tickets bought in the UK but have not yet been claimed. This news hasn't sent me into a frenzy wondering if I might be one of the winners because I know you have to buy a ticket to win a prize! But I am musing about the six people out there who, having bought a lottery ticket in the hope of a life-changing win, are blissfully unaware of the riches that are now theirs for the taking.

The Apostle Paul appears to view the first-century Christians in Ephesus in much the same way. In his short letter to them, he mentions "grace" no fewer than twelve times, "riches" five times and "inheritance" four times. He commends them for their faith and love but clearly sees them as blissfully unaware of the life-changing riches they already have in Christ that could revolutionize their fruitfulness if only they could grasp them.

He prays an absolutely fascinating prayer for them:

> I keep asking that the God of our Lord Jesus Christ, the glorious Father, may give you the Spirit of wisdom and revelation, so that you may know him better. I pray that the eyes of your heart may be enlightened in order that you may know the hope to which he has called you, the riches of his glorious inheritance in his holy people, and his incomparably great power for us who believe (Ephesians 1:17-19a).

Note that he doesn't ask God to give them more hope or riches or power. No, he asks that God will *open their eyes* to the incredible hope, riches and power that they *already* have.

They are simply unaware of what they already have in Christ. They may be aware intellectually, but Paul is specifically wanting to see "the eyes of their *heart*" opened. Those great truths have to make the journey from head to heart if they are to have a real effect.

I'm fairly confident that most Christians already know that it is "by grace.... through faith" (Ephesians 2:8) that they now have a wonderful relationship with Jesus. I'm equally convinced that most Christians could give me a good definition of "grace."

But in my experience, both in my own life and after decades of having the privilege of teaching others, most of us are just like the Ephesians. When it comes to understanding what God's grace means practically in our day-to-day life, we don't know what we already have. We need to have the eyes of our hearts opened to the riches available for us to take hold of.

And that's the journey that *The Grace Connection* is intended to accompany you on. Because when Christians really "get" grace—in their hearts, not just their heads—they describe it in terms such as "life-changing" and "transformational." And they become significantly more fruitful as disciples of Jesus as they co-operate with Him to reach this world.

We are going to consider what it means to *experience* God's grace every day so that our love for God and others becomes our sole motivation. We'll look practically at the things that get in the way and how to deal with them.

I hope you'll be enthralled and amazed as you encounter afresh the incredible grace of your Father towards you. It's far better than winning a lottery prize!

I know for sure that His Spirit of wisdom and revelation is poised and ready to open the eyes of your heart. So, before you plunge into the rest of this book, may I invite you to pray an adapted version of that wonderful prayer of Paul:

> *Glorious Father, the God of our Lord Jesus Christ, please give me the Spirit of wisdom and revelation, so that I may know You better. I pray that the eyes of my heart may be enlightened in*

order that I may know the hope to which You have called me, the riches of Your glorious inheritance in Your holy people, and Your incomparably great power for us who believe. Amen.

THE GRACE & FREEDOM PROJECT

This book is one of the components of *The Grace & Freedom Project*, a collaboration between a number of leading producers of discipleship and devotional resources.

There are some wonderful additional resources you can take advantage of:

*   *The Grace Course*: an 8-week small group video-based study with Leader's Guide and Participant's Guide.

*   *The Wonder of Grace:* 8 introductory videos (part of *The Grace Course* but can also stand alone).

*   *Daily Nuggets Of Grace* YouVersion Devotional: a 56-day (8-week) daily devotional designed to accompany you on your journey through *The Grace Course* or this book.

*   *The Wonder Of Grace: A 40-Day Devotional Journey* by Rich Miller: a 40-day devotional book by Rich Miller designed to be used directly after *The Grace Course* or this book to help you process the principles you learn and put them into practice.

Scan the QR code to find out more or go to:

www.GraceAndFreedomProject.com

CHAPTER 1

FREE!

GRACE—TOO HUGE TO DEFINE

I remember being taken on a school trip to the Planetarium in London when I was about ten years old. For the first time, I began to appreciate the sheer mind-boggling size of our galaxy, which pales into insignificance compared to the whole universe, which is a speck of dust compared to the whole of space out there. It was as if the more I learned about it, the less my mind could contain it. It's just so HUGE.

Grace is the same. Every Christian knows about it. We sing about it at church—in fact, John Newton's 250-year-old hymn, *Amazing Grace*, is the most popular Christian hymn of all time and is performed around ten million times a year (I think I have probably sung it nearly that many times myself!). All of us would no doubt wholeheartedly agree that "amazing" is an apt word to describe it.

But whatever we already know about grace, none of us are doing much more than scratching the surface. It's just so HUGE.

I have been a Christian for exactly 50 years and have spent much of that time in leadership positions at church. But looking back, I now see that for most of that time I didn't know grace as much more than a theological concept. If you had asked me what it was, I'd have given a reasonable answer. I'd have said it was "undeserved favor" or I'd have repeated the acronym I'd been taught as a new Christian: "God's Riches At Christ's Expense."

Of course, I was so grateful for what God had done for me in sending Jesus to die in my place. But that was in the past, and grace did not seem so relevant for my day-to-day Christian life of striving to be the best Christian I could be and feeling like I constantly let God down.

Over the course of a couple of years, I kept being drawn to the story Jesus told that we tend to call "The Parable of the Prodigal Son." It seemed that every sermon I heard or book I read seemed to reference it. God used it to revolutionize my understanding of His grace and to help me make a real heart-connection with it, rather than grace being just a concept in my head. It's no exaggeration to say that understanding His grace in my heart totally turned my Christian life upside down.

This new heart-connection changed my daily relationship with Father God, helping me understand Him as the loving Father He is. It helped me get off the treadmill of "trying harder" and beating myself up when I felt that I had failed. It opened doors to greater fruitfulness than I had ever known, and seemingly without the great effort I had imagined.

Now, don't let me give you the impression that I'm now floating around on a cloud and every aspect of my life is joy and light with people flocking to Jesus everywhere I go! No, I still face all kinds of struggles, temptations, and disappointments. But the basis on which I approach these things has changed. When I go wrong, I no longer spin off into the rough for weeks but come straight back into the arms of my loving Father.

Peter urges us to "grow in the grace and knowledge of our Lord and Savior Jesus Christ" (2 Peter 3:18). I hope that you will find this book a practical way to do just that and that it will help you connect with God's amazing grace in your heart, not just your head, so that you will become an even more fruitful disciple of Jesus.

And of course, because grace is so HUGE, that's something that all of us can keep working on every day for the rest of our lives.

THE STORY OF TWO BROTHERS

Let's set the scene by considering that astonishing story Jesus told. It's set on a rich farming estate. Even though I've been gripped by it for well over a decade, each time I look at it, I seem to uncover some new facet that helps me uncover a little more of God's grace. You will find it in Luke 15:11-31:

> *Jesus continued: "There was a man who had two sons. The younger one said to his father, 'Father, give me my share of the estate.'*

A father's inheritance would usually come to his sons after his death, but this son just couldn't wait. He was in effect saying, "Dad, I wish you were dead."

> *So he divided his property between them. Not long after that, the younger son got together all he had, set off for a distant country and there squandered his wealth in wild living. After he had spent everything, there was a severe famine in that whole country, and he began to be in need.*
>
> *So he went and hired himself out to a citizen of that country, who sent him to his fields to feed pigs. He longed to fill his stomach with the pods that the pigs were eating, but no one gave him anything.*
>
> *When he came to his senses, he said, "How many of my father's hired servants have food to spare, and here I am starving to death! I will set out and go back to my father and say to him: Father, I have*

sinned against heaven and against you. I am no longer worthy to be called your son; make me like one of your hired servants." So he got up and went to his father.

THE YOUNGER BROTHER

Jesus is clearly painting a picture of someone whose behavior was the worst imaginable in his culture. He showed no respect whatsoever for his father. According to his older brother, he blew money on prostitutes. Then, when he had nothing left, he stooped so low as to take a job looking after the animals that to Jews represented the height of uncleanness: pigs. It's difficult to imagine how Jesus could have portrayed him any worse or less deserving of his position as a son in this wealthy, land-owning family.

He himself knew that he had blown it completely, so he decided to return to his father, not expecting to be received any more as a son but hoping simply for a job as a hired hand, one who would have to earn anything that might come from the father.

> *But while he was still a long way off, his father saw him and was filled with compassion for him; he ran to his son, threw his arms around him and kissed him.*

Note that the father ran—in that culture, wealthy men never did that. Love for his son overcame all the social norms.

> *The son said to him, 'Father, I have sinned against heaven and against you. I am no longer worthy to be called your son.'*

Was it true that his sin made him no longer worthy to be called a son? Yes, undoubtedly. But, of course, nothing could change the fact that he was a son, and always would be. But watch how the father reacts. He doesn't seem even to be listening to the words of his son's well-rehearsed confession. The father knew the son's heart and that's all that mattered.

> But the father said to his servants, 'Quick! Bring the best robe and put it on him. Put a ring on his finger and sandals on his feet. Bring the fattened calf and kill it. Let's have a feast and celebrate. For this son of mine was dead and is alive again; he was lost and is found.' So they began to celebrate.

The son expected to be disowned or at best to be severely punished—and that would have been just. It's what he deserved. Yet the father immediately embraces this smelly, dirty, broken individual, puts the best clothes on him and throws a party to end all parties!

Meanwhile back at the farmhouse, the servants bring the three things that the father had ordered them to fetch. And, this being a parable, each of them is loaded with significance.

The robe would not have been any old robe but the best robe in the house, probably the father's own robe. It symbolized that the son had once again been given the right to enjoy the place of "right standing" with the father. He was completely restored.

The ring would have been a signet-type ring that would make a mark on official documents and could be instantly recognizable as the father's mark. Without that mark or seal, there would be no authority behind the instructions in the document. The ring symbolized power and authority to carry out the father's business. This boy, who had squandered his father's wealth in wild living, was essentially being handed the passwords and security keys to the father's account in an exclusive private bank for high net worth individuals. He was being trusted to run the father's business once again. He could tell people what to do, and they would have to do it because he had the father's ring on his finger.

The third thing the servants bring—sandals—may not sound terribly important. But in a Jewish household at that time, the only people allowed footwear in the house were the father and

5

his sons. The father was declaring in no uncertain terms that the boy, despite everything he had done, was still his son, entitled to the rights of a son.

So what is grace? No definition that you or I could come up with could do it justice. So I'm simply going to invite you to pause and take in that scene from Jesus' story.

A son who has behaved in the worst way imaginable returns and his father, who clearly represents God, has no thought of doing anything other than embracing him and celebrating his return. A child utterly bereft throws himself on the mercy of his father who picks him up, dusts him down, and restores him. This is grace.

This son, who had completely and utterly blown it, who had no right whatsoever to expect anything from his father except possibly what he might be allowed to earn, who doesn't deserve any favor whatsoever, stands there looking no doubt totally bemused in his rich robe, with his ring of authority and the sandals that mark him out as one of the family. This is grace.

If you have never made a decision to give your life to Jesus in response to God's love for you, there's no time like the present. The Father is looking out for you. When He sees you, He will run out and embrace you—and call for the robe, the ring, and the sandals. Will you put them on?

Those of us who have been Christians a while know this story well. We tend to relate it to the first time we came to Him, gave our lives to Him and accepted His free gift of grace. But what about now? Does this part of the story have anything to say to us as we live our Christian lives today or does it just reflect a one-off moment in the past?

What is the worst thing you have ever done? Have you got it in your head? What if you did it again or worse and then sincerely came back to God? What reception would you get from Him? The logic of this story is that you would be treated in exactly the same way as this boy.

This is grace. And, yes, it genuinely is amazing.

Does the thought that you as a Christian could behave in the worst way imaginable and then come back to God with the relationship still secure, not sit quite right with you?

Let's step back and look at why Jesus told this story in the first place. The context is that He was clearly setting Himself up as a religious teacher, but the way He behaved was nothing like what people expected from religious teachers. He was always mixing with the "wrong" crowd, tax collectors and so-called "sinners," and the religious people complained, saying "This man welcomes sinners and even sits down to eat with them."

In response, Jesus told a series of stories about things that were lost and found. This is the third and by far the most comprehensive.

The whole point of the story is this: it is not our behavior that puts us into a right relationship with God; it's His grace.

As we will see, it's not that the son's behavior did not matter. It did. Sin has consequences. But the ending of his relationship with his father was not among them. That's what it means to be a child of God.

God gives you freedom to fail. He is rooting for you and has given you everything you need so that you do not have to fail. But even if you fall flat on your face and make a complete mess, your Heavenly Father will always be there to welcome you back and pick you up, no matter how badly you have messed up. This is genuinely shocking.

"HYPER-GRACE"

Since the earliest times, people have pushed this Biblical truth too far to the point of turning it into an untruth. They have said that, since by God's grace we are saved through faith and our sins are forgiven, our behavior doesn't really matter. This line of thinking has been called "antinomianism" (which means "anti-law") and nowadays tends to be called "hyper-grace," "hyper" meaning "excessive." Maybe it's starting to sound a little like that's where I'm heading.

Jesus' parable does not explain what had to happen in order for our holy Heavenly Father to exercise this amazing grace. The Son of God Himself had to die. That fact alone shouts loud and clear that God does not—indeed cannot—simply brush sin under the carpet and ignore it. He is holy and all sin has consequences.

> *My dear children, I write this to you so that you will not sin. But if anybody does sin, we have an advocate with the Father—Jesus Christ, the Righteous One. (1 John 2:1)*

Jesus died to set us free from sin. And He is now our "advocate," our defense lawyer, should we slip into sin. Whenever we are accused, He steps in and proclaims that the consequences of our sin have been dealt with; it is on this basis that the Father can welcome us home and restore us completely.

As 1 John 2 states, the idea is that we will not sin. Sin is never OK and always has consequences; it's just that those consequences do not include ending your relationship with your Heavenly Father.

Martyn Lloyd-Jones was probably the most famous Christian teacher of his day. He was the minister of Westminster Chapel in London in the middle of the last century. He was known for his absolute commitment to interpreting the Bible faithfully, and he said something very interesting to preachers about grace:

> *"There is no better test as to whether a man is really preaching the New Testament gospel than this, that some people might misunderstand it and mis-interpret it that it really amounts to this: that because you are saved by grace alone, it does not really matter at all WHAT you do, you can go on sinning all you like..."*

Note that he says that interpreting Gospel preaching as meaning it doesn't matter how you behave is to misunderstand it. But his point was that **if you don't find some people misinterpreting your teaching that way, then you are not actually preaching the Gospel of grace.** He goes on to say even more directly (and in capital letters!):

> *"I would say to all preachers: IF YOUR PREACHING OF SALVATION HAS NOT BEEN MISUNDERSTOOD IN THAT WAY, THEN YOU HAD BETTER EXAMINE YOUR SERMONS AGAIN, and you had better make sure that you really ARE preaching the salvation that is offered in the New Testament."* [1]

As we continue our exploration of grace, we will see why God set up the Old Testament Law, and what Jesus meant when He said that He did not come to abolish it but to fulfill it. We will see that there are significant consequences for believers who deliberately persist in sin, and that they are as much in need of understanding the true nature of grace as Christians who are stuck in legalism.

When we really get hold of grace in all its wonder, we will not want to go anywhere near "pervert[ing] the grace of our God into a license for immorality" (Jude 1:4). Instead, we will find ourselves empowered to walk in freedom from sin. And here's the point: we will choose to do just that, not because we are scared of incurring the wrath of God, but simply out of love for Him. And when we do fall into sin, as all of us will from time to time, we will be quick to confess our sins and turn away from them, thus experiencing God's grace afresh because when we confess and repent, He will "forgive us our sins and purify us from all unrighteousness" (1 John 1:9).

We will look in Chapter 8 at some truly shocking words that Jesus speaks to a woman in the church at Thyatira who appears to

---

1. D. Martyn Lloyd-Jones, Romans, An Exposition of Chapter 6, The New Man, (Grand Rapids: Zondervan, 1973), pages 9–10.

have been an early proponent of hyper-grace. She was leading others into sin and Jesus warns her that, if she does not repent, the consequences will include sickness and death. As we shall see, because God is love, everything He does, including judgment, comes from love.

It is only understanding God's grace in all its fullness that will enable us to walk in balance so that we do not become legalistic Pharisees on the one hand, or "anything goes" hyper-grace evangelists on the other.

THE OLDER BROTHER

Let's continue with Jesus' story:

> *Meanwhile, the older son was in the field. When he came near the house, he heard music and dancing. So he called one of the servants and asked him what was going on. 'Your brother has come,' he replied, 'and your father has killed the fattened calf because he has him back safe and sound.'*
>
> *The older brother became angry and refused to go in. So his father went out and pleaded with him. But he answered his father, 'Look! All these years I've been slaving for you and never disobeyed your orders. Yet you never gave me even a young goat so I could celebrate with my friends.*
>
> *'But when this son of yours who has squandered your property with prostitutes comes home, you kill the fattened calf for him!'*
>
> *'My son,' the father said, 'you are always with me, and everything I have is yours. But we had to celebrate and be glad, because this brother of yours was dead and is alive again; he was lost and is found.'*

There is another character in the story who is often overlooked but, in many ways, is the one that Jesus was specifically addressing. There was an older brother who did not throw everything back in his father's face. He stayed and worked hard. He always toed the line and did what was expected of him. He clearly represents the religious people of the day, the ones who thought they could please God by doing the right things, by behaving the right way.

He was completely unable to get his head around the concept of grace. To him, it's quite straightforward: you earn the father's favor by what you do. When his brother returned after all that he had done and, instead of being turned away or at the very least severely disciplined, he had a party thrown for him, this older brother was incandescent with rage. You can almost hear him spluttering, "But, but, but.... All these years I have done everything right. I've played by the rules. And you never threw a party for me. It's totally unfair!"

He didn't understand that the father's love and acceptance had as little to do with his good outward behavior as it was with the other son's bad outward behavior. It had nothing to do with behavior. It was all about the father's love and grace.

This elder brother had an eye on the inheritance that he would one day receive in return for "slaving away" day after day as he put it. We imagine fathers taking their sons around the estate and saying, "One day son, all this will be yours." That's what this son was thinking. But this father says, "Everything I have is yours. Look around you. It's already yours. Everything I have is yours."

He could have been enjoying everything the father had for years, but instead he slaved away thinking that he would have to earn the father's approval and his inheritance. In fact, because the father loved him, the inheritance was there all along for him to enjoy.

What a tragedy to go through life slaving away for something that in fact you've already got. But most Christians I know are like the older brother. We do not know what we already have – or who we already are. Although theologically we know that the Christian life is about grace and not about obeying rules, we live in practice as if it's about how we behave. We know we are saved by grace but, although we would never put it like this, we end up thinking we have to maintain that salvation by what we do. In practice, we show that what we actually believe is how we behave determines our standing with the Father.

Some years ago, we contracted The Barna Group to do a scientific survey of American Christianity. We asked followers of Jesus to respond to six statements, one of which was "The Christian life is well-summed up as trying hard to obey God's commands." What would you say? We were astonished to discover that 82% of those surveyed agreed with that statement (including 57% who strongly agreed).

The staggering point of the story that Jesus is telling is that your acceptance by God has nothing to do with how well or how badly you behave. It's nothing to do with your behavior at all. It's entirely down to His grace.

Left to my own devices, I know I would be very much like the older brother. Thinking back to when I was a teenager who had just become a Christian, when I went wrong and sinned – usually it was something like lustful thoughts – I didn't realize I could come straight back to God like the younger brother. I somehow felt I had to earn my way back into God's favor. Yet I didn't dare approach Him because I felt I had let Him down so I would spin off into the rough for weeks. When I finally did crawl back, I didn't feel OK until I had had three really good quiet times in a row! That is not how God wants us to be. It robs us of the joy of our relationship with our wonderful Father.

There is a story Jesus told that we tend not to hear very often, perhaps because we struggle to work out what it means. It's about how the owner of a vineyard chose to treat hired laborers (see Matthew 20:1-16). In the story, he hires some workers in the marketplace early in the morning and offers them the standard payment of one denarius for a day's work. The owner goes out a little later and hires more workers promising to pay them "whatever is right." He goes out three more times and hires even more workers, the final time being "the 11th hour," when there is only an hour left to work.

When it comes to paying them, they all receive the same wage of one denarius no matter how long they have worked. The workers hired initially—even though they have received exactly what they had been promised—are outraged. The owner's response is, "Am I not allowed to do what I choose with what belongs to me? Or do you begrudge my generosity?" (Matthew 20:15 ESV).

God's generosity often appears outrageous—and it is! But He is God and that is His prerogative. This is grace. And it is the sacrifice of God's Son that makes it possible for us to experience it today.

When you know that it's His grace rather than your performance that makes you pleasing to God, it's incredibly liberating and, as we shall see, it inspires you to behave well but with an entirely different and much better motivation.

LEGALISM

The younger son traded the place of grace and privilege that he had been born into and chose to walk away from relationship with his father. The elder brother didn't do that. Or did he?

In fact, it wasn't just the younger son who was having an identity crisis and had removed himself from intimacy and joy with the father. Neither of them stayed in relationship with Him.

The younger brother found himself "in a distant land" with the pigs. Although the elder brother never left home physically, in his heart, he was a long way away too. In the story, Jesus places him not with the father inside the home, enjoying fellowship as you might expect. Instead he is out in the fields with the hired servants, working hard or as he himself describes it, "slaving away."

This was a dishonorable place for the elder son to be. Instead of taking his place at the father's side and enjoying the favor and blessings of being in the father's company that were his by right, he had in effect taken the identity of a hired servant. Ironically this was the very same identity that the younger son was heading towards, thinking it was the best he could get in the circumstances.

The father's presence alone wasn't enough for the elder son. Rather he preferred to strive for what the father could give him; he was trying to make his father bless him by seeking to do everything right externally. But internally his heart was far away.

The younger brother walked away from his identity as son but joyfully received it back through grace because he chose to turn back to the father. The older brother—who represented the religious people—walked away from it too but did not turn back. The father's grace was available to him just as it had been to his brother—but he didn't experience it because he chose not to turn away from his wrong thinking and turn back to his father.

Jesus was showing the religious people that if they thought that legalistic outward behavior was what it took to earn God's favor, they were terribly deceived.

WHAT MOTIVATES US?

There's a paradox here. What we actually do in this life is crucially important. Paul tells us that, at the end of the age, there will be a day when what we have done—our "works"—will be tested. He uses the image of a building and says that Christ is the foundation and that we have a choice of how we build on that foundation:

> Now if anyone builds on the foundation with gold, silver, precious stones, wood, hay, straw- each one's work will become manifest, for the Day will disclose it, because it will be revealed by fire, and the fire will test what sort of work each one has done. If the work that anyone has built on the foundation survives, he will receive a reward. If anyone's work is burned up,

he will suffer loss, though he himself will be saved,
but only as through fire. (1 Corinthians 3:12-15 ESV)

So there is a foundation of Christ laid by God's grace, and we all have a choice as to how we build on it. When these works are tested, those that are of no value, the ones done in our own strength or which are designed to make us look good—the Bible calls them "wood, hay, straw"—will be burned, while works that are of value, those God wants done and are done in His strength and for His honor—"gold, silver, precious stones"—will remain.

I don't know about you, but I'm not interested in one day watching much of my life go up in smoke.

Romans 8:1 assures us that there is no *condemnation* for those who are in Christ Jesus. Even if your work is burned up, you are still saved but "only as through fire," turning up before God with nothing but a pair of singed eyebrows! But the big question is, will there be any *commendation*? Will the things we do in this life actually be of any value for eternity? The religious people thought that their religious works were good in themselves, but Jesus told them that, since they were doing things just to impress other people, they had already received their reward: the approval of other people. But there would be no reward from God.

So how do we build with gold, silver, and precious stones?

Do you think you can you look at what someone is doing and tell whether it is pleasing to God or not?

Sometimes you can, but by no means always.

Two people can be doing exactly the same thing—feeding the poor perhaps, spending an hour a day reading the Bible and praying. One will be delighting God, the other not.

What's the difference?

When God chose David to be King of Israel, his family couldn't believe it because he was the youngest and smallest. His oldest brother thought he was a pest. But Samuel said, "The Lord sees not as man sees: man looks on the outward appearance, but the

Lord looks on the heart" (1 Samuel 16:7b ESV). Towards the end of the Old Testament, God makes a promise that He will write His laws not on tablets of stone but on our hearts (Jeremiah 31:33).

What is important to God is not so much *what* we do but *why* we do it. God has never taken pleasure from people just obeying a set of rules outwardly if they are not doing it from the heart.

That's the whole point of 1 Corinthians 13, the great "love chapter" that is read at most Christian marriage ceremonies.

> *If I speak in the tongues of men and of angels, but have not love, I am a noisy gong or a clanging cymbal. And if I have prophetic powers, and understand all mysteries and all knowledge, and if I have all faith, so as to remove mountains, but have not love, I am nothing. If I give away all I have, and if I deliver up my body to be burned, but have not love, I gain nothing. (1 Corinthians 13:1-3 ESV)*

The difference is what's happening inside. God judges the thoughts and attitudes of our hearts. It is not to do with our behavior *per se*. It's all about our motivation. And if that motivation is not love, then what we do, no matter how good it looks, is worth precisely nothing. It's wood, hay, or straw.

Jesus tells us that some will come to Him at the end of time and say they did amazing things like driving out demons and performing miracles in His name. Are those wood, hay, and straw or gold, silver, and precious stones? Well, Jesus says He will say to them, "I never knew you. Away from me, you evildoers!" (Matthew 7:22).

WHAT WE DO COMES FROM WHO WE ARE

Let's understand a key concept: what we *do* comes from who we *are*. Can I invite you to pause with me and consider two pictures?

First, picture the younger son at the point that he collapses into his father's arms and casts himself on his mercy. He can scarcely believe his father's grace as he realizes that, even though he richly deserves it, he will not be punished. He knows that he is forgiven and accepted, but he also knows that he is dirty, smelly, and broken. He is acutely aware of his failure and deeply ashamed of what he has become. This is how many Christians see themselves. Forgiven but believing they are still essentially the same no good rotten people they always were.

It's as if our understanding of the Gospel stopped with Good Friday: Jesus died for my sins and I'm going to go to Heaven when I die. But nothing much changes right now.

But the father does not leave the son there.

Here's the second picture. The same son just a matter of minutes later is dressed in the finest robe with the ring on his finger and the sandals on his feet feasting on the finest food. He is still aware of his past failures, yet it is dawning on him that he has been not just forgiven but completely restored to his position as son, with free access to everything his father owns along with great power and authority. He knows he doesn't deserve it at all. He realizes he is totally dependent on the father. It's almost unbelievable but it is actually happening.

Which picture most accurately represents how you see yourself in relation to God? In my experience, most Christians get stuck on the first picture, knowing they're forgiven but still feeling like miserable sinners, constantly letting God down.

May I encourage you to move on to the second? We need to make it past Good Friday and through to Easter Sunday. I know you celebrate Easter Sunday but what do you celebrate? That Jesus rose from the dead. He did, of course, but the whole point is that *we* rose from the dead with Him and became someone completely new; we need to know that we are now holy ones, saints, that we share God's very nature (see 2 Peter 1:4). And that's not all. We have also ascended with Christ to the right hand of the Father, the ultimate seat of power and authority in the whole universe.

Like the younger son, we have been completely restored to the place of authority and honor.

In order to be free to be motivated by love, we have to know that we are more than just forgiven. We need to know that we are completely restored and deep down inside absolutely acceptable, a delight to God.

And we can stay in that place of utter amazement at the Father's goodness and grace and retain the healthy awareness that without Him we can't do a single thing of any eternal significance.

This concept that our acceptance by God and our new identity has nothing to do with our behavior goes against the way you think it should work, doesn't it? It's not what many of us have learned as we've grown up as Christians.

We have tended to be like the elder brother, acting as if what we do is the primary thing:

"What must I do to be accepted by God?" "If you're a Christian, you're already accepted by God!" "Yes, but what should I *do*?"

Most churches have been happy to come up with a list of things to do: read your Bible every day; come to church every week. Are those good things? Of course! But the problem is that discipleship often ends up becoming a load of rules. And we struggle to obey those rules because we've gotten things backwards. We think that God is most "into" rules, when actually He's most concerned about relationship.

As part of the research done by The Barna Group, we asked people to respond to this statement: "Rigid rules and strict standards are an important part of the life and teaching of our church." Even though we used words that typically people would recoil from— "rigid" and "strict"—66% of Christians agreed with that statement. Two thirds!

Now, of course, most churches teach about grace. But often, they also give the impression that we have to work hard and toe the line if we want God to smile at us. And often we hear teaching about grace through our own clogged filters and still hear "law."

But what we do comes from who we are, not *vice versa*. The starting point is knowing who we are in Christ: God's loved, accepted and secure children.

Read any one of Paul's letters to the churches and see how far you get before he gives an instruction on what to do or how to behave. You'll get half way through at least. The first half is all about what has already been done, what you already have, who you already are in Christ. Paul knows that if you grasp that, the rest will flow naturally. "If you love me, you will obey my commands" (John 14:15 NCV).

Over the years I've talked many times to a guy who was diagnosed as paranoid schizophrenic but found his freedom simply by listening to our teaching and taking himself through *The Steps To Freedom In Christ*. He went from someone who was in and out of mental institutions and on lots of medication to someone who keeps introducing people to Jesus. He called me because he had got into sexual sin. He already resolved that God still loved him, and he dealt with the condemning voices. He had also broken off the relationship to ensure the sin did not repeat. Then he said, "I used to think God was a guy with a big stick. But now I know that He loves me. The reason I want to stop sinning is because I don't want to keep hurting Someone who loves me so much."

Come back to that picture of the younger brother standing there bemused because he had the full rights and privileges of a son restored yet knew he didn't deserve it one bit. How do you think he will act from that point on? He knows that he doesn't have to do a thing; his father will always love him. But won't he want to do his very best for his father, to love him back? Will it feel like "slaving away"? No!

God's love and acceptance of you has nothing—nothing!—to do with your behavior. But when you stop trying to "act like you think a Christian should act" and just simply live from the truth of who you now are, you will find you *want* to do what's right and you will!

CHOOSING TO BE A SLAVE

We've seen that both sons had essentially embraced the identity of a hired servant—someone who chooses to work for someone else in return for payment. Yet the word that the elder son uses for "slaving away" carries the meaning that you would expect from the translation, that of a slave with no rights whatsoever who is forced to obey their master without pay.

In Jesus' time, slavery was a daily reality and totally legal. If you were a slave, you were totally owned by your owner who could sell you or do to you whatever they wanted physically, sexually, and in any other way. Just as in the later enslavement of Africans or people-trafficking today, it was a horrific experience where you were totally controlled by someone else and forced to behave however they choose or face terrible consequences.

Yet Paul describes himself as a "slave of Christ" (Romans 1:1 NLT) and Paul implies that Timothy should be a slave to Christ (2 Timothy 2:24). Most English translations choose to translate the Greek word "slave" as "servant" which lessens the impact, but make no mistake, it meant "slave" and would have been understood as such by the original hearers.

Modern readers may understandably balk at the use of such language, thinking that it puts Christ in the position of a slave owner. But let's remember that Jesus came specifically to set us free from slavery to sin and death. As He Himself said, "If the Son sets you free, you will be free indeed" (John 8:36).

In New Testament times, it was very common for Roman masters to reward slaves who had served them well by freeing them. The former slaves then became fully fledged Roman citizens and many went on to do very well for themselves.

It's difficult for us to get our heads around this, but sometimes former slaves chose to stay and continue to serve in the household simply because of the love they had developed for their former masters.

From the outside, what they did day-by-day would not have looked any different. But there is a world of difference between doing what you do because you choose to and doing it because you are forced to. And that is the concept behind Paul's use of the language.

In Christ you have been set free. He hates people being enslaved against their will by others. But when you truly understand His wonderful loving nature, you may choose of your own free will to work for Him and do whatever He wants, knowing that He will do nothing to harm you and that you are free to leave at any time.

Jesus has significant works that He has prepared in advance for you to do, but He doesn't force you in any way to do them. He will love you whatever you do.

However, as you make a choice to serve Him *just because* you love Him, you'll find it becomes a real pleasure to do the work He gives you to do.

WHAT MOTIVATES YOU?

In 2 Corinthians 5:14, Paul says, "For Christ's love compels us." God wants our motivation to be love and nothing but love. But we can easily end up motivated by other things:

Guilt—I don't want God to be upset with me so I try my best to avoid doing wrong. But then I do what's wrong anyway and end up feeling even more guilty and trapped in a joyless cycle of self-condemnation.

Shame—I know I am a disappointment to God and to others but feel that if I can just be a better person maybe He'll think I'm worthy of His love.

Fear—I'm scared that God might be angry with me. I've heard the promises, but they don't really seem to apply to me. Maybe I'm not a Christian at all. Maybe I've committed the unforgivable sin.

Anxiety—life is full of dangers, and I need to make sure that I avoid them. I know God promises to look after me but I'm not sure He really means it, so I need to make sure that I keep a close eye on things too.

Pride—I know I don't measure up to God's standards but then again who does? I feel much better if I compare myself with other people. I've really studied doctrine and theology and made sure that mine is absolutely right. I measure what others say against it.

We will go on to look at each of these "false motivators" and have the opportunity to root them out, ensuring that it's love for Christ that compels us and nothing else.

MAKING THE GRACE CONNECTION

There is no great hurry to finish this book. You don't have to rush through it. After all, what will you do when you have finished it— find another book to read?

I would encourage you to slow down and ensure that the precious time you are spending on understanding grace results in a genuine, life-changing heart connection with your loving Father. He is waiting for you. He loves it when you spend time with Him. There is no condemnation for you.

At the end of each chapter, you are encouraged to take some time out and process what you have read. Why not read it again slowly first? This is where you are likely to make the grace connection. It's a heart thing, not a head thing.

So find yourself somewhere quiet, clear your mind and pray:

> **Glorious Father, the God of our Lord Jesus Christ, please give me the Spirit of wisdom**

and revelation, so that I may know You better. I pray that the eyes of my heart may be enlightened in order that I may know the hope to which You have called me, the riches of Your glorious inheritance in Your holy people, and Your incomparably great power for us who believe. Amen.

Find yourself a means to make some notes and take all the time you need to respond to these few questions.

1. The father gives the younger son three gifts which symbolize things that God has given to you. Which gift is most meaningful to you? Why?

2. If you knew for sure that God's acceptance of you and love for you did not depend on how well you behaved, how might that change the way you live?

3. Consider the following statements. To what extent do they reflect what you feel? Score them between 0 and 10 where 0 is "not at all" and 10 is "That's exactly how I feel." Note: this is about how you feel rather than a test of your theological understanding!

    • What I have done is too bad for God to forgive me or accept me back;

    • God loves other people but He can't really love me;

    • I can behave however I like because Jesus has forgiven me;

    • I have to live up to a certain set of standards for God to be pleased with me;

    • God loves me more when I work hard for Him.

According to the Bible, none of these statements are true. For the statements that you have scored the highest, can you find one or more verses from the Bible that show them to be false?

Imagine how different your life could be and how different your relationship with God would be if you were genuinely able to score a zero on each of those statements. In the coming days, read the verses you have identified and affirm your commitment to believing what God says is true rather than what your feelings are telling you.

CHAPTER 2

UNASHAMED!

In the time of Jesus, leprosy was a fairly common infectious disease. People would have been used to seeing lepers begging or simply living out their miserable isolated existence, ostracized from normal society, forbidden from approaching people lest they pass on the disease.

> *A leper came to Jesus, beseeching Him and falling on his knees before Him, and saying, "If You are willing, You can make me clean" (Mark 1:40 NASB).*

This man would have had a mass of ulcerating skin all over his body. He would have looked repulsive, smelt terribly, and been on a relentless course toward a slow and agonizing death once the disease began to ravage his mind. To make his situation even worse, he would have been well aware what the Bible itself said about him:

> *The leprous person who has the disease shall wear torn clothes and let the hair of his head hang loose, and he shall cover his upper lip and cry out, 'Unclean, unclean.' He shall remain unclean as long as he has the disease. He is unclean. He shall*

> *live alone. His dwelling shall be outside the camp.*
> *(Leviticus 13:45,46)*

There were some very good reasons for these regulations, of course, that had to do with protecting others from this hideous, contagious disease. But can you imagine reading this about yourself in the very Word of God, "He is unclean. He shall live alone"?

How would you feel about yourself? What words would you use to describe yourself? Unlovable? Dirty? Alone? Contaminated? Worthless?

We may not suffer from this particular disease, but we may identify with some of those words or others like them when we think of how to describe ourselves. Maybe we feel that we are different to everyone else. Or that if people knew what we were really like, they would reject us.

This is shame, which is the first "false motivator" we want to take a look at so that we can ensure that it's love for Jesus—and nothing but love for Jesus—that drives us on in our Christian life.

As we shall see, all of us are affected by shame to one degree or another. But God has provided the remedy.

THE ORIGIN OF SHAME

Originally in the garden, before Adam sinned, Genesis tells us, "Adam and his wife were both naked, and they felt no shame" (Genesis 2:25). They knew they were children of God and had an intimate relationship with Him. They serve as a picture of the relationship with Him that God intended us to have.

After Adam and Eve sinned, what was the most obvious change?

> *"The eyes of both of them were opened, and they*
> *realized they were naked; so they sewed fig leaves*

together and made coverings for themselves"
(Genesis 3:7).

They felt something they had never experienced before: shame. The result? They wanted to cover their naked bodies. All of a sudden, they had a sense that they were not good enough.

At this point, let's digress a little to consider the Biblical story of Adam and Eve itself. If we are going to draw some fundamental conclusions from it, can we really trust it?

I'm not a scientist, and I have steered away from debates about exactly how God created the world and how human beings came about. They can all too easily stray into the realm of "foolish controversies, genealogies, dissensions, and quarrels" that Titus 3:9 (ESV) tells us are "unprofitable and worthless." It's not that the question is unimportant. It's just that none of us can prove it beyond doubt either way.

I was nevertheless absolutely fascinated to learn that in the 1980s, it became clear to scientists that our mitochondrial DNA shows definitively that all of us are descended from the same woman. Scientists have named her "Mitochondrial Eve."

Furthermore, analysis of men's Y chromosomes has confirmed that we are all descended from the same man, whom scientists have dubbed "Y-chromosome Adam."

This does not in itself prove that the Biblical story of Adam and Eve is literally true. Most scientists believe, for example, that the man and woman in question lived in different places at different times (and if you want to understand why, search for 'Y-chromosome Adam' and 'Mitochondrial Eve').

But it does prove that the core Biblical principle that all of us are descended from the same man and the same woman is true.

And there is nothing in the scientific evidence that proves they could not have lived in the same place at the same time. In fact, an article in *Nature* stated, "The Book of Genesis puts Adam and Eve together in the Garden of Eden, but geneticists' version of the duo —the ancestors to whom the Y chromosomes and mitochondrial

DNA of today's humans can be traced—were thought to have lived tens of thousands of years apart. Now, two major studies of modern humans' Y chromosomes suggest that 'Y-chromosome Adam' and 'mitochondrial Eve' may have lived around the same time after all."[1]

Buy why, you may quite reasonably be wondering, am I including a short digression into the field of genetics in a chapter called "Unashamed!"?

Consider this statement from the Apostle Paul: "sin entered the world through one man, and death through sin, and in this way death came to all people" (Romans 5:12). He clearly teaches that we are all descended from one man and that, crucially, this man was the source of all sin. Consider this further statement: "just as through the disobedience of the one man the many were made sinners, so also through the obedience of the one man the many will be made righteous" (Romans 5:19).

If we do not accept that we are all descended from the same original "one man" whose disobedience made us all sinners, then the death and sacrifice of the "one man" Jesus Christ does not make sense.

Debates about creation versus evolution have undermined the impact of the Biblical account of Adam and Eve for some Christians and have thus weakened a crucial foundation of the whole Gospel message. I hope knowing that science has clearly validated the essential fact—that we are all descended from the same man—will give you the confidence to accept at face value the principles the story communicates, even if you question exactly what process God used to create Adam.

As I consider the story and other Biblical passages related to it, some key principles stand out to me.

---

1. "Genetic Adam and Eve did not live too far apart in time", Nature.com, 6 August 2013 (retrieved on 6 March 2024).

Before the beginning of time, the Father, the Son, and the Holy Spirit already enjoyed a beautiful loving relationship, and God's great desire was to include others in that.

God's love moved Him to create incredible universes, amazing galaxies, and this wonderful planet. And to create human beings.

He gave us a task: to work with Him to look after the world.

But God didn't make us as robots who had to do what He told us to. Out of love, He gave us the ability to decide for ourselves how we live our lives.

So Adam, the first human being, was totally free to accomplish the mission God had given him in any way he chose. God didn't burden him with rules but said just one thing. He told him not to eat fruit from a certain tree. And He explained why: "for when you eat from it you will certainly die" (Genesis 2:17).

This wasn't some kind of test to see how well Adam behaved. Genuine freedom includes genuine consequences for the choices we make. And, out of love, God wanted Adam to avoid the unpleasant consequences of a bad choice.

But God's enemy, Satan, deceived Eve. She and Adam chose to disobey God. Like the younger son, they turned their backs on their Father and walked away.

And, just as God had warned, there were huge consequences, not just for them but for their children, their children's children, and all their descendants right down to us.

Adam and Eve did indeed die. They didn't die physically—at least not straightaway. They died spiritually. In other words, they lost their spiritual connection to God and all that came with it: their significance, their intimacy with God, and their security. They were cut off from the fellowship with God they had enjoyed.

A CHANGE OF IDENTITY

Adam and Eve's sin displeased God and made them guilty before Him. Guilt is about *what we do*: I did something wrong, therefore I am guilty.

But there was a more fundamental consequence. They had taken a step that changed their entire identity, and also the identity that God intended all of us to have. Because of the disobedience of one man, Adam, "the many were made sinners" (Romans 5:19).

Shame is about *who we are*. It's about our very identity. Shame says not that I *did* something wrong but that I *am* what is wrong.

When the younger son returned to his father, full of shame, it affected his identity: "I am no longer worthy to be called your son."

Adam, Eve and all of us were made "sinners." In the New Testament, the word "sinner" is used many times. It is a shorthand way of referring to those who are spiritually dead, disconnected from God as Adam now was, and all of us would be too.

It's important to understand that being a sinner is a condition, a state of being, an identity. We didn't become sinners the first time we sinned. It's the other way around. Because we inherited Adam's characteristics, we were *born* spiritually dead—disconnected, cut off from the life of God—and therefore our default setting was to sin, to do things our way rather than God's way. We sinned because we were sinners. We were doomed to hurt ourselves, those around us, and pretty much everything we touched.

Shame is the painful emotional experience that comes from believing that there is something very wrong not so much with what we have *done* but with who we *are*. And because of Adam, there actually was something wrong with us.

If we are to deal with shame, it has to be done at the level of our fundamental identity. We will see how God has done that for us, but first let's understand more about how shame affects us.

Shame has to do with our identity. That's why it affects us so deeply. We try to cope by hiding, covering up, or just hoping it won't happen again, but just like those fig leaves, our coping mechanisms don't work.

If you had asked me a few years ago if I was affected by shame, I'd probably have said something like, "Not hugely." But I've since realized it's a bigger issue for me than I thought.

Dr. Neil T. Anderson, founder of Freedom In Christ Ministries, and I were invited to speak at a large Christian conference. To be more precise, Neil was invited, and I tagged along to carry his bag!

I was new to all this and suddenly found myself mixing with lots of "big names" from the Christian world. Every morning, we attended a prayer meeting with the other speakers but, feeling a little overawed by the company I found myself in, I didn't pluck up the courage to pray out loud or share anything with them. But on our final morning, I made a huge effort. I stood up and said how nice it had been to be there with them all. At the end, one of the 'big names' beckoned to me. "My moment has come," I thought. He put his arm on my shoulder and whispered, "By the way, your fly is undone." And so it was!

I hope that story brings a little smile to your face today. But when I think about it, it still brings a flush to my cheeks.

And I have realized that embarrassment, or trying to avoid feeling embarrassed, is actually a big deal for me. Anyone would feel embarrassed in the story I just recounted but I realized that embarrassment was more serious than that in my life. It was preventing me from relating properly to people, stopping me from taking opportunities to share my faith in Jesus, and just generally making me feel the need to try to prove I was OK or as good as other people (because I didn't feel I was).

Embarrassment is actually a mild form of shame.

There's a huge difference between the intensity of shame that the leper must have felt and my embarrassment, but both of us are experiencing the effects of the sin of "the one man" which changed our fundamental identity. Our life experiences tend to determine how acute our sense of shame is.

SHAME IS INTENSIFIED BY SHAME-BASED CULTURES

It's worse if we were raised in a shame-based culture.

All societies try to find ways of discouraging us from doing things that are not acceptable. Western societies tend to use guilt for this. We are pressured to conform by the threat of punishment, such as disapproving words and looks, the law courts or teaching that God will punish us. We will consider guilt in the next chapter.

Other societies, particularly Eastern ones, use shame rather than guilt. Control is maintained by creating a culture where, if you do not conform to social norms, you yourself are not acceptable. Making sure you do what is socially acceptable becomes the main cultural value. The fear of being rejected and ostracized is a powerful motivator.

I heard the story of a missionary in an Eastern culture who was puzzled by something he observed. Every morning, the friend of a divorced Muslim lady would come round to her house and feel her hair to see if it was damp. He was told that the reason for this was so that she could tell if her friend had committed adultery. The religious belief in that society was that having sex outside marriage makes you unclean and that you must bathe and wash your hair in order to be clean again. But what puzzled the missionary is why, if the woman was going to be disobedient enough to commit adultery, her friend thought she would be obedient enough to take a bath.

He learned that it was inconceivable that she would neglect to wash because her uncleanness would make even the ground she walked on cursed. In other words, being in a state of ritual uncleanness was more unthinkable than committing adultery!

In a shame-based culture what matters most is being clean, being acceptable, particularly in the eyes of other people. It's not so much a question of whether you have done something wrong or right, but whether you have done what others expect. If you feel that you don't hit the mark, you experience shame.

Some families and religious institutions—even Christian ones—can create mini shame-based cultures. A church leader or parent may overuse the words "ought to" and "should" to make you feel that you have to behave in a certain way to be an accepted part of the church or family or to be a "good Christian." They may say things like:

> "You should be ashamed of yourself!"

> "You're a disgrace to the family or to the church!"

> "Why can't you be more like your brother or sister?"

> "You'll never amount to anything"

> "I wish you'd never been born."

If we believe the world's lies that we have to be beautiful or slim or whatever to fit in, we can feel tremendous shame if we think we don't measure up.

Even those who excel athletically, academically or in their chosen field can live a shame-based life if all they ever get is applause and approval when they do well. The message that can come across loud and clear: You are not worth anything in and of yourself. You are only valuable and worthy of approval if you perform well.

I generally did well at school but that left me with a sense that I always had to hit standards to feel good about myself. And no one can hit them all the time. When you don't do so well, the words of encouragement stop; the pats on the back are gone; you are met with disapproval and disappointment because your performance wasn't so good. This is a crushing message and can set you up for a lifetime of battling shame.

SHAME IS INTENSIFIED BY PAST EXPERIENCES

We can also be predisposed to feel shame because of things we've done that we regret. Addictions and any sin that degrades our bodies or causes others to look down on us are a source of shame.

In John 4, we find Jesus sitting by a well at midday whilst His disciples buy food.

A woman approaches, no doubt surprised to find someone else there at the hottest part of the day. Custom demands that a man should withdraw a good distance away from a woman on her own and not even make eye contact with her. In any case, they are enemies. He is a Jew, and she is a Samaritan.

Shockingly, He speaks to her and asks for water, and then they get into quite a conversation during which He says: "Go, call your husband, and come here." The woman answers him, "I have no husband." Jesus says to her, "You are right in saying, 'I have no husband'; for you have had five husbands, and the one you now have is not your husband. What you have said is true" (John 4:16-18 ESV).

Now we understand why she comes to the well at that time. She is full of shame.

Look at what Jesus does with His knowledge about her sinful lifestyle. He doesn't use it in any way. He simply treats her with kindness and respect.

And this was the sinless Son of God, the only person who had the right to condemn her for how far she had fallen.

We can also feel shame because of things other people did to us, particularly if we were abused in some way in childhood. Maybe we even feel it was somehow our fault or that we deserved it. But children are never to blame for the shameful acts of perpetrators.

If that's you today, I am very, very sorry that you suffered so terribly. But more importantly, so is Jesus, the One who came specifically to bind your broken heart and set you free.

I have lived a fairly sheltered life, but over the years, I have had the opportunity to sit with people as they go through *The Steps To Freedom In Christ*. I have heard tragic stories of the sick things people have done to fellow human beings, very often when they were children. Some of it is sexual, some just plain cruel. Some of it is occult in nature.

Too often those victimized by child molesters feel it was their own fault or that they somehow deserved it. That is a terrible deception. But too often the victim is the one that experiences the shame, not the one truly responsible.

The Samaritan woman's life was totally changed through her encounter with Jesus, her encounter with grace. She went back to the very people she wanted to hide from and told them about Jesus. And many believed in Him. No one has fallen so far or been so deeply wounded that Jesus cannot resolve their shame and use their lives for His glory.

THE "LESS MESS"

Shame's basic message is that there's something wrong with *us*, that we are the problem. It puts us into "the less mess." We feel help*less*, worth*less*, meaning*less*, power*less*, hope*less*. So we hide, we wear masks, we avoid, we pretend. And we never feel truly accepted.

We develop strategies to try to alleviate shame and to cover up and hide. Some of the more common include:

- Lying;
- Blame-shifting by making everyone but us appear to be the problem;

- Pretending everything's okay and we're doing great when we know we're not;
- Criticizing others harshly in order to make them appear inferior to us;
- Compensating for shameful deficiencies in one area by seeking to excel in others;
- Moralizing by preaching hard against ways we ourselves have behaved and are ashamed of;
- Self-medicating in order to blunt the sting and numb the pain of our own shame;
- Compromising moral or biblical values to fit in and avoid the shame of rejection;
- Striving for perfection in our behavior or our looks to compensate for that painful belief that in reality we fall far short of who we should be.

But like Adam and Eve's fig leaves, none of these things work.

God has a better way! His way to remove *dis*grace is grace.

GOD'S REMEDY FOR SHAME

Let's come back to that leper. This leper, in violation of all common decency and propriety, approached Jesus and asked him a question. The obvious question to ask is, "Will you heal me?" But in fact, he asked something much more fundamental, "Will you make me clean?"

He knew that the root issue was not the actual physical illness but his very identity.

"Moved with compassion, Jesus stretched out His hand and touched him, and said to him, 'I am willing; be cleansed.'" (Mark 1:41 NASB)

Jesus touched him and made him clean. He didn't need to touch him to heal him of leprosy. But how long had it been since that man had felt the gentle touch of another human being?

The younger brother who messed up massively in the story we looked at in the last chapter must have felt immense shame as he returned to the family home with his tail between his legs. Despite everything, the father embraces him and completely restores his identity as son.

That's exactly what Jesus wants to do for you today: reach out to you, embrace you, and remove your shame.

He wants you to come out of hiding and stand unashamed before Him and before other people. Accepted, loved and secure. No matter what you have done or what people have done to you.

How can that be possible?

THE GREAT EXCHANGE

As we've seen, because of our ancestor Adam's actions, we were all born with a different fundamental identity to the one God intended us to have. We were sinners. And being a sinner was a condition, a state of being.

Paul puts it this way: "we were by nature objects of wrath" (Ephesians 2:3). Jeremiah said our heart, the very core of our being, was "deceitful above all things and beyond cure" (Jeremiah 17:9). Isaiah rubs salt in the wound: "All of us have become like one who is unclean, and all our righteous acts are like filthy rags" (Isaiah 64:6).

We were not the people God intended us to be, and there was nothing we could do about it. Our sense of shame is a consequence of that.

But I mentioned that God had a remedy and here it is:

> *"While we were still sinners, Christ died for us"*
> *(Romans 5:8).*

Look at that verse again. Note that it is written in the past tense. Clearly, if we know Jesus, we are not sinners anymore according to Paul.

The Old Testament law contained a whole set of rituals for cleansing. They never could—and were never intended to—remove our defilement but pointed towards the sacrifice that would, that is Jesus.

2 Corinthians 5:21 (ESV) reveals how this works: "For our sake He made Him to be sin who knew no sin, so that in Him we might *become* the righteousness of God."

On the cross, Jesus, who was totally blameless, became sin for our sake. God took all our shortcomings, failures, rebellion, and shame—and laid them on Christ. He didn't die just to forgive us, to pay the penalty for our sin. A clean slate is great, but it's deeper than that. He also took on Himself our defiled, unclean nature and destroyed our inner contamination. And then He rose from the dead to new life.

When we surrender our life to Jesus, a great exchange takes place. We don't just get our sins forgiven. We actually *become* someone very different. We *become* the righteousness of God.

Your heart is no longer deceitful and beyond cure. Ezekiel's amazing prophecy is fulfilled: we get a new heart and a new spirit (see Ezekiel 11:19).

We are no longer by nature objects of wrath. Peter tells us that now we actually share God's divine nature (2 Peter 1:4). Two thousand years ago, you and I and all those who are in Christ died on the cross with Christ. Our old unclean, shameful self was killed. Dead. Gone.

Just think about that—what was wrong with us died! The shame of who we used to be is gone!

In short, we've become a whole new person. We now have a totally new, clean, wonderful identity. And instead of calling us "sinners," the Bible's standard word for those who are in Christ is "holy ones" (often translated "saints"). Paul addresses his letters, for example, to "the holy ones in Ephesus," or to "the holy ones in Corinth."

Yes, you are now a holy one. Holy means set apart for God. Special. Like a wedding dress that you don't wear on any old day. It's set apart for one special purpose. Deep in the core of your being, your very identity has changed. From someone disconnected, cut off from God, to someone who is accepted, significant, and secure in Christ.

Our shame has been completely taken away. Once and for all. Past, present, and future! You're not contaminated anymore. You're not unacceptable. You're clean. You're presentable. You can take off your mask and let down the walls. You *can* show yourself to God and to others with no shame whatsoever! Here's God's invitation to you:

> *Therefore, brothers and sisters, since we have confidence to enter the Most Holy Place by the blood of Jesus, by a new and living way opened for us through the curtain, that is, his body, and since we have a great priest over the house of God, let us draw near to God with a sincere heart and with the full assurance that faith brings, having our hearts sprinkled to cleanse us from a guilty conscience and having our bodies washed with pure water. (Hebrews 10:19-22)*

We don't have to run away any more. We don't have to hide, no matter what's in our past, or even in our present, because we have a new, clean identity in Christ. We're invited to come near to God in the Holy of Holies because we *are* holy ones!

Don't be tempted to think that this invitation to draw near is conditional, that it depends on doing all the things you think a good Christian should do. That would be like living under the old system of continuous ritual cleansings and sacrifices. No further sacrifice is needed. And that's that!

TAKING HOLD OF OUR NEW IDENTITY

This issue of ongoing shame in our lives as Christians is not due to the fact that we used to be sinners, though that is its origin. It's caused by not knowing who we are *now*.

Like the leper, we say to Jesus, "Will You make me clean?" And Jesus says to us, "I've already done it. You *are* clean! You are not contaminated anymore. You are not unacceptable. You are clean. You are presentable. Take off the mask and tear down the walls!"

The big question we all face is this: Are you going to believe what God's Word says about you? Or are you going to believe what your past experiences tell you about yourself?

Where are you on that?

In Luke 17, He healed ten lepers at once. Again He didn't say "Be healed" and this time He didn't even say, "Be cleansed." He simply said, "Go, show yourselves to the priests" (Luke 17:14). Luke tells us, "And as they went they were cleansed." There's something significant in His command to go and show themselves to someone else. For those who feel unclean and ashamed, opening themselves up and showing themselves to others is too painful to contemplate. It's the last thing they want to do. It feels safer to hide behind protective masks and walls than risk the pain of rejection.

I remember one lady who had been terribly abused for a decade or more in childhood looking, for the first time, at the awful things that had been done to her square in the eye rather than hiding them away in the depths of her consciousness. She was quiet for a long time and then looked at me and said, "They did those things to *me*, Steve." I was able to say gently, "Yes, they did. So what?" We had been talking about who she now is in Christ—pure, holy, clean. She thought about it and said with a smile, "Yes, you're right. Why should I let it bother me? I'm a child of God!" That was a key turning point. She went on to run a really fruitful ministry helping others who had been abused in the same way.

YOUR NEW NAME

One morning, while on holiday with my family in Spain, I was reading a passage in Revelation that says that those who overcome will be given a white stone with a new name on it (Revelation 2:17). I was struck by that and felt God asking, "What would you like your new name to be?" I had always struggled with the sense of not being good enough and my mind being full of condemning thoughts, so I immediately knew I'd like my new name to be "Free From Condemnation."

That evening after dinner we walked down to the local beach as the sun was setting, and our girls ran down the beach towards the sea. A little later they came running back to us with their hands full of smooth white quartz pebbles, saying "Look at all these white stones. We could each write our names on one." God was letting me know that "Free from Condemnation" is already my name. I don't have to wait for it.

I still have my white stone with "Free From Condemnation" written on it.

There is a recurring theme in the Bible of people being given new names. God changed "Abram," which meant "exalted father," to "Abraham" which means "father of a multitude." Abraham's new name reflected the way God planned to use him. Jesus gave one of His disciples, Simon, an additional name, "Peter" which means "rock." This reflected God's plan to make this most unstable and un-rock-like character a fundamental building block of His Church.

In the Bible, names are much more than labels. They are a reflection of a person's identity, and God is all about giving us a new identity. Consider Isaiah 62:2-4:

> *The nations shall see your righteousness, and all the kings your glory, and you shall be called by a new name that the mouth of the LORD will give. You shall be a crown of beauty in the hand of the LORD, and a royal diadem in the hand of your God, You shall no more be termed Forsaken, and your land shall no*

more be termed Desolate, but you shall be called My
Delight Is In Her, and your land Married.

Did you know that God has given you a new name? Many of them
in fact. Take a look at the list at the end of this chapter. Every
single one of them describes who you now are. They may not
feel true right now. But they are true. At the deepest level of your
being. Because of God's grace.

Let's allow God's grace to bring us out of disgrace.

Let's learn to live as the holy ones we are!

MY NEW NAME

- My new name is Beloved (Colossians 3:12)

- My new name is Chosen (Ephesians 1:4)

- My new name is Precious (Isaiah 43:4)

- My new name is Loved (1 John 4:10)

- My new name is Clean (John 15:3)

- My new name is Presentable (Luke 17:14)

- My new name is Protected (Psalm 91:14,
  John 17:15)

- My new name is Welcomed (Ephesians 3:12)

- My new name is Heir (Romans 8:17,
  Galatians 3:29)

- My new name is Complete (Colossians 2:10)

- My new name is Holy (Hebrews 10:10,
  Ephesians 1:4)

- My new name is Forgiven (Psalm 103:3, Colossians 2:13)
- My new name is Adopted (Ephesians 1:5)
- My new name is Delight (Psalm 147:11)
- My new name is Unashamed (Romans 10:11)
- My new name is Known (Psalm 139:1)
- My new name is Planned (Ephesians 1:11-12)
- My new name is Gifted (2 Timothy 1:6, 1 Corinthians 12:11)
- My new name is Enriched (2 Corinthians 8:9)
- My new name is Provided For (1 Timothy 6:17)
- My new name is Treasured (Deuteronomy 7:6)
- My new name is Pure (1 Corinthians 6:11)
- My new name is Established (Romans 16:25)
- My new name is God's Work of Art (Ephesians 2:10)
- My new name is Helped (Hebrews 13:5)
- My new name is Free from Condemnation (Romans 8:1)
- My new name is God's Child (Romans 8:15)
- My new name is Christ's Friend (John 15:15)
- My new name is Christ's Precious Bride (Isaiah 54:5, Song of Songs 7:10).

MAKING THE GRACE CONNECTION

Remember, there really is no hurry to finish this book. The slower you process these truths, the deeper they are likely to go and the stronger the connection you will make with them. Would you benefit from reading this chapter again? If so, go for it!

If you're ready to ask the Holy Spirit to help you connect with the Biblical truths we've considered, find somewhere quiet, clear your mind, and pray:

> **Glorious Father, the God of our Lord Jesus Christ, please give me the Spirit of wisdom and revelation, so that I may know You better. I pray that the eyes of my heart may be enlightened in order that I may know the hope to which You have called me, the riches of Your glorious inheritance in Your holy people, and Your incomparably great power for us who believe. Amen.**

God takes us from shame to grace; from humiliation to dignity; from rejection to acceptance; from isolation to belonging; from alienation to intimacy. Take all the time you need to respond to these few questions (and write your answers down).

1. Read this passage slowly, trying to put yourself in the place of the leper who approached Jesus:

   And a leper came to him, imploring him, and kneeling said to him, "If you will, you can make me clean." Moved with pity, he stretched out his hand and touched him and said to him, "I will; be clean." And immediately the leprosy left him, and he was made clean. (Mark 1:40-42 ESV)

   Why do you think he did not ask Jesus to "heal" him?

What do you think it meant to the man for Jesus to touch him?

Is Jesus *willing* to make you clean? *Can* He make you clean? Does He even need to make you clean or are you already clean?

2. Have you considered your core identity to be that of a "sinner," even though you have chosen to follow Jesus? What difference might it make in your life to understand that your identity has completely changed and that you are now a "holy one"?

3. Take a good look through that amazing list of your new names. Read it out loud if you can. All of them apply to you if you know Jesus but take some time to allow the Holy Spirit to impress upon you one or more names that He particularly wants you to take hold of. Declare confidently: "Thank You, Jesus, that my new name is.... I choose to believe that this is true even if it doesn't feel true."

CHAPTER 3

INNOCENT!

FAILED TO LIVE UP TO EXPECTATIONS?

I love corny jokes. Here's one of my all-time favorites:

The inflatable boy took a pin to the inflatable school. The inflatable principal called him out in front of the whole school and said to him, "You've not only let me down, and let the whole school down. Above all, you've let yourself down."

Sorry 'bout that.

I think the main reason I find this funny is that it reminds me of the kind of thing teachers at my school actually said when somebody did something wrong. The objective was to make the erring pupil feel guilty to discourage others from doing similar "naughty" things. Guilt was consciously being used as a method of maintaining discipline and order.

What if you were asked to write the ending to the story of the two brothers starting at the point where the younger brother returns home and asks the father to receive him back as a hired laborer— would you portray the father differently from the way Jesus did?

Shouldn't the father expect the son to be thorough in his apology?

Shouldn't the father have been portrayed as at least a little angry, maybe turning his back or looking the other way as his son approached? Shouldn't the son be made aware of how he offended the father and abandoned the family? Shouldn't the son have to prove himself for a time to earn trust and only then be allowed to spend money again? Maybe you think that the way the father so quickly forgave his son and restored him to the family was a bit foolish, a little premature. Wouldn't the father have been wiser to make the son prove the sincerity of his repentance for a while before having a party thrown for him? Maybe a better strategy would have been to make his son feel really guilty about what he had done, at least for a while.

If you, like me, were brought up in a Western society that mostly uses guilt rather than shame to persuade people to behave well, I suspect you might have at least some sympathy with this line of thinking.

When I was small, if I didn't do what my mum suggested, she would sometimes pretend to cry in a humorous way—no harmful intention and no harm done. But it made me feel a little guilty and usually motivated me to behave in a way that would avoid that feeling.

In a guilt-based society, when we conform to what is expected, we are made to feel good. If we mess up and don't reach a particular expectation, we are made to feel bad.

IF you do your homework....
THEN you can go out to the movies later.

IF you serve on Sunday morning ....
THEN you'll be seen as a good member of this church.

IF you have a Quiet Time every day....
THEN God will be pleased with you.

And that approach is highly effective at motivating us to "behave," especially for a firstborn like me who is keen to follow the rules.

So, our whole motivation in daily life ends up being trying to reach certain standards in order to please God, a parent, a spouse, an employer, or a church leader. Or we try hard to adhere to our own set of "rules" or standards that we have developed, all to avoid feeling guilty.

We try really hard but often fall short. We end up walking around with the sense that we are failing miserably as sons and daughters of God, or as parents, workers or whatever. We end up in a near-permanent state of beating ourselves up.

A pastor friend of mine told me about a dream he had in which he saw his own gravestone. He saw that it carried the inscription, "He failed to live up to expectations." It made him realize how conditioned he was to try and live up to expectations rather than to give and serve out of God's grace and love. He said it was a struggle to come out of that way of thinking but when he did, in his words, "Liberation was sweet!"

Is guilt a significant motivator in your life? If so, the liberation that Jesus' grace offers will be equally sweet for you.

The Church has been particularly good at using guilt to motivate us. As a young Christian in my teens, I used to believe that I had to try really hard to please God, who I thought was watching me with an eagle eye. It's almost like I had confused Jesus with Santa Claus! You know, "You better watch out, you better not cry, you better not pout, I'm telling you why... *Jesus Christ* is coming to town. He's making a list, checking it twice, gonna find out who's naughty and nice...." So we try really hard to do right and make God happy, afraid that if we don't perform well, He will ignore us or reject us or even bring some horrible tragedy into our lives. If we feel we check every box on our spiritual "To Do" list, we might feel OK. But when we slip up and do something on our spiritual "To Don't" list, we feel God shakes His head in disappointment and disapproval.

"I don't pray enough; I failed to read the Bible in one year, again; I don't give enough money; I'm a flop at sharing my faith; I don't have the spiritual gifts she does; I don't seem to hear from God like him; I'm not as fruitful as she is...."

When we are motivated by guilt, we become like the elder brother. We end up slaving away in a doomed quest to please, when we could be enjoying everything the father had all along.

WHAT IS GUILT?

Let's try to understand guilt, starting by asking what it actually is.

We tend to think of guilt primarily as a feeling, as in "I feel really guilty for saying that." But in fact, true guilt has nothing to do with feelings. It's about hard facts.

Guilt is at root a legal term, used in a courtroom where a judge or jury, after hearing the facts of the case, comes to a decision that the charge against the defendant is true and pronounces them guilty.

Guilt is defined in relation to the legal authority who has laid down the laws. If we break the laws of that legal authority, we are guilty. If we do not, we are innocent.

Think about the two criminals who were crucified alongside Jesus:

> One of the criminals who hung there hurled insults at him: "Aren't you the Messiah? Save yourself and us!" But the other criminal rebuked him. "Don't you fear God," he said, "since you are under the same sentence? We are punished justly, for we are getting what our deeds deserve. But this man has done nothing wrong." (Luke 23:39-41)

We don't know exactly what crime the criminals had committed— they were probably rebels or robbers—but they themselves knew that they had been justly found guilty of breaking the law of the land. The law demanded physical death by crucifixion for their particular crimes so they were simply getting what they deserved. And they seem to have had no argument with that.

In many cases, however, a defendant may not *feel* guilty; their family may not *feel* they are guilty; even the public may not *feel* they are guilty. But if they committed the crime, they *are* guilty.

In other words, true guilt and guilt feelings are different things. True guilt is based on fact not feelings. And guilt feelings (or lack of them) are not a reliable guide to true guilt.

ARE *YOU* GUILTY?

There is a much higher court than the highest court in your country—the court of God Himself. We will all have to stand before God's throne at the end of time. Ultimately this is the only court that will matter because its judgments will have eternal consequences:

> Then I saw a great white throne and him who was seated on it. The earth and the heavens fled from his presence, and there was no place for them. And I saw the dead, great and small, standing before the throne, and books were opened. Another book was opened, which is the book of life. The dead were judged according to what they had done as recorded in the books. The sea gave up the dead that were in it, and death and Hades gave up the dead that were in them, and each person was judged according to what they had done. Then death and Hades were thrown into the lake of fire. The lake of fire is the second death. Anyone whose name was not found written in the book of life was thrown into the lake of fire. (Revelation 20:11-15)

We may well be law-abiding citizens, innocent before the law of the land, but the crucial question is this: where do you and I stand in relation to this heavenly court? Are we guilty before God?

In this book, I will emphasize the love of God. After all God is love. But that love is in perfect harmony with another fundamental aspect of His character: His holiness.

I have worked for two decades with a gifted illustrator who has produced hundreds of cartoon illustrations for our key discipleship resources. I once asked him to come up with one to illustrate God's holiness. He went through a few iterations but none of them worked—they all seemed so trivial in comparison to their subject matter. In the end we both concluded that it was impossible to come up with something that could come anywhere near. God's holiness is, quite literally, unimaginable to us.

The Old Testament often refers to Him as "holy, holy, holy," the word repeated three times to emphasize the unimaginable extent of His holiness. This is what A.W. Tozer says:

> "We cannot grasp the true meaning of the divine holiness by thinking of someone or something very pure and then raising the concept to the highest degree we are capable of. God's holiness is not simply the best we know infinitely bettered. We know nothing like the divine holiness. It stands apart, unique, unapproachable, incomprehensible and unattainable." [1]

Even though we can never fully grasp God's holiness, even a slight grasp of it is enough for us to understand that it would be impossible for this holy, holy, holy God to tolerate sin, to gloss over it, to say it didn't matter. He wouldn't be holy if He did, let alone "holy, holy, holy."

We have seen how our ancestor, Adam, was created perfect with the capacity to choose. God didn't burden him with a whole load of rules but told him in effect that he could carry out his commission in any way he chose. There was just one thing that God told him not to do because He knew it would harm him and others: he was not to eat from a certain tree. Deceived by God's enemy, Satan, Adam chose to disobey God, and that disobedience is the essence of what the Bible calls sin.

And as we have seen, "By the one man's disobedience the many were made sinners" (Romans 5:19 ESV). When Adam sinned, he became guilty before God and a consequence of that is that you and I and all his descendants were made guilty before God too. Whether we felt guilty or not, we were all born with true guilt before God and that Heavenly Court. And our subsequent sinful actions soon added to our true guilt.

---

1. *The Knowledge of the Holy*, Chapter 21, A.W. Tozer, 1961

Paul tells us, "For the wages of sin is death, but the gift of God is eternal life in Christ Jesus our Lord" (Romans 6:23). We could do nothing about all this—without an intervention from outside, we could expect only death. The only possible way out was for God to do something. And He did, through Jesus. Before we understand how Jesus dealt with our true guilt, let's consider briefly an important question that may be troubling you: what is the position of a baby that dies in the womb or shortly after birth?

The Bible makes no explicit statement about this but most Christians who search the Bible for an answer to this question, myself included, come to the conclusion that, through some mechanism that we don't understand, God, who is supremely just, is able to save those children through the sacrifice of Jesus. When you see how loving He is and you also see how much value He puts on free will, I find it inconceivable that He would not find a way to do that for those who have been unable to make their own choice. If this is a question that is particularly relevant for you, focus on God's love and inherent fairness. We can release our children into the hands of our incredible Father God who can be totally trusted always to do the right thing. Even though the Bible does not specifically address the question, it does very clearly tell us about God's incredible character. He is love. He is perfectly just. And He is the source of all wisdom. One day we will understand this mystery but for now we need to leave it with our loving Father. We really can trust Him.

GUILTY NO MORE

We have seen how God, "made Him to be sin who knew no sin, so that in Him we might *become* the righteousness of God" (2 Corinthians 5:21 ESV). Jesus' death and resurrection enabled us to have that incredible new identity—we are no longer sinners but holy ones. We are the righteousness of God!

But what about our guilt?

When you say the Lord's prayer, you may say "Forgive us our sins" or "forgive us our debts" because the versions in different gospels are slightly different. But most are agreed that Jesus' core meaning was most likely to be "debts."

There is a strong relationship between guilt and debts. If you are found guilty of breaking the law by driving too fast, it will usually lead to a financial penalty.

Scales are often used to symbolize justice—as guilt weighs down one side, payment needs to be made on the other until they are both balanced again. And biblically, our guilt before God is the same thing as having a debt to Him.

In New Testament times, if someone owed money to someone else, a legal document was drawn up itemizing exactly who owed what to whom, what the repayment terms were, and what the consequences for default would be. It was called a certificate of debt. If you have a mortgage, you probably get sent the modern equivalent once a year.

If someone couldn't repay the debt, their property might be seized, or they themselves could be taken into slavery.

Because of Adam's rebellion, we were all born with a certificate of debt to God. Last time I checked, the USA had a national debt of around 33 trillion dollars and a population of around 330 million. That's a debt of $100,000 for every American citizen. Imagine a baby born today. Through no fault of its own but just by being born American and because of the spending of previous generations, it immediately has a debt of $100,000!

Our holy, holy, holy God could not just sweep our debt under the carpet and say it didn't matter. Sin always matters. Sin always has consequences that have to be paid for. But He did resolve it and here's how:

> *When you were dead in your wrongdoings and the uncircumcision of your flesh, He made you alive together with Him, having forgiven us all our wrongdoings, having canceled the certificate of debt*

consisting of decrees against us, which was hostile
to us; and He has taken it out of the way, having
nailed it to the cross. (Colossians 2:13-14 NASB)

God did two significant things. First He made us alive with Christ, and gave us that incredible new identity. Then God wrote *"paid in full"* across our certificate of debt. He could do that only because Jesus, His own Son, was nailed to the cross and died as a payment for our sin, to balance the scales of justice. Because Jesus is God, His death is enough to pay for the sins of all people across all of time.

Far from sweeping our sin under the carpet, this God of love chose to pay a terrible price. Our certificate of debt was nailed to the cross with Jesus and totally dealt with.

How can Jesus' death on the cross cancel out my certificate of debt and resolve my guilt? Normally a guilty Roman criminal had to pay for their own debts by spending the allotted time in prison. However, it was technically possible to find someone else who would take your place in the cell and serve out the required time on your behalf as your substitute.

That is what Jesus has done, potentially for every person who has ever lived or ever will. His sacrifice is enough to balance the scales for every sin because He is that unimaginably holy God. And if you had been the only person in the whole of history who needed God to do all this, I am certain that He would have done it all just for you. That is how much He loves you.

God does not impose the payment He has made upon us. Every person has the choice whether or not to receive this gift, but if you do, that's it. It is finished. Done and dusted.

According to this passage, how many of our sins have been forgiven? All of them! Past, present, and future. So how much guilt before God do we still have for our sins? None. Absolutely none! We are totally debt free!

Paul says: "There is therefore now no condemnation for those who are in Christ Jesus" (Romans 8:1). Now means *now* and no means *no*!

God has forgotten our sins, in the sense that He will never raise these issues and use them against us again. The best a human court can do is declare us "not guilty." God's grace goes further than that. As far as God is concerned, it's as if what you and I did never took place. He declares us "innocent"! And that's a legal fact.

In Christ, all of God's expectations of you have been met in full. You don't need to try harder or compare yourself to others. You have nothing to prove, no debt to pay off. Your guilt is gone. Forever.

"Failed to live up to expectations" can never be applied to you. In Christ, all God's expectations of you have been met in full. God *does not have* a list, and He *is not* checking it twice to see who is naughty and nice. What *does* exist is the Lamb's Book of Life in which your name is written if you've chosen to follow Jesus.

This declaration of "innocent" is not just for when we first came to Christ. God's grace is for every moment of every day. For those in Christ Jesus, no sin we commit can ever take away one bit from the full and complete sacrifice Jesus paid for us. Even though we still sin, we remain holy ones. Despite our sin, we are still forgiven. Our guilt is still gone. Forever.

You are innocent! And if you still *feel* guilty? Then your feelings are lying to you. Guilt and guilt feelings are not the same thing, remember.

Either your conscience has not yet fully grasped the wonder of Christ's total forgiveness, or you're inadvertently listening to the whisper of your enemy, Satan. In either case, the answer is to make a choice to believe what God tells you in His Word is true. You are not just "not guilty." You are innocent!

A FULLER UNDERSTANDING

If I were to ask you why God sent Jesus, His only Son, to die for us, how would you explain it? For most of my Christian life, I'd have said, almost without having to think about it, "to forgive my sins." And of course, as we've just seen, that's right. But it's not the whole story.

Look at the story of Adam and Eve after their rebellion and its dreadful consequences. There's very little about guilt and forgiveness or an angry God in that story. Yes, Adam sinned and made us all sinners. But the primary consequence of that sin was spiritual death, not anger and condemnation from God.

As the story continues, God doesn't come across as some kind of angry figure, who feels wronged, or who turns His back on the people He created. Not at all. He didn't leave Adam with a feeble fig leaf but provided clothes for him and Eve. And right away He put into motion a plan to restore us, even though He knew it would lead to the death of His Son.

God is love. And His heart is not to condemn but to make things right, whatever it takes.

Let's look at three direct quotes from Jesus in which He Himself tells us why He came.

In Luke 19:10 Jesus says: "For the Son of Man came to seek and to save the lost."

God is love. In His love, God moved to pursue and rescue us who were lost. Not to have us burn ourselves out trying to please Him.

In John 10:10 Jesus says, "I have come that they may have life, and have it to the full."

Adam lost *life*. Jesus came specifically to give us that life back—by reconnecting us to God in order to change our very identity and make us holy ones.

In Matthew 20:28 Jesus explained, "The Son of Man did not come to be served, but to serve, and to give his life as a ransom for many."

A ransom was paid to buy someone out of slavery. Jesus came to give His life not just to forgive our sins, but also to buy us out of slavery to death, to the flesh, to sin and to Satan.

I hope you're getting the idea. In three different verses where Jesus explains specifically why He came, forgiveness of sins is not a major emphasis. Kinda surprising!

Let's try the verses from John that we use the most in our Gospel presentations:

> *"For God so loved the world that he gave his one and only Son, that whoever believes in him shall not perish but have eternal life. For God did not send his Son into the world to condemn the world, but to save the world through him." (John 3:16-17)*

No mention of sins or guilt or forgiveness. It's about *life* again. And John says specifically that God did not send Jesus to condemn the world but to save it.

I am not at all saying that we weren't guilty and that Jesus didn't die for our sins. It's clear that we *were* guilty. And Jesus *did* die to forgive our sins. The point I'm trying to make is that, when Jesus, Paul and the Biblical writers explained the good news, guilt and forgiveness were not the focus of their explanations. So why does guilt loom so large over most of us?

It's a historic and cultural issue. In many so-called Christian countries, the Church and the state became so intertwined that they were practically the same thing. It's one thing to threaten citizens with jail or a whipping when they don't obey the rules. But it's so much more effective if you can threaten them with an eternity in hell! The Church was very happy to act as a kind of police officer for the state, warning the populace that God was watching closely and keeping tabs.

This was at best a distortion of the Biblical Gospel message. And at worst it was a disgraceful and cynical manipulation in the name of Christianity.

But the result is that the concepts of sin, guilt, and punishment took center stage in our understanding of the Gospel. This has tended to skew even our understanding of God Himself. On one level we know that He is love. But in practice it's all too easy to think of Him as that Santa Claus caricature or as a school principal with a big stick looking to see if we put a foot out of place. If we're honest, many of us have been taught to think of Him as a hard taskmaster who is borderline obsessed with how we behave.

And that's why, even though we know on one level that we're saved by grace alone through faith, when it comes to living as disciples day by day, many of us are followed around by that cloud of guilt or that nagging feeling we're not doing enough or not doing it right. It's like a low-grade fever of feeling guilty that is always there in the background.

Let's note in passing that our faulty understanding of God has had serious consequences. It has affected negatively how we approach those who don't yet know Jesus. Because we have seen God as a nit-picking, strict, hard-to-please taskmaster obsessed with sin, we have approached others the same way.

Instead of welcoming everybody as God does, the Church often comes across as condemning people for their behavior: for the way they dress, the way they vote, the issues they support, and so on and so on. And we have come across as a bunch of kill-joys focused on sin, condemnation and judgment. And that is not good news.

STRATEGIES WE USE BUT DON'T NEED

If we continue to carry guilt feelings, even though we are in fact innocent, we may try one of three strategies to make ourselves feel better.

We can try to feel good about ourselves by **doing good things**. I know you know already that we are not *saved* by good works—but when it come to our day-to-day lives, it's easy to think that God changes the rules. We can subtly slip into thinking that to *remain* in God's favor, to be sure of His love for us, we have to perform well spiritually, doing things like reading the Bible, attending church regularly, giving money to the church, feeding the hungry, and so on.

As a young Christian I was taught to have a "quiet time" every day, and one of my friends took it upon himself to check up on me. Whenever I would see him, he would ask "How are your QTs?" I am so grateful for the care he showed me, and his desire to help me grow as a Christian.

However, I ended up creating a rule in my head that I MUST have a quiet time with God for half an hour every day. My motivation for doing it was simply to avoid feeling guilty for breaking the rule. And religious rules produce a dead, dry, stale religion rather than a real growing relationship with God. So my quiet times became, well, quiet!

Now, is setting apart time to pray and listen to God every day a good thing to do? Absolutely. It's a great thing to do, and it's difficult to think that anyone could grow as a disciple without a regular discipline of that type.

Despite my mixed motivation, God was able to use the times I spent with Him every morning. But over the years I became increasingly frustrated that most mornings they felt like a burden rather than a joy. One day I was brutally honest with God (as if He didn't already know!) and asked Him, "Do I really have to do this?" And, to my surprise, I sensed Him say "No, you don't."

I felt a liberty to let go of the pressure of "having to" and for the next couple of years, I stopped that routine so that I could get it out of my system. It's not that I didn't spend time with God during that period, but I made a deliberate effort not to do it if it was simply to avoid feeling guilty. And I'm pleased to tell you that I did eventually get to the point where I knew that I didn't have to have a quiet time and that nothing would change in terms of God's love for me if I didn't.

Guess what! Nowadays it's very rare indeed that I don't start my day with a quiet time. And I do it simply because I want to start the day focusing on my loving Father. I now enjoy those times so much more, get much more out of them, and tend to spend much longer on them. So much nicer! So much more helpful!

Proverbs 8:34 (ESV) reads, "Blessed is the one who listens to me, watching daily at my gates, waiting beside my doors." Instead of asking God, "Do I *have* to spend time with You?," to which the answer is "No," what if I asked Him, "Do I *need* to spend time with You?" I would hear a definite "Yes!" If I don't give God the opportunity to speak to me daily, I will lose my way.

I had fallen into the trap of thinking I had to load up one side of the measuring scale of my life with good works in order to counterbalance the guilt I felt was piled up on the other side.

But there is no guilt on the other side to balance out. We are innocent! Let's not make the mistake the elder brother made. Let's stop "slaving away" and just enjoy our Father and all He has.

Another strategy to help assuage those guilt feelings is **falling back on our religious background or upbringing**. When John the Baptist called the Jewish leaders "a brood of vipers" and told them they needed to repent, they made themselves feel better by protesting that they were "children of Abraham" (see Matthew 3:1-10). John retorted that God could turn rocks into children of Abraham if He wanted to!

Maybe you've been a good Baptist, Catholic, Methodist, Presbyterian, Anglican, Lutheran, or whatever, all your life. You have lived up to the standards required and might even be "a pillar of the church." And maybe you try to outweigh your feelings of guilt by falling back on that.

The apostle Paul did the same at one time:

> *If someone else thinks they have reasons to put confidence in the flesh, I have more: circumcised on the eighth day, of the people of Israel, of the tribe of Benjamin, a Hebrew of Hebrews; in regard to the law, a Pharisee; as for zeal, persecuting the church; as for righteousness based on the law, faultless. (Philippians 3:4b-6)*

But he came to this conclusion: "Whatever were gains to me I now consider loss for the sake of Christ" (Philippians 3:7). Or, in the words of Shania Twain, "That don't impress me much!"

The point, of course, is that your religious background does not increase your standing before God even a bit. Because in Christ you already have the highest standing. And no guilt.

A similar way we can try to counter those guilt feelings to feel better about ourselves is to compare ourselves favorably to others: "Well, at least I don't... like so and so." And we fill in the blank with some kind of sin that we deem worse than anything we have ever done.

Let's allow Jesus to answer that one in His own words:

> *"Two men went up to the temple to pray, one a Pharisee and the other a tax collector. The Pharisee stood by himself and prayed: 'God, I thank you that I am not like other people—robbers, evildoers, adulterers—or even like this tax collector. I fast twice a week and give a tenth of all I get.' But the tax collector stood at a distance. He would not even look up to heaven, but beat his breast and said, 'God, have mercy on me, a sinner.' I tell you that this man, rather than the other, went home justified before God. For all those who exalt themselves will be humbled, and those who humble themselves will be exalted." (Luke 18:9-14)*

The bottom line: we are innocent! If we feel guilty, we need to align our thinking with what is already true rather than trying to outweigh guilt feelings through doing good things, claiming our religious heritage, or comparing ourselves to others.

In Luke 7:36-50 we find a story that may help us really get this. A strict religious leader called Simon had invited Jesus over for supper. Simon probably thought it was all going rather well, but then his worst nightmare began to unfold. A prostitute walked in uninvited. She stood by Jesus and broke down in sobs, her tears showering Jesus' feet. She bent down to try to dry His feet with her hair, kissing His feet in the process. Then she produced an expensive bottle of perfume, no doubt purchased from her immoral earnings, and poured it all over Jesus' feet. "Er... anyone for an hors d'oeuvre?" I can imagine Simon saying.

Simon and the prostitute form quite a contrast. Simon was confident in his religious background and all the good things he did. He saw himself as a fine, upstanding member of society. He didn't realize his guilt before God. He certainly didn't feel guilty.

She, on the other hand, knew that she was guilty. She made a living by selling her body. She knew her life was a mess. Jesus didn't gloss over that and referred to her "many sins," but He graciously received her act of remorse and repentance. He didn't tell her to go away and clean up her life.

At supper, Jesus contrasted the prostitute's loving actions with Simon's negligence in affording Jesus customary kindnesses such as greeting guests with a kiss and washing the dust off their feet as they arrived. Then He made a significant public declaration:

> *"Therefore, I tell you, her many sins have been forgiven—as her great love has shown. But whoever has been forgiven little loves little." Then Jesus said to her, "Your sins are forgiven." The other guests began to say among themselves, "Who is this who even forgives sins?" Jesus said to the woman, "Your faith has saved you; go in peace." (Luke 7:47-50)*

A law-abiding man of good standing, who has a great religious pedigree and fine religious actions to match, retains his true guilt before God. A woman who up to that point had been engaged in what her society would have seen as the ultimate sinful life is declared innocent by the Son of God. Jesus told her that her faith had saved her.

What is the difference between them? It's not the amount of sin that each had committed. It's not even the seriousness of the sin that each had committed. It's quite simply that one responded to Jesus in *faith*. And the other did not.

It's the same with the two robbers who were crucified with Jesus. Both were guilty before God. Yet one of them responded to Jesus in faith and was immediately pronounced "not guilty." Jesus promised that he would be with Him in paradise later that very day.

The apostle Paul explains, "For it is by grace you have been saved, through faith—and this is not from yourselves, it is the gift of God" (Ephesians 2:8).

Being declared innocent is a pure grace gift from God. It is activated by faith when we turn to Him in sheer desperation and ask for salvation.

By faith in Jesus, we stand in grace: forgiven, justified, at peace with God. Jesus says to you too, "Your sins are forgiven. Your faith has saved you. Go in peace."

Knowing that we are now holy ones whose certificate of debt for sins past, present, and future has been totally dealt with on the cross by the holy Son of God, we can simply rest in the Father's love and enjoy Him.

DOESN'T SIN MATTER?

We've seen how Jesus approached the woman at the well, and the woman who gatecrashed Simon's party—with nothing but grace, respect, and love. But in neither case did He imply that their sin was OK; He just didn't come to them with condemnation.

Because of the way we've learned to focus on sin, guilt, and forgiveness, this can make us uncomfortable.

How does God want us to feel when we sin, if not guilty?

What does He want us to do when we realize we have sinned?

And if we're already forgiven for sins past, present, and future, can't we just live the rest of our lives doing whatever sinful behavior we like without worrying about it?

Let's look a little more into this and start with serious sins that Paul could see in the Corinthian church. They were a bit of a mess —there was jealousy, quarreling, sexual immorality, drunkenness, and class discrimination to name just a few of their issues. Unlike the younger brother, they clearly did not yet realize the problem and were certainly not "coming back home" in repentance.

Paul certainly did not say, "Well, we live under God's grace so it doesn't really matter." Quite the opposite. He took it very seriously indeed. Paul understood the consequences of sin and agonized over how to approach them. In the end, he decided to write them a tough letter. The actual words he used are lost to history, but we do know that his strategy worked because in a subsequent letter that we do have, he said this:

> I... rejoice, not that you were made sorrowful, but that you were made sorrowful to the point of repentance;... For the sorrow that is according to the will of God produces a repentance without regret, leading to salvation, but the sorrow of the world produces death. (2 Corinthians 7, 9a,10 NASB)

He describes two possible reactions the Corinthians might have had when his tough words revealed they were off track: "sorrow that is according to the will of God" and "sorrow of the world."

Worldly sorrow is what Judas experienced after he had betrayed Jesus—he found himself filled with guilt with no hope. Paul says that worldly sorrow leads to death. Instead of trusting in the One who was going to the cross for him, Judas turned away and hanged himself. Worldly sorrow is what we experience when we continually revisit sin that has already been dealt with on the cross and beat ourselves up for it.

But Paul's aim was not to make the Corinthians experience worldly sorrow. He wanted them to experience "Godly sorrow" that would lead to "repentance without regret" and "salvation."

To understand Godly sorrow, look at the Apostle Peter who had betrayed his best friend at His greatest hour of need by denying Him three times and felt terrible about it.

In John 21, we see Jesus cooking breakfast for Peter and the rest of the disciples. He could have raised the issue in front of the other disciples to make Peter feel even guiltier than he already did, just to make sure he never did it again. But Jesus didn't even mention this monumental failure.

Instead, after the meal, Jesus asks Peter if he loves him. Peter says he does. But Jesus asks him again. Then He asks him a third time, one time for each of his previous denials. Then, rather than demoting him to "last place" in the disciples' leadership ranks, Jesus honors him in front of the others and restores him: "Tend My lambs," "Shepherd My sheep," "Tend My sheep."

He could have used guilt to motivate Peter, but He didn't. He used grace. And this grace meant that Peter was able to experience godly sorrow—"a repentance without regret"—and could move forward.

God does want you to understand that all sin has consequences, but He doesn't want you to be weighed down with guilt, no matter what you've done or what you're caught in right now. He wants that sense of Godly sorrow to pull you into His arms, where you will find the same welcome the younger son received.

Sin is not OK. All sin is harmful. All sin has consequences. But Jesus knew that heaping guilt on does not help. Honestly, I can't think of a single occasion when Jesus used guilt to try to motivate someone to behave better. God's heart is not to condemn. His heart is to make things right.

WHEN WE SIN

If we claim to be without sin, we deceive ourselves and the truth is not in us. If we confess our sins, he is faithful and just and will forgive us our sins and purify us from all unrighteousness. (1 John 1:8-9)

Although our identity is now "holy ones" rather than "sinners," we still live in a fallen world, have some of our old thought patterns, and have an enemy who tempts us. That means we will all still sin from time to time.

When we do, God wants us to experience Godly sorrow, which produces a "repentance without regret." In other words, God wants your sense of sorrow not to drive you away from Him but to drive you into His arms. There you will find the same welcome the younger son received, and you will be able to draw a line under it and move on.

In that place of love and security, you can *confess* your sins as the younger son did. Confession means simply that we agree with God that we have sinned. But you can also at that point agree with Him about something else: that you are forgiven in Christ; that there is now no condemnation whatsoever for you (at least not from the only Person who matters).

And you can then choose to *repent*; that is, change your mind about your sinful actions, and turn away from them, seeking His strength to walk as the holy one that you now are.

This is what James calls "submitting to God." But he tells us not only to do that but also to "resist the devil" (James 4:7). The biggest issue with sin is that it opens a great big door of influence to the enemy in our lives that will stop us from being fruitful. We need to close that door by submitting *and* resisting. If you know Freedom In Christ, you'll be aware of *The Steps To Freedom In Christ*, which is a kind, gentle way to do this. *The Grace Course* contains *The Steps To Experiencing God's Grace*, a similar process where you can deal with barriers to grace in your life.

When we respond to our sin appropriately, by confessing and repenting, by submitting to God *and* resisting the enemy, God immediately cleanses us from *all* evil and unrighteousness. And our intimacy with Jesus and other people is restored.

And there will be no regret. No beating ourselves up. No going round and round in circles.

It may take some time for your conscience to fully grasp the wonder of Christ's forgiveness and total cleansing and to learn not to listen to the condemning whispers of your enemy, Satan. But you will be able to do that as you focus on the truth that, "There is therefore now no condemnation for those who are in Christ Jesus" (Romans 8:1 ESV). This is not just religious talk or wishful thinking; it is *truth*.

God doesn't want you to *feel* guilty for your sins when you are innocent! He wants you to rejoice. He wants to restore your joy.

Does this sound just too good to be true? Well, it *is* good. And it *is* true! For those in Christ Jesus, God loves you before you sin; God loves you after you sin; God even loves you in the midst of your sinning, though He never loves your sinning.

Remember, your sins *are* forgiven; your faith *has* saved you; you *can* go in peace.

CAN WE KEEP ON SINNING?

"Hang on a minute!" you may be saying, "If God just accepts us back with no questions asked, doesn't that mean we can just do whatever we like?"

That's an important question. Among the seven letters to churches in Revelation, there is just one, the church in Thyatira, that is commended for its love. But they seem to think that grace means you can do whatever you like, and they're allowing sexual immorality and idol worship.

Jesus' words about the consequences of this for the ringleader make for uncomfortable reading:

> *"Behold, I will throw her onto a sickbed, and those who commit adultery with her I will throw into great tribulation, unless they repent of her works, and I will strike her children dead." (Revelation 2:22-23a ESV)*

This is Jesus speaking! Maybe you can't conceive that He would use this kind of language. And it's tempting to skip over verses like this. But think about it. God is love. Therefore, everything He does, and everything He says, must come from love, even words like these. Let's try to understand how.

Out of love God has laid down boundaries in order to *protect* us. He told Adam not to eat from the tree because He knew the consequences. And it's because God *loves* this woman and this church that he tells her not to continue sinning. His intent is that they will *not* suffer, will *not* die.

If I see one of my kids up a tree moving along a branch that I know is going to break, what should I do? I'm going to start shouting and running towards them. To my child I'm going to look and sound angry. But actually, I'm expressing love, and any parent would do the same.

When we truly understand the consequences of sin, we'll also understand why God takes it so seriously. We'll look a little more at this in the next chapter.

John helps us understand more:

> This is the message we have heard from him and proclaim to you, that God is light, and in him is no darkness at all. If we say we have fellowship with him while we walk in darkness, we lie and do not practice the truth. But if we walk in the light, as he is in the light, we have fellowship with one another, and the blood of Jesus his Son cleanses us from all sin. (1 John 1:5-7 ESV)

If someone persists in sin and is really not bothered by it, I would have serious questions about whether they actually know Jesus at all. If we are walking openly with our Father, we will *want* to live in the light.

GRACE—THE MOST POWERFUL MOTIVATOR

So can you do whatever you want? Read these verses slowly:

> For the grace of God has appeared that offers salvation to all people. It teaches us to say "No" to ungodliness and worldly passions, and to live self-controlled, upright and godly lives in this present age. (Titus 2:11-12)

It's *grace, not guilt,* that's the most powerful motivator to live a righteous life.

When you truly "get" grace, you won't for a minute want to use it as an excuse to keep sinning. So if you are asking whether it's OK to sin, you're missing the point. Don't beat yourself up but persevere in your journey to understand God's grace in all its glorious fullness.

In the next chapter, we'll understand practically how grace really does lead us to live godly lives. We'll see that Jesus died to set us free, not just from the *consequences* of sin, but also from the *power* of sin in our lives.

MAKING THE GRACE CONNECTION

If you are aware that guilt is prominent in your thinking and you are prone to guilt feelings, take your time to allow the truth to penetrate into your conscience.

We are going to consider two beautiful pictures of God's forgiveness. Find somewhere quiet, clear your mind, and pray:

> **Glorious Father, the God of our Lord Jesus Christ, please give me the Spirit of wisdom and revelation, so that I may know You better. I pray that the eyes of my heart may be enlightened in order that I may know the hope to which You have called me, the riches of Your glorious inheritance in Your holy people, and Your incomparably great power for us who believe. Amen.**

Snow

Thousands of years ago, God made a promise through Isaiah the prophet:

> *"Come now, let us settle the matter," says the LORD.*
> *(Isaiah 1:18)*

That promise is written in the future tense but now through Christ has been fulfilled. If you belong to Jesus, you can now say this:

> Though my sins were like scarlet,
> they are now as white as snow;
> though they were red as crimson,
> they are now like wool.

Say those words slowly a couple of times.

Think about a time you experienced a fresh fall of snow or imagine what that would be like. Think about how snow covers absolutely everything and makes it beautiful.

God has forgiven your sins and changed you into the purity, brightness and beauty of freshly fallen snow. The red stain of your sins is turned to beautiful, pure white by the precious blood of Jesus.

The Deepest Ocean

Here's another promise written before Jesus came:

> *You will again have compassion on us; you will tread*
> *our sins underfoot and hurl all our iniquities into the*
> *depths of the sea. (Micah 7:19)*

Again, read it in the past tense as it now applies to you:

You will always have compassion on me;
You have trodden my sins underfoot
and hurled all my iniquities into the depths of the sea.

God has crushed your sins like a heavy boot totally obliterates a cigarette butt.

And He has hurled your twisted wickedness (that's what iniquities are) into the deepest part of the sea. The deepest part of the sea is the Mariana Trench in the Pacific Ocean. It's almost seven miles under the surface of the sea, deeper in the ocean than Mount Everest is higher than sea level.

God has placed your sins there, and there they will stay. Nobody goes to the bottom of the Mariana Trench to fish and neither should you!

Take some time to thank God that Jesus destroyed the certificate of debt against you and has dealt with every single one of your sins so that you can live as the holy one you now are.

CHAPTER 4

VICTORIOUS!

FULLY EQUIPPED

I spent a lot of my early years as a Christian asking God for more. More power. More love. More victory over sin. Until I came across a verse that shocked me:

> *His divine power has given us everything we need*
> *for a godly life through our knowledge of him who*
> *called us by his own glory and goodness.*
> *(2 Peter 1:3)*

I must have read it many times before, but I noticed for the first time that it is written in the past tense. Which means it states very clearly that we have *already* been given everything we need to live a godly life. Another verse, also written in the past tense, helped to confirm this:

> *Praise be to the God and Father of our Lord Jesus*
> *Christ, who has blessed us in the heavenly realms*
> *with every spiritual blessing in Christ.*
> *(Ephesians 1:3).*

He has *already* given us every spiritual blessing. There's no question of God needing to give us more. If something appears to be lacking, it must be something on our side, not His.

Does that surprise you as much as it did me?

Perhaps the first practical application of that in my life was when I was caught in a sin that I couldn't seem to get out of. I was watching the wrong sort of stuff on TV late at night. After watching something totally inappropriate, I'd say something like, "Sorry, Lord God, please forgive me. Please help me. Please give me power to resist temptation." Or in other words, "Please give me more than I already have."

But God didn't seem to answer that prayer, and the next day or week I'd do it again. And again. And end up feeling completely hopeless.

It's all very well understanding that Jesus has removed all of our guilt (as we saw in the last chapter) but if we find ourselves caught in a sin that we don't seem to escape from, it's difficult not to wallow in guilt and allow it to continue to be a false motivator in our lives. The answer, of course, is to get out of that vicious cycle of sin-confess, sin-confess, sin-give up.

I didn't think that was possible. But one day a preacher called Frank came to our church, and described exactly the situation I was trapped in. Then he said, "Do you want to know how to get out of that?" I really, really did and waited with bated breath for his next sentence.

"It's quite simple. Just stop."

"Hmm...," I thought, "Thanks for nothing, Frank! I've tried that several times and it doesn't work. In fact, it was the very first thing I tried."

But he went on to show from Romans 6 that if the Bible says that the power of sin is broken in our lives as Christians, it really is, whether it feels like it or not. I remember going home from church that day feeling confused. I went upstairs, knelt down, and said something like, "Lord God, it says in Romans 6 that the power of sin is broken in my life. That really doesn't feel true. But I choose to believe it."

To my surprise, I walked away from that issue then and there and, although I've been tempted, I've never fallen for it again. The remedy to being stuck in a sin doesn't always come as quickly as it did to me at that time, but I now know that all of us who are holy ones really do have everything we need to deal with sin and live the life that God has for us. And if that doesn't seem true, it's not a question of God needing to do something more. It's about our understanding who we are and what we have in Christ.

FREE OR SLAVES?

Consider this key verse:

> It is for freedom that Christ has set us free. Stand firm, then, and do not let yourselves be burdened again by a yoke of slavery. (Galatians 5:1)

Notice three things:

- Again it's written in the past tense. Christ has *already* set us free.
- The responsibility to stand firm in that freedom is given firmly to us—it's not about asking God to do anything more.
- And the sobering thing: if we don't learn to stand firm, we can lose our freedom and end up as slaves again.

When Paul talks about "freedom" he focuses on two things: freedom from sin and freedom from the demands of the Law. It's a word borrowed from the language of slavery, which was a brutal reality in the Roman Empire so it would have been very familiar to his original readers.

The idea that someone can be totally owned by someone else who can do to them—or force them to do—whatever they choose is horrifying. If you were in that position and were suddenly given your freedom, why would you ever want to return to being a slave?

It's equally ridiculous that, having been set free from the compulsion to sin and from having to obey rules and regulations, we would willingly go back to that. And yet, we do.

But the great news is that, if we realize we have allowed ourselves to be "burdened by a yoke of slavery," it is totally resolvable. We can stop settling for second best. We can take hold of our freedom again and continue our journey of growing as disciples of Jesus who bear much fruit.

Even after I had escaped my sin-confess cycle and taken hold of my freedom in Christ, I'm not sure I understood how I had done it or, to be more precise, why what I did was so effective. I now understand more, and in this chapter, want to help us understand why all of us can break that sin-confess-give up cycle and can experience being "more than conquerors" (Romans 8:37) in daily life.

FREEDOM FROM SIN

The most comprehensive teaching in the Bible about all this is found in Romans chapters 6 to 8. It's absolutely critical that we understand it.

A confession: I thought I might be able to improve on the Apostle Paul's teaching by taking just a few key quotations out of those chapters and explaining it all a little more concisely than he was able to do. You won't be surprised to learn that I soon discovered that Paul had a much better grasp of this than I do—and is a much better teacher than I am! So I think I'll allow him to speak for himself. Would you care to accompany me on a journey through Romans 6 so that we can let this crucial teaching sink into our minds and permeate our lives?

Up to this point in the book of Romans, Paul has been outlining how sin came into the world through one man, Adam, and how it affected every single one of his descendants, who all became subject to death. He has explained that Jesus' death dealt with the *penalty* of sin and brought justification and righteousness as free gifts to those who would receive them.

At the end of Chapter 5, Paul stresses that no matter how bad the consequences of Adam's sin were God's grace "abounded." In other words, God's grace was bigger. So with that great truth ringing in our ears, let's join him in Romans 6:

> *What shall we say then? Are we to continue in sin that grace may abound? By no means! How can we who died to sin still live in it? Do you not know that all of us who have been baptized into Christ Jesus were baptized into his death? We were buried therefore with him by baptism into death, in order that, just as Christ was raised from the dead by the glory of the Father, we too might walk in newness of life. For if we have been united with him in a death like his, we shall certainly be united with him in a resurrection like his. (Romans 6:1-5 ESV)*

He has been talking about Christ's death but now he moves on to focus on Christ's *resurrection*. He wants us to realize that we are free not only from the *penalty* of sin—accomplished when Jesus died—but also from the power of sin over us—accomplished when Jesus rose to life.

What I mean by "the power of sin," of course, is the compulsion to keep returning to sin even though we know it's harming us and others, and even though in our heart of hearts we don't want to.

As I write this, it is the week before Easter. For many years after I became a Christian, I had a persistent nagging feeling that I didn't really understand what Easter was about. I somehow sensed that I wasn't "getting it."

Of course, I joined in on Good Friday to remember the death of Jesus on the Cross and celebrate the fact that He dealt with the penalty of sin—our true guilt before God—by cancelling our certificate of debt. I understood that in some way we had died with Him. I was fine with Good Friday. It was Easter Sunday that got me.

What would you say Easter Sunday is about? What do we celebrate on that day? If you had asked me at that time, I'd have said that we celebrate the fact that Jesus rose from the dead. I didn't take it any further than that.

But notice Paul's emphasis. Of course the fact that Jesus rose from the dead is central to his argument but it's not the final thing. The point of Jesus' new life was so that "we too might walk in newness of life."

Once I understood that Easter Sunday is all about the fact that *we* have been raised to new life with Christ, it all fell into place!

"If we have been united with him in a death like his, we shall certainly be united with him in a resurrection like his." We didn't just *die* with Christ—we now *live* with Him. Not just in the sense of "I'm going to go to Heaven when I die", but right now on this earth we have a totally new quality of resurrection life.

We have become completely new creations. We are holy ones. God's Spirit lives in us. Right now! And it's this "walking in newness of life" that enables us to deal with the *power* of sin.

The concept of "life" is fundamental throughout the Bible. God warned Adam that if he ate from the tree, he would die. When he did eat, he didn't die physically (at least not immediately) but he did die spiritually. He lost that abundant spiritual life that God designed us to have—that connection to God, that sense of significance, security, and acceptance. So it's no surprise that, when Jesus was explaining why He had come, He said it was so that we "may have life, and have it to the full" (John 10:10).

The reason that we find it much easier to identify ourselves with Jesus in His death rather than in His resurrection is, of course, our historic and cultural emphasis on sin and guilt. But all of that was dealt with on Good Friday. Let's move on to live in the glorious truth of Easter Sunday! This is where we'll find the way out of slavery to sin. This is where we'll learn to live in our glorious new identity as holy ones.

> *We know that our old self was crucified with him*
> *in order that the body of sin might be brought to*

*nothing, so that we would no longer be enslaved
to sin. (Romans 6:6 ESV)*

Yes, we walk in newness of life, and we are now holy ones at the deepest level of our being. But we still live in a physical body, and we still face temptations and urges to return to sinful ways. Paul says that they are, however, "brought to nothing" so that we no longer have to give in to the compulsion to sin.

Paul mentions "the body of sin" here and talks a lot about a related term, the "flesh," in Romans 6 to 8.

He is not saying that our physical bodies are inherently sinful or evil or anything like that—the words he uses for "body" and "flesh" are used positively in other contexts. But he is using the body and the flesh that covers it as a metaphor for the drives and impulses towards sin that we all still have, even though we are now holy ones.

"Flesh" is a literal translation of the Greek word "sarx" which refers to the flesh on our bodies. Our word "sarcophagus" is a combination of "sarx" and "phagein" so literally means "flesh-eating"—quite a graphic description of the function of a stone coffin!

Metaphorically "the flesh" came to mean the part of us that wants to be self-reliant rather than dependent on God, the part of us that has a tendency towards sin even though we are new creations. I think of it as "what comes naturally to a fallen human being."

Because "flesh" is a rather archaic-sounding word in English, until recently some Bible translations *interpreted* the word as "sinful nature" rather than translating it literally.

I totally understand why they did this, but the use of the word "nature" (which is not there in the original text) causes a potential problem. It might lead Christians to believe that their very nature is sinful when the Bible is clear that we are now holy ones and share God's divine nature (2 Peter 1:4). We do still have all our old self-reliant thought patterns and tendencies ("the flesh"). But these are not who we are. They are not part of our *nature* but will die with our physical body while we go on to eternal life.

If the translators had interpreted "sarx" as something like "sinful tendency" then I would have no issue at all—it's that word "nature" that is potentially misleading. Thankfully most translations have now moved away from referring to the flesh as "sinful nature" (generally reverting to "flesh") but if you do come across that phrase in your Bible, it's good to know that the original writer did not at all intend to say that your very nature is sinful. If you are in Christ, the truth is the direct opposite of that. You are a holy one!

And that means that, even though we still have the flesh, we don't have to follow its urges any longer. We can choose at any moment to live by the Spirit rather than the flesh (Galatians 5:16). We are back in the same position Adam was before he sinned: we have a genuine choice.

Let's return to Paul's argument as he gets to the crux of his first point:

> For one who has died has been set free from sin. Now if we have died with Christ, we believe that we will also live with him. We know that Christ, being raised from the dead, will never die again; death no longer has dominion over him. For the death he died he died to sin, once for all, but the life he lives he lives to God. So you also must consider yourselves dead to sin and alive to God in Christ Jesus. (Romans 6:7-11 ESV)

Paul's point is that, just as Christ will never be subject to death again, so we need never be subject to slavery to sin again.

If someone you know dies, that ends your relationship with them. Now, exactly who does Paul say has died in these verses? We have! We died with Christ, and our death to sin has ended our relationship with sin.

So, here are two key questions for you:

Have you died with Christ?

Have you been set free from sin?

If you said "yes" to the first question, I hope you said "yes" to the second question too! In fact, if you are following Paul's logic, you must: "For one who has died has been set free from sin."

Based on this, Paul gives us three instructions and the first is, "Consider yourselves dead to sin and alive to God in Christ Jesus." That verb "consider" is written in a tense that we don't have in English. It's the present continuous tense so it means something like, "keep on considering, every day, all of the time."

You have to make the choice—and keep on making the choice—to believe the truth that you are alive in Christ and dead to sin; that you have a genuine choice; that when sin makes its appeal, you have the power to say "no" to it.

A famous Christian writer, Watchman Nee, struggled for nine years to work out how to "consider himself" dead to sin so that he didn't keep returning to sin. He thought it was like some mind-over-matter thing—like he had to keep "considering" it to be true even though it wasn't, as if that would make it true. But that just didn't work. He was still caught in sin. And he got to the point where he was ready even to give up his ministry if he couldn't sort this issue out. One day, he had a lightbulb moment and suddenly understood that all he had to do was believe what was actually *already* true. That he was dead to sin and alive to God.

And that was it. Suddenly he knew the truth. And the truth set him free, and he was able to make good choices. From that point on he would go around saying, "Praise the Lord that I am dead!"

My friend Mike Quarles was a pastor and an alcoholic. He had tried everything he could think of to escape from the grips of alcoholism. He listed them at one time:

1. Consistent Quiet Time

2. Bible Study

3. Fasting

4. Visitation Evangelism

5. Christian Twelve Step Program

6. Accountability group

7. Hundreds Of AA meetings And Five Different Sponsors

8. Christian Counselors

9. Christian Psychiatrist

10. Secular Psychiatrist

11. Christian Psychologist

12. Secular Psychologist

13. Addictions Counselor

14. Flew To New Jersey And Spent Three days With an Addictions Specialist

15. Secular Treatment Center

16. Christian Treatment Center

17. Read Every Book On Addiction I Could Find

18. Healing Of Memories Session

19. Baptism Of The Spirit Session

20. Casting Out Of Demons Session (Twice)

21. Public Confession

22. Group Therapy

23. Took The Drug Antabuse

24. Disciplined By My Church

25. Rigid Schedule With Every Minute Planned

26. Hundreds Of Hours Studying Scriptural Principles

27. Memorized Chapters Of Scripture

28. Discipleship Groups

29. Prayer

30. Promises To God And My Wife

But nothing worked.

Finally, at rock bottom, he was persuaded to listen to some talks by someone whose theology he knew he disagreed with. This is how he describes what happened:

> I was driving along listening to the third tape, which was "Co-crucifixion is Past Tense." Bill Gillham was teaching on our death with Christ. Romans 6:6,7 says, "For we know that our old self was crucified with Him so that the body of sin might be done away with, that we should no longer be slaves to sin—because anyone who has died has been freed from sin." What is this? I have died with Christ, and I have been freed from sin? That's what I need, but how do I make that true in my life? Then Gillham was saying, "It is not something you do, it is something that has been done; our death with Christ is past tense, the old person that we were 'was crucified' and 'anyone who has died has been freed from sin'." And then he said, "You 'died to sin' (Romans 6:2), you are 'dead to sin' (Romans 6:11). I know you don't act dead to sin, you don't feel dead to sin, you don't even look dead to sin, you think that is just a positional truth, that's just the way God sees me, that's just what God says about me. Listen, the way God sees you is reality. What God says is the truth."

> It was at that moment that the lights came on, and in that moment I knew the truth. I knew I had died with Christ and the old sin-loving sinner had died and was no more. Oh I had believed the lie and acted like it for all these years, but that

85

was not who I was. I now knew the truth was that I was dead to sin whether I acted like it, felt like it, looked like it, or anyone else believed it—because God said I was. I also knew the truth that I was free, ".... because anyone who has died has been freed from sin" (Romans 6:7). Jesus said, "Then you will know the truth and the truth will set you free" (John 8:32). I had believed the lie that I was a hopeless, helpless alcoholic and had lived in bondage all the years that I believed it. But less than 24 hours away from a drunk, I knew without a shadow of a doubt, that I, Mike Quarles, was a child of God who was "in Christ" because I had died with Christ, was dead to sin and had been freed from sin. Free at last, free at last! Praise God I was free at last!!!!!!!!![1]

And he was. God went on to use Mike powerfully. For many years he worked with Freedom In Christ Ministries equipping churches to help people caught in addiction find their freedom.

When I first met Mike, I asked him why he became an alcoholic in the first place, and he explained that his father was very strict and used to call him a "lousy no-good bum." He said that even as an adult, every day he heard his father's voice ringing in his head, and it was to counter this pain that he used alcohol. I said something like, "So now that you are free, presumably you don't hear that voice in your head anymore?" and Mike surprised me when he said that actually he sometimes still did. If hearing his father's voice was what caused the alcoholism and he still heard it, I didn't understand how he was now free. I must have looked very confused because he added, "The difference now is that I know it's not true. So it doesn't bother me."

---

1. Retrieved from https://freedfrom.wordpress.com/testimonies/mike-quarles-testimony/ on 25 March 2024. Mike has written many books on addiction.

It really is *knowing* the truth that sets us free. And conversely it's *not* knowing the truth that keeps us in bondage.

So, is Paul saying that we don't have to sin? Yes, he absolutely, definitely is! God has made you a holy one and called you to live a holy life—and He's made it genuinely possible for you to do that. At any given moment, you are free to make the right choice. That's the freedom for which Christ set you free!

To be perfectly honest with you, even though I too have come to the amazing revelation that I am now alive to God and dead to sin, very often I wake up in the morning and feel very alive to sin and dead to God. And I'm sure the Apostle Paul did too. His encouragement to us is to ignore our feelings and stick to the facts (as crazy as that may sound!). Whatever we *feel*, the truth is that we *are* now alive to Christ and dead to sin. This is not something we need to strive to *make* true. It just *is* true. We simply need to make a choice to agree with God's Word and live accordingly.

Paul is not saying that we're going to be living a life of sinless perfection and I am not saying that either. From time to time we are going to make a bad choice. One day we will be given wonderful new bodies and the flesh will be no more. But for now, we still have the flesh and the reality is that we will give in from time to time, and we will fall for temptation from time to time: "if we say we have no sin we deceive ourselves" (1 John 1:8 ESV).

But here's the wonderful news: when we do go wrong, it doesn't in any way change who we are or how much God loves us.

THE CONSEQUENCES OF BAD CHOICES

There may be a question in your mind at this point along the lines of, "Well, if I'm already forgiven when I sin and it doesn't change my relationship with God or who I am in Him, then does it really matter if I sin a little here and there?" And let me be honest with you. Once you get hold of grace and the truth of your forgiveness, it's easy to start going down that path and many do.

But beware! It's a blind alley that will lead you right into the hands of the enemy.

We tend to think the problem when we sin is that we've disappointed God, that we've let Him down, that we are guilty. But there's a much more significant issue. Paul goes on to explain very clearly why continuing to sin is a massive problem. Here's his second instruction to us:

> Let not sin therefore reign in your mortal body, to
> make you obey its passions. (Romans 6:12 ESV)

Though we have died to sin and ended our relationship with it, sin is still very much alive. It's like a nasty "ex" trying to get back into our lives. If we let down our guard and allow it in, we can rekindle our relationship with it, and the consequence is that it will "reign" in our bodies where Jesus alone should be Lord. And when it reigns, it will keep drawing us back, and we will feel powerless to resist.

Have you noticed that Paul talks about "sin" almost as if it's a person? He may or may not be directly equating it with Satan here, but sin is definitely a spiritual warfare issue. In John 14:30 (ESV), Jesus talks about the way Satan works. He uses legal language, saying to his disciples, "I will no longer talk much with you, for the ruler of this world is coming. He has no *claim* on me..."

In Ephesians 4:26-27, Paul says that if we let the sun go down on our anger (which is not in itself a sin but just an emotion), we allow it to turn into the sin of unforgiveness and at that point we give the devil a foothold—a place of influence—in our lives.

Sin is the mechanism Satan uses to get a claim on us. That is the issue with continuing to sin. Footholds of the enemy stop us from being fruitful, hinder our intimacy with the Father, and hold us back. They allow our nasty "ex" to reign in Jesus' place and turn us back into its slaves, so that we keep returning to sin even though we don't want to.

So how do we stop giving sin permission to reign in our bodies?

Here's the third instruction:

> *Do not offer any part of yourself to sin as an*
> *instrument of wickedness, but rather offer yourselves*
> *to God as those who have been brought from death*
> *to life; and offer every part of yourself to him as an*
> *instrument of righteousness. (Romans 6:13)*

If you have a car, you can choose to use it either to give someone in need a ride to church, or to deal drugs. In the same way, we have a choice as to how we use our bodies. We can either present ourselves to sin or to God. There's no middle ground. Every day we make that choice.

James gives us a similar instruction:

> *Submit yourselves, then, to God. Resist the devil, and*
> *he will flee from you. (James 4:7)*

If we open the door to the enemy through sin, we allow sin to reign in our bodies, to become our master. Our natural reaction is to apologize to God, ask for His forgiveness, and determine to do better next time. That's good, but it isn't enough.

Confession is part of submitting. But we mustn't stop there. We finish the job by actively resisting the devil and reclaiming the place of influence that our sin gave him.

Our worldview can get in the way of understanding this biblically. We're not living in a world where it's just God and us. And it isn't a battle just between us and our flesh. Throughout the Bible, from the garden of Eden in Genesis to the last battle in Revelation, we learn about evil spiritual beings who oppose God and His people. Satan's objective is "to steal and kill and destroy" (John 10:10). And he will use any foothold you give him through sin to hold you back.

If we've grown up in the West, we might acknowledge the existence of the devil and demons theologically, but our worldview predisposes us to ignore the reality of the spiritual world when it comes to living our daily lives. So even though we have the spiritual authority to deal with the spiritual world, we get duped into doing nothing. Our passivity means the devil keeps a foothold in our lives.

On the other hand, if you've grown up in a different culture, you might have a far greater awareness of the spiritual realm, but the chances are it's one rooted in fear that gives far too much power to the devil and the demonic.

Suppose I was shown into a room, told that I must under no circumstances open the green door in the corner, and left alone. Obviously I wonder why on earth I can't open the door and what is behind it. Suddenly I hear a cute little voice from behind the door saying, "Help! Let me out, I'm trapped!" I say, "I've been told I mustn't open the door. Who are you?" The response I get is a soft attractive voice saying, "Come on, please open the door. It's perfectly safe. Don't you want to see what's in here? You do, don't you? Please."

So, I make sure no one is looking and open the door. And out comes a huge dog which sinks its teeth into my leg and won't let go. The voice now turns mean. "That was stupid! What were you thinking, you failure? Aren't you ever going to learn?"

Now, this dog is invisible. All I know is I did something wrong and now I'm in pain and feel terrible. Who do I get angry with—the dog? No, because I don't know it's there. I get angry with myself.

I confess: "Father God, I opened the door. Please forgive me!" Does He? Of course. In fact I'm already forgiven.

But I'm still walking around, limping, with an invisible dog hanging off my leg telling me I'm a failure! And the more I seem unable to get out of the cycle, the more the enemy accuses me and the more shame I feel for what I've done. God's power to enable me to live righteously is short-circuited. It makes it difficult for me to resist further temptation or make the right choice.

So what should we do? Start by confessing: "Father God, I opened the door. I'm so sorry." We then need to finish what James says to do by actively resisting the devil and taking back the foothold we've given to the enemy that allows sin to reign in our body. I need to tell the dog to let go of my leg and be gone, then close the door to stop other dogs from coming in. But why would a big scary dog obey little old me?

Because of who I now am. We've seen that we have died with Christ and risen with Him to newness of life. But there's even more!

And God raised us up with Christ and seated us with him in the heavenly realms in Christ Jesus, in order that in the coming ages he might show the incomparable riches of his grace, expressed in his kindness to us in Christ Jesus. (Ephesians 2:6-7)

We have also ascended with Him to the right hand of the Father, the ultimate place of power and authority, and right now in Him we are "far above all rule and authority, power and dominion, and every name that is invoked, not only in the present age but also in the one to come" (Ephesians 1:21).

When we issue a command to the enemy, provided we have first dealt with any right we have given him to reign in our bodies, he can only obey. Most Christians have simply not been taught this. But it's actually quite straightforward. *The Steps To Freedom In Christ* and *The Steps To Experiencing God's Grace* are great ways to submit to God and resist the devil. We ask the Holy Spirit to show us where there are footholds of the enemy in our lives. We then renounce them and repent of them. To renounce something is to declare to God, and to the unseen spiritual world, that our agreement with, allegiance to, and our participation in that thing is over. To repent means to change our mind about our sin and turn away from it. It's a kind, gentle method that I use every year.

Once you renounce that sinful, shameful practice and stop allowing sin to use your body for its evil purposes, you will find God's strength to do what's right.

You see, the idea of having been set free by Jesus is to *stay* free. But you are free not to stay free. And if you choose to use your freedom in order to indulge in sin, you will find that it will turn you into a slave again. It will master you.

Jesus said some very sobering words: "Very truly I tell you, everyone who sins is a slave to sin" (John 8:34).

When you talk to Christian young people, they often want to know, "How far can I go in this area? Is this a sin? Can I do this? Can I not do that?" The pertinent question isn't, "How far can I go?" The real issue is, "Can I stop?" Because if you can't, you are a slave to sin. You have allowed sin to reign in your body. You've presented your body to sin as an instrument of unrighteousness. Even though Jesus set you free, you have allowed yourself to become burdened again by a yoke of slavery.

In any area of our lives, we are either free or we are a slave. It's an on-off switch: either you're free or you're not. Freedom isn't something that you gradually grow into. Freedom is something that you take hold of.

Let's consider one more verse from Romans 6 which brings this section to an intriguing conclusion:

> For sin will have no dominion over you, since you are
> not under law but under grace. (Romans 6:14 ESV)

We've understood that sin will have no dominion over us—that we no longer have to be slaves to it—but what has that got to do with law and grace?

The implication is that if we *were* under law, that is to say if our religion were about keeping to a set of rules, sin would have dominion over us. Why? We'll come back to that intriguing truth in a later chapter. For now let's consider a key principle when it comes to our behavior.

WHAT WE DO COMES FROM WHO WE ARE

Think about the huge contrast between the two sons at the end of the story we looked at in the first chapter.

When the younger son returns home, he discovers his true

identity as a son who is loved for who he is, not for what he has done. Even though he's behaved in the worst way imaginable, he now knows that the father loves him anyway, and he still has his place as a son. He has done nothing to earn it—it's sheer grace.

But the elder son refuses to come and celebrate. Instead, he continues to "slave away" with the hired servants in the fields, believing that if he is going to get anything at all from his father, he has to work to get it. He is not living out the identity of a son but that of a slave. In his last words in the story, we hear him defending himself on the basis of his performance, striving, and hard work.

Jesus told the story of the two sons in response to an accusation from the religious teachers that his behavior wasn't pleasing to God. And of course our behavior is important. The critical question in discipleship is, how do you get someone to behave in a way that is pleasing to God?

The Pharisees' answer was to give them lots and lots of laws, lots of things to do. And many of our discipleship programs tend to do that too.

But God's answer is to give us a whole new identity. Because what we do comes from who we are.

With our emphasis on doing, when Paul says "consider yourself to dead to sin," we tend to think he meant something like "you're not really dead to sin but if you consider that you are, you might have a chance." No! Paul is saying that you really are dead to sin and simply need to realize that truth. Then you will live accordingly.

Paul also says "our old self was crucified" (past tense) but our emphasis on doing has meant that most of us have understood it as "we must try hard to crucify our old self." We try and try to put the old self to death, and we can't do it. Why not? Because it's already dead! You cannot do for yourself what Christ has already done for you.

When Paul says, "You were once darkness, but now you are light in the Lord; walk as children of light" (Ephesians 5:8 NASB), we tend to read it as, "I must try hard to walk as a child of light" rather than what it plainly says. When you know that you *are* a child of light, you will *live* as a child of light. Automatically. Because what you do comes from who you are.

I now know that the very best starting point when it comes to helping someone grow into a fruitful disciple is to encourage them to embrace the truth about who they now are in Christ. This frees them from a sense of trying to act like they think a Christian should act and serving Jesus comes naturally rather than being a joyless trudge of "trying harder."

When someone has an issue in a marriage, for example, we look for great advice in the Bible. Where do we find it? Always in the second half of Paul's letters. The trouble is, if they have not processed the first half of Paul's letters, where he unfailingly teaches about who we now are in Christ, they simply cannot put into practice the good advice in the second half. We send people straight to the "doing" instructions, but Paul always precedes them with the "being" truths of who we are in Christ.

I once spoke at a church which had a thriving discipleship ministry based on Freedom In Christ's resources and teaching. It was run by a wonderful couple who had an amazing story. They told me that their marriage had broken down, seemingly irretrievably, and they had separated. Even though they were headed towards a divorce, they both kept coming to church, avoiding each other by going to different small groups.

Their church announced one day that all the small groups were going to go through the *Freedom In Christ Course*. Both the husband and wife were hugely impacted by the teaching and submitted to God and resisted the devil during *The Steps To Freedom In Christ* element.

Having resolved issues from their past, dealt with footholds of the enemy in their lives, embraced their identity in Christ, and forgiven each other during the process, they both independently realized that they loved each other, and the issues that seemed so intractable just faded away. At the point I met them, they had been back together for several years, were very much in love, and were leading a very fruitful discipleship ministry in their church.

A fruitful disciple is not someone who is trying to become pleasing to God, or trying to become a child of God. Your fruitfulness is likely to increase hugely when:

- You know that you are already pleasing to God, already His child—because of Christ.
- You know that you are not working for your salvation but working out your salvation.
- You obey God's commands, not because you feel you ought to out of a sense of obligation—but because you really want to, and know you will be able to, because you are free to make good choices.

Think about a beautiful butterfly. It used to be a creepy, crawly caterpillar, but by the amazing process of metamorphosis, it changed into a totally different creature. And it can fly! You used to be a sinner doomed to fail, but you have been transformed into a beautiful new creation in Christ. And you can fly above the flesh and sin.

However, if a butterfly gets caught in the rain, it's a sad sight. With wet wings, it ends up crawling slowly along the ground, acting just like a caterpillar. Even though we're not caterpillars anymore, we can go back to crawling in sin. Butterflies are supposed to fly free, but instead can end up *acting* like caterpillars. We are holy ones, but we can act like sinners.

If we do sin, we are free from condemnation. God never comes to us and says, "You are a sinner!" In fact, I think He says something which is pretty much the opposite of that: "Hey, you're not a sinner, you're a holy one. So why are you acting like a sinner?"

And when you, a holy one, act out of character and sin, it doesn't change God's love for you even a bit. Or the fact that His arms are open to you Or the fact that you are a holy one. But it does affect your fruitfulness.

We are genuinely free from the law of sin and death. At any given moment we have a real choice either to walk by the flesh or to walk by the Spirit.

And we're free from the law. In other words, we're free from having to behave in a particular way. God doesn't demand that we obey any rules. As Paul says in 1 Corinthians 10:23 (NASB): "All things are permitted." You don't have to "act like a Christian" anymore.

So why don't we just go out and do whatever we want to do, whatever the flesh puts into our minds—like the younger son did to start with? Let's read the whole verse: "All things are permitted, but not all things are of benefit. All things are permitted, but not all things build people up." If we offer the parts of our body to unrighteousness, we allow the enemy to rule in us, and we end up in that wretched sin-confess cycle where we don't bear any fruit.

What is freedom? My conclusion is this: all God has ever wanted is a people who will obey Him, not because they *have* to but because they choose to. And freedom is being in the position to do just that. Which is where you find yourself right now, unless (of course) you have offered parts of your body to unrighteousness and returned to slavery to sin.

But if you've done that, don't settle for second best! Resolve it! "Put on the Lord Jesus Christ and make no provision for the flesh" (Romans 13:14 ESV).

Continually work on your understanding of the truth about sin: how damaging it is to us. It promises you all this wonderful stuff, but at the end of the day it leads to bondage.

Recognize that legalism is bondage too. Working hard to obey rules, or because you think that God needs you to, or because people want you to, again leads to bondage. Serve God, to the best of your ability, not because you feel you have to but simply because you love Him so much and are free to make a good choice.

THE SERIOUSNESS OF SIN

Do not be deceived: God cannot be mocked. A man reaps what he sows. Whoever sows to please their flesh, from the flesh will reap destruction; whoever sows to please the Spirit, from the Spirit will reap eternal life. (Galatians 6:7-8)

Our actions have consequences. God loves us and tells us what is good for us and what is bad for us. If we choose to do what is bad for us, we will face consequences.

There is a tendency in our society and in the Church to minimize the seriousness of sin. To talk of "going wrong" or "making a mistake" rather than using Biblical language such as "sin" and "iniquities." Maybe you think I may have been slipping into that. Let me redress the balance.

When God made a covenant with Israel, it included blessings for obedience and curses for disobedience (see Deuteronomy 28). These curses included disease and plague.

Paul told the Corinthians that the sickness and death they were experiencing in their church came from "eating and drinking judgment on themselves" (1 Corinthians 11:28-30) because they were handling the bread and the wine wrongly.

King David was walking on his rooftop when his attention was captured by the sight of a beautiful woman bathing. He discovered that her name was Bathsheba, and that she was married to Uriah the Hittite, one of the commanders in his army. Despite that, David had Bathsheba brought to his palace and slept with her. She let him know some time later that she was pregnant. In a panic, David tried to hide what he had done by having Uriah brought home in the hope that he would sleep with his wife and think the baby was his own. But Uriah's sense of duty made him refuse to take things easy while his troops were facing danger so he slept elsewhere. David then had Uriah deliberately placed on the front line so that he was likely to be killed—which is what happened. David married Bathsheba, and her baby, a son, was born. David must have thought that he had got away with it but then Nathan the Prophet turned up. He helped David see how sinful his behavior had been.

> Then David said to Nathan, "I have sinned against the LORD."
>
> Nathan replied, "The LORD has taken away your sin. You are not going to die. But because by doing this you have shown utter contempt for the LORD, the son born to you will die." (2 Samuel 12:13-14)

And the baby boy did indeed die.

David's sin wreaked havoc in the lives of many people and in his own life.

After realizing exactly what he had done, he wrote Psalm 51. You may well find what he wrote quite astonishing:

> For I know my transgressions,
> and my sin is always before me.
> Against you, you only, have I sinned
> and done what is evil in your sight;
> so you are right in your verdict
> and justified when you judge.
> (Psalm 51:3-4)

He does not mention the people he hurt at all: the woman he forced to have sex with him; her husband whom he killed; the innocent child who died as a direct result. I don't think for a minute that he was making light of what he had done to them but he realized that above every other consideration, "Against You, You only, have I sinned."

Whoever else we hurt and whatever other damage we do, our sin's most serious effect is on our relationship with our Father God. When we sin, we declare our independence. We declare our lack of trust. We throw what He has done for us back in His face.

Sin is devastating for our own lives and for the lives of others. But above all for our relationship with God.

Now, in realizing that, don't lose sight of the fact that God has forgiven us and our relationship with Him is still intact. He is not the guy with the big stick looking to see if we have put a foot out of place—He is our loving Father looking anxiously for us to return.

But we must not allow those truths to make us think that sin is somehow not serious. If you're ever tempted to think that, take a moment to consider what needed to happen for our forgiveness and unconditional acceptance: the torture and death of the Son of God Himself.

THE WAY OUT OF TEMPTATION

Let's recap. We live in a fallen world, and we have an enemy who will assault our mind relentlessly in order to persuade us to sin and gain a foothold in our lives. Even though Jesus has set us free, and we have everything we need to live a godly life, we face daily pressure to sin and surrender our freedom.

Satan has observed your behavior over the years, and he knows where you are vulnerable. That's where he will attack. Your temptations will be unique to your specific area of vulnerability.

So, how can we resist temptation when it rears its ugly head?

Every temptation is an attempt to get you to live your life independently of God. The basis for that temptation is often legitimate needs for acceptance, significance, and security. The question is: are those needs going to be met by responding to the world, the flesh and the devil, or are they going to be met by God who promises to meet all your needs according to his glorious riches in Christ Jesus (see Philippians 4:19)?

Every temptation is based on a lie. Does money really give you permanent security? No! Can another person really fulfill your need to be accepted? Not completely. Does getting people to like you really make you significant? Of course not. We might ask King David, "Your Majesty, was a moment of lust and sexual gratification with Bathsheba worth the awful consequences?" Of course it wasn't. But wouldn't it have been good if he had realized that in advance? Getting these truths firm in our minds is crucial.

We have a very specific promise from God that we don't ever have to give in to temptation:

> No temptation has overtaken you except what is common to mankind. And God is faithful; he will not let you be tempted beyond what you can bear. But when you are tempted, he will also provide a way out so that you can endure it. (1 Corinthians 10:13)

I used to get really irritated with that verse because it didn't seem that there was a way out. The temptation was just so intense. "Where is it then, God?" I used to think.

I now know that this way of escape, the "fire exit" if you like, is always right at the beginning of being tempted. You have to recognize the exit and take it immediately.

Suppose you are struggling with online porn. It's late at night, you're alone and a thought comes into your head, "Why don't I just check how many likes I got on that post I made earlier?" You go online and another thought appears, "Well, I'm not tired, I'll just keep scrolling." Before you know it, you're on a porn site. Again.

Now, you can rationalize as much as you like, but actually as soon as you went online, the intention to end up on a porn site was there. Where is the way of escape? It's right at the beginning—when the tempting thought first comes into your mind. That's your opportunity to "take captive every thought to make it obedient to Christ" (2 Corinthians 10:5). Whether you admit it to yourself or not, the innocent-seeming thought prompting you to check your social media post was not innocent at all. Deep down inside you knew where it would end.

When next you're out strolling on the rooftop of your palace and you happen to glimpse an attractive person bathing, and a thought comes into your mind to find out who they are, learn to look away immediately and do not google them or check them out on social media!

If you can learn to recognize that innocent-seeming thought for what it actually is and throw it out, you can continue walking in freedom. But if you don't recognize and discard that tempting thought straightaway, it will lead to sin, which gives ground to your enemy.

It starts with fantasy and daydreaming about the attractive person. But Jesus was clear that lust is exactly the same as adultery. I got some great advice from a friend of mine a number of years ago. He said that when he is tempted to look for too long at an attractive member of the opposite sex, he declares, "Jesus is my Lord and Sarah is my wife!" And it seems to work for me too even though my wife's name is Zoë (sorry!).

You may find it helpful to think of your mind as an airport where you are the air traffic controller. A lot of thoughts ask for permission to land. But you have complete control over which will land and which will be turned away. You have to decide right at the outset, however. You have to learn to take charge of your mind. The moment you give a tempting thought permission to land, the chances of your being able to turn it away reduce significantly.

Suppose you are aware of an attraction to a work colleague, perhaps someone who works for you. One day your boss asks you to attend a conference, and you are to take the most appropriate person from your team with you. Who are you going to choose? Thoughts are circling in your mind asking for permission to land. This is the moment where you can take the way of escape— right at the outset. But you have to be aware enough of your own vulnerabilities to recognize what is going on. Then you will do whatever it takes to make sure that you and this particular colleague are not the ones who go to the conference together.

But if you don't do that, and you find yourself telling this attractive colleague, "There's a conference coming up in a couple of weeks' time—can you make it?," then you can rationalize as much as you like ("Well, they are the best qualified"). But, the truth is that you are being drawn to spend time with them inappropriately, and it's the start of a slippery slope.

Once that process is underway, your chances of turning it around diminish rapidly. It's not that you couldn't stop it, but it becomes more and more difficult.

The bottom line is that there is a way out of every temptation you face. At any given moment you can avoid falling into sin. It requires a constant commitment to believing the truth, being relentlessly honest with ourselves, and taking radical action to avoid sin.

What are the temptations you face most often? Are you aware of the innocent-seeming thoughts the enemy feeds you to persuade you to fall for them?

Have you worked out that sin never delivers what it promises? You may temporarily feel better but in the long run it will make you feel much worse.

And don't fall for the lie that always accompanies the temptation, the one that says that your specific sin is "no big deal."

DRAW NEAR TO THE THRONE OF GRACE

Yet even when we go wrong, we are still under God's grace—not some legalistic system that demands a punishment. And if we have allowed sin to reign, we know how to resolve it:

1. Submit to God *and* resist the devil;
2. Know that you are now dead to sin and alive to God;
3. Make the choice every day not to let sin reign in your body by offering every part of your body to God rather than to sin.

In any area of your life, you are either free or you are a slave. You don't *grow* into freedom. You *take hold* of it.

If you are struggling with a deeply ingrained issue, it's good to get some support from mature Christian friends. We all need support and encouragement to hang on to the truth. My wife and I had the privilege to walk alongside a lady who resolved huge issues in her life. Afterwards she came up with this helpful phrase: "You alone can do it but you can't do it alone."

She recognized that she already had everything she needed but also that she needed help and encouragement from others to use what she had been given. As we supported her, we never tried to "do it for her" but essentially reminded her who she was and what she had in Christ. And we saw her blossom as she learned to act as the child of God she was.

It can help to have someone who agrees to hold us accountable. Maybe they will call once a week and ask how we are doing. Just knowing they're going to call and ask the question can be really helpful in avoiding temptation.

Before we finish this chapter, I want you to hear some powerful, refreshing words of grace about Jesus, who is our great High Priest:

> *For we do not have a high priest who is unable to sympathize with our weaknesses, but one who in every respect has been tempted as we are, yet without sin. (Hebrews 4:15 ESV)*

He totally gets it. He understands! He knows what it's like to live in this fallen world with temptation on every side. He didn't fall for it himself, but He knows your weaknesses. And He doesn't condemn you for them. He actually sympathizes with you.

> *Let us then with confidence draw near to the throne of grace, that we may receive mercy and find grace to help in time of need. (Hebrews 4:16 ESV)*

His heart is always that we should draw near with confidence, not crawl in like miserable worms. If we've gone wrong, we'll find nothing but mercy, forgiveness and understanding. If we're facing temptation, we'll find grace to overcome.

God loves you so much. No matter where you are right now, He has things for you to do and fruit for you to bear.

What you *do* comes from who you *are*. And you are a pure, holy child of the Living God. You are victorious. In fact, you are *more* than a conqueror in Christ!

Draw near. Receive mercy. Find grace to help in your time of need.

MAKING THE GRACE CONNECTION

There were two caterpillars talking when a butterfly flew past. Looking up at it, one said to the other, "You'll never get me up in one of those things!"

We can all too easily be butterflies who are behaving like caterpillars.

Could today be the day that you take hold of the truth of who you have become and start to fly with God?

> **Glorious Father, the God of our Lord Jesus Christ, please give me the Spirit of wisdom and revelation, so that I may know You better. I pray that the eyes of my heart may be enlightened in order that I may know the hope to which You have called me, the riches of Your glorious inheritance in Your holy**

people, and Your incomparably great power for us who believe. Amen.

Taking The Fire Exit

The Bible promises in 1 Corinthians 10:13 that there is a way out of every temptation you face. At any given moment, you can avoid falling into sin. It requires a constant commitment to believing the truth and a willingness to take charge of your mind. Spend some time thinking about the following questions, allowing the Holy Spirit to guide you.

- What are the temptations that you tend to fall for most often?
- For each one, what are the seemingly innocent thoughts the enemy feeds you to persuade you to fall for them?
- What lies are behind the tempting thoughts?
- The way of escape, the "fire exit," is always right at the beginning of the process of being tempted. For each of your temptations, what would it look like for you to take it?

Breaking Sin-Confess Cycles

If you are frustrated that you return again and again to the same sins, I invite you to speak out loud the declaration below (which is based on Romans 6 and James 4). It will help you resolve to live out of your new identity in Christ instead of depending on your own strength. Speak it out every day as long as it takes.

> **I declare that I am now a new creation in Christ. I am dead to sin and alive to God. I confess the sin of** [specifically name the habitual sin] **and turn away from it.**

I declare that the sin of [specifically name the habitual sin] does not rule me any longer and I renounce its control of me. Jesus, who lives in me, is my loving Master and Ruler and all that I am now belongs to Him.

Thank You, Jesus, that You have made me a saint, a holy one, so I can glorify You in my body. Therefore I refuse to offer my body to be used to commit unrighteousness. Instead, I submit all that I am to my Heavenly Father who raised me to life with Christ.

I now gladly offer the parts of my body: my heart; eyes; ears; mouth; tongue; hands; feet; sexual organs; mind; understanding; mental powers; emotions; imagination and reasoning to God, and I choose to use the parts of my body only for righteousness, completely relying on the power of His Holy Spirit within me to accomplish this.

So I submit myself completely to God and resist the devil who must flee from me now (James 4:7).

CHAPTER 5

COURAGEOUS!

WHAT HAS GOD PREPARED FOR YOU TO DO?

One of my favorite verses is Ephesians 2:10: "For we are God's handiwork, created in Christ Jesus to do good works, which God prepared in advance for us to do."

The Greek word used for "workmanship" literally means a work of art. I like to think of God as a sculptor carefully chiseling away at my life so that something beautiful gradually emerges from a featureless block of stone. Perhaps you might prefer to think of yourself as a breathtaking painting appearing on a canvas or a beautiful poem or a complex novel.

God's primary focus is on what we are *like*—our character—because what we do should spring naturally from who we *are*. But this verse goes on to tell us that He has been thinking about what He wants us to do since before the beginning of time. God has planned some specific things for you and me to do, and He's preparing us for them.

You might want to pause for a moment to consider this truth: Almighty God Himself has looked at you and in His love and wisdom has carefully prepared things specifically for you to do. He knows you so well and has taken pains to ensure that they are exactly right for you. He doesn't *need* your help but in His grace, He invites you to work with Him. Your life is going to be the most fruitful and satisfying when you do that!

In my experience, God tends to reveal to us only gradually exactly what these good works are. He gives us a direction to head in and, as we respond in faith, we learn more and more about what He has in mind. And He uses the experiences we go through—even the negative ones that He didn't plan—to prepare us for these good works, to chisel away at His work of art.

FEAR—THE ENEMY OF FAITH

One of the works God had prepared in advance for a young man called Joshua was to lead the Israelites across the River Jordan and take the land that He had promised them. It was a very scary prospect because the land was full of people who didn't want to move out. Some of them were very large and had a nasty array of weapons!

We get a pretty good idea about how Joshua was feeling by what God says to him: "Just as I was with Moses, so I will be with you. I will not leave you or forsake you. Be strong and courageous" (Joshua 1:5-6a ESV).

God then repeats Himself: "Only be strong and very courageous" and adds an instruction, "being careful to do according to all the law that Moses my servant commanded you. Do not turn from it to the right hand or to the left, that you may have good success wherever you go" (Joshua 1:7 ESV).

God then repeats Himself yet again: "Be strong and courageous. Do not be frightened, and do not be dismayed, for the Lord your God is with you wherever you go" (Joshua 1:9).

So three times in nine verses God tells him to be strong and courageous. Why? Precisely because He knows that Joshua was feeling quite the opposite—weak and frightened. How could Joshua be strong and courageous? Not in his own strength or abilities but simply in the fact that God Himself promised to be with him.

Because God is always working on our hearts to make us an even better work of art, our Christian lives will always involve facing fear.

Fear is the enemy of faith. But paradoxically it can really help us to build our faith as we learn to trust God more and more. Walking by faith boils down to making a daily choice to act as God would have us act regardless of scary circumstances. The writer to the Hebrews helps us see the world as it actually is when he tells us, "He has said, 'I will never leave you nor forsake you.' So we can confidently say, 'The Lord is my helper; I will not fear; what can man do to me?'" (Hebrews 13:5-6 ESV)

But if we allow it to, fear will hem us in and make us change course away from God's calling on our lives. Fear is another of those false motivators that, if we allow it to, can govern our major decisions in life.

In this chapter we will consider how God's perfect love—His grace—can cast out fear. We'll see that courage comes from our relationship with the God who is love. And that courage is not the absence of fear: it's making the right choice in the face of that fear.

WALKING BY FAITH

I'm not a natural leader. And I have no formal theological training. So it seems ridiculous to me that one of the things God prepared in advance for me is to be President of Freedom In Christ Ministries International at this time. I'm not entirely sure what God's purposes are in this, but I suspect it's to make crystal clear to anyone looking on that whatever good He does through Freedom In Christ, it's down to Him and not to me.

As I write, the ministry is facing huge financial uncertainty. Again! And this is entirely normal. Neil Anderson, the founder of the ministry, has reminded me several times over the years that God wants us to walk by faith, and if we are not constantly having to do that, there may well be something wrong.

One great piece of advice I received is, "Don't doubt in the darkness what God has shown you in the light." In other words, just because things are difficult now, don't assume that you heard wrongly from God. Trust what He said to you when things weren't so tough and persevere through. Difficulties we encounter are not necessarily things to be "prayed out of the way." They can be there in order to grow our faith and help us persevere.

The truth is that, if we are doing what He has told us to, then He will provide. There is absolutely no reason to be concerned. But it is a challenge to persevere when everything around you screams that God is not real and He won't provide. It is a constant battle not to panic but to remind ourselves that, since we have discerned through prayer some specific things that God wants to do through us, we can absolutely expect Him to provide everything we need.

As I say, this is normal. Having lived like this for many years, I am able to look back at how God has worked in the past. Let me share one story.

A couple of years ago, we discerned that God wanted us to employ a certain person full-time, and there was no spare income to cover the cost. I really struggled with the decision to make a job offer to someone who would then go on to give up their existing job and had a family to support. It is one thing for me to make a decision to give up my own source of income in response to what God tells me to do. Quite another to ask someone else to do that.

Zoë and I have a wonderful team of intercessors who pray for us, and I shared with them how I was struggling to know what to do. By the end of that day, one of them (who is based in a different country) emailed me to say that someone had called him to ask what needs Freedom In Christ had. He had shared a number of local needs and this particular need too. Immediately, this amazing person said they would give a large amount to the need—which amounted to about 40% of the salary we needed for one year. It was incredible and so encouraging—a gift of that size is very rare. Nevertheless, as I thought about it, I realized that it wasn't actually enough—yes, it would cover a few months but then what?

The following day I got another email from my intercessor telling me that the donor had called again saying they sensed from God that they weren't giving enough and would double their previous pledge. He also told me that they had transferred the money already to our account. When we checked our account, we were expecting an amount of 80% of the first year's salary, but it was almost exactly 100%! The donor had quoted the amount of the gift in our currency but given it in a different currency—one of us had clearly got the exchange rate wrong but God had not!

It is not just the provision itself that encourages me. To see God show us so clearly that we had heard correctly reminded me that there will never come a time when we are not to walk by faith.

A few months ago, another of our intercessors had a picture God gave them to encourage us to continue walking by faith when finances do not seem sufficient for our needs. It is a picture of sliding electric doors such as you might find in an office building. They seem solidly shut as you walk towards them, and there is not even a handle you can use to open them. But as you approach— and always at the last minute—they suddenly open to let you through. It's rather like Moses' experience at the Red Sea. All he had to do was point his staff at the sea and it parted, rather like electric doors, and he and the Israelites were able to walk on through.

WHAT IS FEAR?

Fear is an emotional reaction that comes from the perception of impending danger or harm. It triggers a physical response in our bodies that is activated when we are confronted with something that appears to be dangerous or harmful.

It's not wrong to feel fear. In essence, fear is simply what we feel when we are alarmed. It is a natural God-given mechanism designed to protect us. If someone comes at us with a gun, for example, it is helpful to experience a strong emotion that will cause us to run away or defend ourselves.

So fear in itself is not a bad thing. We need to have a healthy fear of things that could harm us.

Healthy fear is fear that makes sense. Stuff like you don't try and pet a snarling, frothing-at-the-mouth dog. You don't walk in the middle of a road where there are fast cars. You don't put your hand into a fire. That kind of thing.

The problem comes when the fear is not a reasonable response to what is happening. For example, having a fear of all dogs, or fear of driving a car, or fear of any naked flame. That is when the fear is not reasonable or healthy.

When we give in to unhealthy fears—situations which make us feel frightened when we don't need to be—we find that they close down our lives to one degree or another. They work like the coils of a boa constrictor or python. These snakes do not subdue their prey using venom but use slow suffocation. The snake bites its victim to gain a hold and then rapidly coils itself around its victim's torso. As the victim breathes out, the coils tighten so that they are unable to take as deep a breath as before. After several times of exhaling and the snake's tightening coils, the victim suffocates, unable to breathe at all.

Someone who is afraid of heights takes an alternative route to work in order to avoid crossing a bridge. Or if that's not possible, they leave that job and take a new one closer to home. They won't go to certain places because it would entail crossing a bridge. It becomes more and more restricting.

Unhealthy fears gradually squeeze the joy out of living, reducing the victim's world into a smaller and smaller place.

More severe fears are known as phobias. They are usually the result of trauma, negative modeling from parents or other important adults, or lies that we have believed from the evil one. Sometimes they can become so suffocating that victims develop agoraphobia (literally "fear of the marketplace") where they become increasingly fearful of going anywhere because they think they might have a panic attack. Their world may shrink down to just their own house or room.

Most of us don't have those kinds of phobias. But that doesn't mean we aren't affected by unhealthy fears. It's just that we have learned to accommodate them.

Maybe we fear talking to people about Jesus. So we simply don't do it and have no expectation of doing it, ever.

Maybe we fear not having enough money, so we hold on tightly to what we have and end up working three jobs to the detriment of our family, or a stressful all-consuming job to the detriment of our health.

Many of us have a fear of failure that tempts us not to take risks, like asking a person out for coffee or discipling a young believer.

Maybe we have a fear of Satan and demons. So we walk away from any situation where we think they may be involved.

These fears may simply have become part of our lives so that we think that's just how we are. But they keep us from doing the things God has prepared in advance for us to do.

Fear immobilizes us. It confuses us. It makes it difficult to think straight.

We lose perspective, and it overwhelms us. All you can think about is yourself—your own safety, your own protection, or your own reputation.

Fear also stops us from being motivated by love. By definition, love is focused on others but when fear grips you, all you can think about is yourself.

But God has not given us that kind of cowardly spirit. He has given us a courageous one. When we act out of fear, we are acting out of character.

What are the top three fears that you face? What difference would it make in your life if you were able to overcome them?

The great news is that every unhealthy fear—no matter how severe—can be resolved in Christ. That doesn't mean you'll never experience the fear. It does mean that you can make the right choice in the face of that fear. Which is the definition of courage.

GOD IS IN YOUR BOAT

After a full day of teaching, Jesus' disciples were no doubt looking forward to settling down for the evening and getting some sleep. But Jesus had other ideas. He told them to get into a boat with Him and cross the treacherous Sea of Galilee. In the dark. They could have refused and said they would wait until morning when the journey would be much more straightforward, but they chose to obey.

When they were some way into their journey, a ferocious storm blew up and high waves crashed over the boat. The boat started to fill up with water, and things were looking pretty bleak.

> *Jesus was in the stern, sleeping on a cushion. The disciples woke him and said to him, 'Teacher, don't you care if we drown?' He got up, rebuked the wind and said to the waves, 'Quiet! Be still!' Then the wind died down and it was completely calm. He said to his disciples, 'Why are you so afraid? Do you still have no faith?' They were terrified and asked each other, 'Who is this? Even the wind and the waves obey him!'* (Mark 4:38–41)

The disciples asked two key questions that we would do well to ask in similar scary situations. After Jesus had demonstrated His power over the storm, they asked, "Who is this?" Well, it turns out that the person with them in their boat was God Himself. Almighty, all powerful, everlasting God. When God Himself is in your boat, you have no reason whatsoever to be afraid. Even if He appears to be asleep!

But the first question they asked was just as important: "Teacher, do you not care that we are perishing?" It's all very well having Almighty God there in your boat. But does He care? About you? And about what's happening in your boat right now?

As part of my role, I have the immense privilege of traveling widely to encourage those considering opening up new national offices or meet with our amazing teams around the world.

In fact, I write this the day after my fourteenth flight in an eight-week period in which I have visited no fewer than six countries on three continents.

Generally speaking, flying itself does not worry me because, having done it so often, I know from experience what a safe form of transport it is. But I must confess, I'm pleased that there are no further flights in my schedule in the coming months!

When I read my government's official advice on some of the countries I travel to, it makes the prospect of traveling there quite scary. Beware of violence, do not drive in certain areas, do not go to certain places, ensure you have been vaccinated against certain diseases, don't trust taxi drivers, and so on and so on. On top of that, I have a tendency to dwell on the worst possible things that could happen—it's not unusual for me to catch myself worrying about how I will get from the airport to my accommodation, whether the food will be OK, and that kind of thing.

So most trips cause me some level of fear—at least in the planning—and, if I'm honest, often when I'm making arrangements for a forthcoming trip, I'd rather call the whole thing off. But I know that this is my God-given calling, that it is something that God has prepared in advance for me to do, and so I go. And, of course, without fail the trips are wonderful, and it's such a privilege to meet amazing people through whom God is working in a marvelous way.

The Covid pandemic forced me to cancel a number of scheduled trips, and I had a couple of years where I did not get on a plane or even venture very far from home. In some ways, I quite enjoyed the enforced time at home that the pandemic imposed on us. I had become quite comfortable in our own little bubble.

As restrictions eased and life looked as if it might gradually return to normal, I was invited to attend a meeting of our Latin American team in Quito, Ecuador. It was exciting but felt like a huge thing to do. I knew four people who died of Covid during the first months of the pandemic, including a close friend and a former colleague, so I was well aware of the real dangers. The prospect of the trip loomed ahead of me, and I was quite apprehensive.

In the weeks leading up to the flight, I had a very painful knee injury and at times could barely walk a hundred yards. I wondered whether I could even make it through the airports. It was tempting to use this as a reason to cancel the trip. Everyone would understand.

A couple of days before I was due to depart, I consulted my doctor about my knee and was prescribed some strong painkillers and another pill to protect my stomach from their side effects.

The day after I started taking the medication, I had a strange sore throat and saw that I had a red patch like an ulcer on the roof of my mouth. The following day, it hurt quite a bit and did not look like anything I had seen before. I took a look at the leaflets that came with the pills and both medications listed "Stevens-Johnson Syndrome" as a serious potential side-effect and said that it typically starts with skin issues in the mouth and a sore throat. Researching further, I discovered that, although it is very rare, people like me who suffer from gout are genetically more disposed to it than the average person. It is classified as a "medical emergency" and can lead to very severe outcomes, including sepsis and death. The major symptoms take a few days to develop. Eek!

I ended up going to the hospital where a doctor told me that it was unlikely I had the condition but recommended stopping the medication. Nevertheless, the weekend before the trip, my brain went into overdrive, and I wondered if I was going to die. Again it would have been easy to call the trip off, and I would have preferred that.

But I set off for London Heathrow airport to catch a flight to Miami where I would pick up another flight to Quito.

I remember very well buckling myself into my seat and listening to the music playing in the plane as everyone got ready for the flight. It felt so familiar yet strangely surreal. I put on a face mask that would hopefully offer some protection from Covid. It restricted my breathing and felt quite claustrophobic.

When the plane took off, I suddenly felt very vulnerable. How many of these people were breathing out a virus that could potentially kill me? Would my knee hold up? I was due to arrive late at night—would someone actually be there to meet me? Knowing that I couldn't get off the plane for another 10 hours or so magnified my lack of control. I felt a rising panic.

In the midst of my personal storm, I faced the same two questions: Who is this in my boat (or in this case in my plane)? And does He care about me?

I reminded myself that God is God and that all things are under His control. And I reminded myself that He loves me and is looking out for me. I spent some time reaffirming my trust in God over all areas of my life and my commitment to serve Him in Freedom In Christ, or in whatever other way He might indicate. I wrote in my journal: "I am determined to trust God and seek Him and obey Him."

Peace returned. And I settled down to enjoy the flight and the rest of the trip which, of course, in retrospect I wouldn't have missed for the world.

We don't need to try hard to overcome our fear. We simply need to remind ourselves of what is actually true: that God is with us in every situation, and that He cares deeply about us. Then we can make the right choice despite our fear.

Jesus had some questions too—for the disciples—the first being, "Why are you so afraid?" They might have pointed out that the storm was fierce and the boat seemed likely to sink (quite reasonable). But there was a deeper reality, a deeper truth. For a start, it was Jesus who instigated the crossing by saying, "Let us go over to the other side of the lake." When that comes from the mouth of the Son of God Himself, is it not in effect a promise that you will reach the other side of the lake?

The other part of Jesus' rebuke was in response to the disciples' panicky question, "Teacher, don't you care that we are perishing?" He asked them, "Do you still have no faith?" He was in essence saying, "Don't you believe that I love you and care about you?" Fear is the enemy of faith.

Faith is making a choice to see the world as God says it is. Rather than seeing the situation as it really was, they were allowing their immediate circumstances to drown out the more significant reality: Jesus was in their boat. They were not on their own. God loved them so much and had great plans for them, and He would see to it that they would be fulfilled.

Jesus cares. He really cares. For you. He showed it by dying the most terrible death imaginable and He would have died for you if you had been the only person in the whole of history who needed Him to. God Himself is with you. God Himself cares for you. No matter what the world throws at you, you have Jesus in your boat. So there's no need to be afraid. No matter what's going on, you can go out there and do the things He has prepared for you to do. In the grand scheme of things, all is well.

The disciples' fear came not only because they set their eyes on their circumstances, but because they doubted both the word of Christ and character of Christ. Those two areas of doubt or unbelief are ultimately at the root of all fears.

Let me repeat the closing words of the previous chapter:

> God loves you so much. No matter where you are right now, He has things for you to do, and fruit for you to bear.

> What you *do* comes from who you *are*. And you are a pure, holy child of the Living God. You are victorious. In fact you are *more* than a conqueror in Christ!

> Draw near. Receive mercy. Find grace to help in your time of need.

Remember just who you are: a child of God with the robe, the ring and the sandals. Remind yourself just Who is in your boat.

Your loving Heavenly Father would say to you once, "Be strong and courageous...." Twice, "Only be strong and very courageous." And again, "Be strong and courageous."

OVERCOMING UNHEALTHY FEARS

There are three grace gifts that enable us to deal a death blow to unhealthy fears. 2 Timothy 1:7 (CSB) tells us about them: "For God has not given us a spirit of fear, but one of *power, love,* and *sound judgment.*"

So how do we get them? Notice that this verse is written in the past tense—we already have them! We just need to learn how to use them.

Power

The first gift God has bestowed on us by His grace is the gift of power. Paul prayed for the Ephesians: I pray that "the eyes of your heart may be enlightened in order that you may know the hope to which he has called you, the riches of his glorious inheritance in his holy people, and his incomparably great *power* for us who believe." Amen!

Paul doesn't pray that you will *receive* that power—he's praying that you will *know* the power you already have. He goes on to say, "That power is the same as the mighty strength he exerted when he raised Christ from the dead and seated him at his right hand in the heavenly realms, far above all rule and authority, power and dominion, and every name that is invoked, not only in the present age but also in the one to come" (Ephesians 1:19-23).

Think about the power that raised Christ from the dead. Now that's power! And he's talking about spiritual power. Which is why he mentions Christ's position in the heavenly realms far above all other powers and authorities, meaning demonic powers.

And you already have it—simply because you are in Christ.

Remember your position. You are seated with Christ at the right hand of the Father far above all power and authority. And that's important because Satan is a real enemy, and he likes nothing better than to get you to act out of fear.

In my experience, tempting me into fear is very much one of his main tactics against me. And knowing how to exercise the power that I have been given in Christ is significant.

I didn't always know how to do that. When I first heard about Freedom In Christ Ministries, I read two books by Neil Anderson: *The Bondage Breaker* and *Spiritual Protection For Your Children*. I took the latter with me as holiday reading for our annual two-week family holiday in France. At this point, I had no idea that I would become involved with Freedom In Christ Ministries—but perhaps the enemy did. The book told the story of a family's struggles with demonic activity and, being brought up with the Western worldview, I found it interesting but somewhat outside my experience. I also found it more than a little unnerving to realize that demons were real and targeted Christians.

One night my elder daughter, then aged seven, came into our bedroom and said that she had had a bad dream. I asked her what it was about, but she didn't want to say. I persuaded her gently to tell me: "There were lots of people in hoods and they killed you and Mummy." Well, we prayed together and committed it to the Lord, and she went back to bed. Now, that was an unusual dream for her to have on many levels. She was not prone to nightmares, and she had never seen any horror films—wherever could such an image have come from? I found it a little scary but after some more praying went back to sleep, only to be woken up a little later by my younger daughter, age five. She said that she was having nightmares. Guess what they were about? Exactly the same thing as my other daughter! She used practically the same words to describe it. Was I scared? You bet! We were staying in an old farm building that, in any case, felt dark and creepy, and now this was happening. I didn't get much sleep the rest of the night but spent most of it praying.

That incident could easily have made me decide that I didn't want anything to do with the demonic or any ministry dealing with it. After all, said the thought in my head, maybe it would put my family at risk.

Thankfully, God showed me that all Satan can do is try to scare us. If we use the armor and weapons at our disposal, he cannot touch us (see 1 John 5:18). I can testify to God's faithfulness over two decades in keeping my family absolutely safe as we have followed what He has given us to do. If Satan could have harmed us or stopped us, he would have. The truth is, he has not been able to.

The enemy will attack us wherever he can find legitimate ground. In my experience, this often happens when I am staying away from home, something I get to do reasonably often. I find, however, that simply having a basic understanding of the way the spiritual world works and of my power and authority in Christ, enables me to prevent the enemy's attacks. Before I leave home for a trip, I make a declaration along the lines of, "I declare that I am head of this household and I commit it to Jesus while I am away. I forbid the enemy from interfering with or attacking my family or any part of my domain while I am away." In the same way, when I arrive at where I am staying, I will make a similar declaration, something like, "I declare that I am staying in this room by legal right. If anything has gone on in this room that has been sinful and given the enemy any ground, I take it away now by covering it with the blood of Jesus, and I command the enemy to leave and stay away." That makes for a good night's sleep.

Given that 50 percent of hotel guests use pay-per-view porn, you can guarantee that the enemy has been given ground in practically any hotel you stay in. It makes sense to take that ground away. It's no big deal. It doesn't take very long. But it makes a real difference. I don't do these things in any kind of superstitious way. It would not be a disaster if I forgot—if I sensed the enemy attacking, that would cause me to remember, and I would do it then.

This taking authority comes from realizing what reality is like and living accordingly, in much the same way as I would take the precaution of turning the electricity off if I were going to do any electrical work at home. If I had known how to make a similar declaration at the time we were on holiday in France, my daughters would not have been troubled by those nightmares.

When you realize that a fear you are experiencing is from the enemy, you can use the power God gives. You can say, "Jesus is my Lord, and I tell every enemy of Christ to leave now."

We are in this spiritual battle whether we like it or not. It is raging all around us. We can't choose to opt out—not if we want to be fruitful disciples of Jesus at any rate. Our only choice is to engage in it and protect ourselves or to ignore it and become a casualty.

Right now, you are seated with Christ Himself at the right hand of the Father far above all other power and authority. And if you know just who you are and what you have in Christ, Satan and his demons are petrified of you. Yes, they quake in their boots when they come across little old you!

Love

The second gift that you already have, by God's grace, is love:

> There is no fear in love; but perfect love drives out
> fear, because fear involves punishment, and the one
> who fears is not perfected in love. (1 John 4:18 NASB)

If you still struggle with the fear that God will punish you or that He is cross with you, it is practically impossible for you to trust His love. So you are thrown back onto your own resources to try to deal with your fears. And that's a scary, lonely place to be.

But if you remember who you are, a beloved child of God, and that "there is therefore now no condemnation for those who are in Christ Jesus" (Romans 8:1 ESV), the fear of His punishment is destroyed.

I once met a church leader who was going through a period of intense criticism from a portion of his congregation during which his house had been struck by lightning. The damage was so severe that he and his family had had to move out. Well, you can imagine what the critical faction in the church was saying: "The lightning strike was punishment from God." He said to me, "I know that it's not punishment from God. All my punishment fell on Christ. He will never punish me. And in any case, we're in a nice hotel being paid for by the insurance company and when we move back in, they will have redecorated the whole of the upper floor of our house. That's not punishment, that's blessing!"

He was surely right. God does discipline us out of love so that we don't make the same mistake again and to develop our character. But He will never punish us.

John reminds us that we depend completely on God's love and that God is love. That is the only reason that we can have confidence on the day of judgment that is coming when we will all have to stand before God's judgment seat.

We need to get rid of any idea that God is like a strict school principal whose main concern is to see whether or not we are behaving appropriately. He is nothing like that at all.

One of the mind-blowing realizations I came to in my own journey of getting to know God as He really is (a journey I am still on!) is that He gives me freedom to fail. He doesn't want me to fail and there are consequences for sin. But when I do fail, I am already forgiven, and when I turn back to Him, He is waiting with His loving arms open to pick me up, dust me down, and set me on my way again. That is an astonishing truth!

When we allow fear of failure to rule us, our confidence before God and others becomes dependent upon how well we feel we have performed.

God said of Jesus, "This is my beloved Son with whom I am well-pleased" (Matthew 3:17 ESV). What had Jesus done to deserve this? Well, God said it right at the start of His ministry. He had done nothing yet!

Perfect love drives out fear. Love and fear are opposites, like oil and water. They don't mix. Either we are standing in God's grace dependent on His love, or we are operating out of fear. "The one who fears is not made perfect in love."

This brings up the question: Can you lose your salvation?

Over the years, I have come across many Christians who are absolutely petrified by the fear that they may have lost their salvation. And many seem to have become so plagued by that question it paralyzes them. It seems clear to me that Satan is using this to keep them in fear "because fear involves punishment, and the one who fears is not perfected in love" (1 John 4:18 NASB).

We've already seen that we are saved by grace through faith. Your salvation is not based on what you do or don't do. That's the whole point of the story of the younger brother. So if you're doubting your salvation because of something you did or didn't do, please go back and read the first two chapters again!

Salvation is not just something you qualify for like winning an Olympic gold medal that can easily be stripped from you if you test positive for drugs, for instance. When you become a Christian, you actually become someone completely different, a whole new person deep down inside.

Having said that, this is a question that Christians have debated for centuries, and people who look at it honestly and openly end up coming to different conclusions. Whichever view you take, you will find a number of passages in the Bible that don't quite fit that view, and that force you to interpret the text differently to the interpretation that a simple, plain reading of it would suggest.

My conclusion is that God has deliberately left something of a mystery here. And where God has left a mystery, I'm content for it to remain a mystery. But that doesn't in any way mean that we cannot enter into the truth that "there is no fear in love; but perfect love drives out fear."

What if you have looked at the passages and come to the conclusion that it is possible to lose your salvation, is that any reason for you to worry?

No! Jesus has promised that no one can take you out of His hands. God promises that whoever turns to Him will not be turned away.

One of the major passages that can be taken to imply that you can lose your salvation is in Hebrews 6. It talks about a group of people who can't be brought back to repentance. If you have any concern that you have lost your salvation, just come back to Jesus in repentance. The mere fact that you return to him in repentance demonstrates conclusively that you are not in the group the writer is talking about. In the passage itself, the writer expresses a confidence that the people he is writing to are not in that group anyway.

You will find the Father waiting for you, longing for you to return. You will find you can come with confidence to the throne of grace and receive grace and mercy in time of need.

"What if I've committed the unpardonable sin, blasphemy against the Holy Spirit?" Well, what exactly is that? The Holy Spirit is the one who convicts the world of sin and is doing that all the time. Those who blaspheme the Holy Spirit are surely those who spurn His conviction and reject the salvation that Jesus offers. This is something that only those who are not yet Christians can do. Consider the younger brother whose behavior Jesus was portraying as the absolute worst possible. Even he receives an amazing welcome from his father when he returns. There is nothing you can possibly do that is too big for Jesus' sacrifice.

If you're worried about this, come back to Jesus right now. You will receive mercy and grace to help in time of need.

Please relax and don't allow the enemy to hold you back. For us there is no punisher. Whatever you believe on the "once saved, always saved" question, you need have no fear whatsoever. If you have been plagued by doubts about your salvation, will you take this opportunity to approach the throne of grace with confidence and walk away from those doubts right now? And don't go back!

Sound Judgment

Which brings us to the third gift of God's grace, which is sound judgment, sometimes translated as "a sound mind."

The spiritual battle we are in is at root a battle between truth and lies. The battleground is our mind.

Fear distorts the truth. In fact, every unhealthy fear is based on a lie. So exercising sound judgment simply boils down—again!—to coming back to God's Word and making a choice to see things the way God sees them; in other words, how they really are. For example, to see that God Himself is indeed in your boat and really does love you.

How can we apply sound judgment to unhealthy fears? It's really all to do with working out whether a particular fear is healthy or unhealthy.

For us to have a legitimate healthy fear of something, the thing that we are afraid of has to have two attributes: it has to be both *present* and *powerful*. In other words, it has to be nearby and have the capacity to hurt us.

Let me give you an example. I am afraid of venomous snakes. Is that a healthy fear? Absolutely. However, right this minute I'm not afraid of venomous snakes. Why not? Because there aren't any near me.

Last month on a trip to Uganda, however, a group of us were walking up a hill one evening when the person in front of me, who lived in Uganda, shouted "Snake!" and I saw something slithery emerge onto the path where I was about to put my foot. Much to everyone's amusement, I leapt into the air and jumped over it. But I was right to be afraid. It was a snake. And, although it was tiny and was more frightened than I was at the encounter, it could potentially have done me damage. It was both present and powerful. My fear was entirely rational.

If I hadn't jumped over the snake but instead stepped on it and killed it (it really was very small), should I be afraid? No. Because even though it may still be *present*, it would no longer be *powerful*. Likewise if I went to the reptile house in a zoo and stood behind a glass partition looking at a spitting cobra, should I be afraid of it? No. It can spit and strike all it wants, but it's behind thick glass. Even though it is undoubtedly *powerful*, it can't reach me. It's not *present* in my space.

The point is this: neutralizing just one of those attributes eliminates the fear. Every unhealthy fear comes from believing that the thing we're afraid of is both present *and* powerful when in fact it isn't.

Jesus said that knowing the truth would set us free, so if you want to be set free from an unhealthy fear, ask God to show you the lie behind it. Then you will be able to renounce the lie and take steps to renew your mind which, Paul says, will transform you (Romans 12:2).

Let's have a look at how this can work in practice. Most unhealthy fears are related to either the fear of death or the fear of other people. If we resolve those two things, we deal with a lot of other fears too. Let's see how!

THE FEAR OF DEATH

I have a terminal illness. You do too. It's called being human. Can you remove the presence of death? No, unless Jesus comes back first, every one of us is going to experience physical death, and none of us knows when death will show up.

But what about its *power*?

Hebrews 2:14,15 (NASB) says that Christ died, "that through death He might render powerless him who had the power of death, that is, the devil, and might free those who through fear of death were subject to slavery all their lives."

And Paul says graphically that death has "lost its sting" (1 Corinthians 15:55).

In order for us to be free from slavery to the fear of death, we need to know the truth that sets us free. Let's look at the truth about death:

> *We will not all sleep, but we will all be changed—in a*
> *flash, in the twinkling of an eye, at the last trumpet.*
> *For the trumpet will sound, the dead will be raised*
> *imperishable, and we will be changed.*
> *(1 Corinthians 15:51-52)*

When our physical body dies, our spirit is still connected to God, and we will be with Him forever in a place where the Bible promises "there will be no more death or mourning or crying or pain" (Revelation 21:4).

Knowing these things in our heart (not just our head) will transform us and enable us to think about our own physical death and—without being morbid—live in the light of it. The Apostle Paul did just that. When he was in prison in Rome with the likelihood of a death sentence coming his way, he wrote this to the Philippians:

> *It is my eager expectation and hope that I will not be at all ashamed, but that with full courage now as always Christ will be honored in my body, whether by life or by death. For to me to live is Christ, and to die is gain. If I am to live in the flesh, that means fruitful labor for me. Yet which I shall choose I cannot tell. I am hard pressed between the two. (Philippians 1:20-23a ESV)*

Paul is torn between staying in his body—which he knows is only a temporary thing—and leaving for the joys of heaven. But whether he lives or dies, he wants Christ to be honored in his body. He has made his body a "living sacrifice."

The reason he gives for staying alive is fruitful labor. He will be able to do more of the things God prepared specifically for him to do.

The bottom line is this: "For to me to live is Christ, and to die is gain." Nothing else works in that equation: "For me to live is my family or my career or my ministry, to die is loss." But when living here in this body is all about Christ and becoming more and more like Him and doing the things He has prepared for us to do, when we die and get to be with Him, things just get even better!

Physical death will open the door for you to be with Jesus in a very tangible way, and to experience all the joys of heaven. Death has no power over us whatsoever!

THE FEAR OF PEOPLE

Proverbs 29:25 (NASB) says, "The fear of man brings a snare, but he who trusts in the LORD will be exalted."

Let's say you've got a huge fear of your boss. He's an intimidating person perhaps but right now you are not afraid of him, are you? Why not? He's not present (presumably!). But when you go to work on Monday morning, there he is.

When you are at the coffee machine, having a cup of coffee with your colleagues, you are not afraid of him because he's over on the other side of the building in his office. Powerful but not present. In fact, you may well want to get off your chest what you think about him. You are well into your story and completely oblivious to the little signs your colleagues are trying to give you. But eventually you turn around and see him standing there hands on hips with a tight smile on his face. Now he is not only powerful. He is also present.

So now the fear is healthy!

Or is it? Because we're told not to fear people. So what can you do to stop your boss from exercising that kind of fear over you even when he's present? You have to get rid of one of those attributes. He's a big guy so you can't do anything about the fact that he's present. So what about powerful?

Well, exactly what power does he have over you in the worst-case scenario? "He might be able to fire me." True. How can you deal with that? Resign! Well, you don't have to write the letter—but if he ever tries to pressure you into doing something that is not right, be willing to resign, knowing that God is your real boss and that He will always provide for you if you choose to do the right thing.

Many years ago, I took what seemed like a huge step and gave up a regular salary to start a business. Discussing it with my business partner at the time, we both agreed that we would always regret not trying. We considered the worst thing that could happen to us—that the business would fail, and we would possibly have to sell our homes. We asked ourselves if we could live with that scenario and decided we could. "We'll just start again and go out and try to get a job" is what we said. We reconciled ourselves with the worst case.

What if you are doing what you know to be the right thing and someone else doesn't like it—what is the worst thing that could happen? They may reject you. They may say nasty things about you. They may just raise an eyebrow or give you a funny look but even that can be enough to shake our confidence and cause us to want to behave differently in the future; in effect, giving them some kind of control over us.

If we are doing the right thing in God's eyes—perhaps speaking honestly about Jesus—do we really want to let the fear of disapproval or rejection set the agenda?

We must never set out to be awkward or objectionable but must be ready, humbly and gently, to do the right thing and trust God with the outcome.

In Psalm 56, David gives us the bottom line. "What can man do to me?" he asks. And then he answers his own question: "Nothing." He didn't write this in the comfort of his palace but while he was in the hands of his enemies! He had resolved that he could face the worst-case scenario if he was walking in obedience. Above it all, God was in charge. The danger from his enemies was *present*, but in light of the Creator of the universe, it wasn't *powerful*.

God doesn't want us to remove ourselves from the presence of people. He wants us to be actively engaged with people, serving as salt and light in a dark and lost world. So, the possibility of someone not liking us and giving us the cold shoulder (or worse) is always present. By exercising the sound judgment that God has already given you, you can resolve even today that, if push comes to shove, you will always obey God rather than people and believe His opinion of you rather than theirs. And you will find that even though they are still present, they are no longer powerful, and you do not have to be afraid of them.

Jesus said, "If anyone comes to me and does not hate father and mother, wife and children, brothers and sisters—yes, even their own life—such a person cannot be my disciple" (Luke 14:26). The New Living Translation helpfully clarifies what He means. It says: "If you want to be my disciple, you must, by comparison, hate everyone else."

We need to come to the point where we resolve that our allegiance to King Jesus comes before anything else. Even if those closest to us disapprove of what we're doing for Him, as long as we know that it's the right thing, we will not be afraid of their disapproval or rejection but will choose to do the right thing.

GOD IS ALWAYS *PRESENT* AND ALL *POWERFUL*

There is just one fear that is always healthy: The fear of God. Why? Because God is always present and all powerful.

Perhaps "the fear of God" sounds like we're supposed to be afraid of Him. But nothing could be further from the truth.

> For those who are led by the Spirit of God are the children of God. The Spirit you received does not make you slaves, so that you live in fear again; rather, the Spirit you received brought about your adoption to sonship. And by him we cry, "Abba, Father." (Romans 8:14-15)

As God's children, the Holy Spirit moves us to cry out "Daddy!" As the younger brother did when he collapsed into his loving father's arms.

What is intriguing to me about the story of Jesus calming the storm is that, although the disciples were clearly very afraid they were going to perish in the storm, they are described as "terrified" only once the storm had died down. What terrified them was seeing the power that Jesus had. Having a healthy fear of God will spur us on to do the right thing despite our natural fears.

Fear of the Lord is, in reality, a profound awe, a realization of our smallness next to His infinite greatness.

God is love. He's on our side! David worked out how to make that truth real. He said, "I sought the LORD, and He answered me, and delivered me from all my fears" (Psalm 34:4 ESV).

"Fear not" is only learned in relationship, when you know the truth about your loving Heavenly Father. That the all-knowing, everywhere-present, all-powerful, and absolutely loving God of grace is in your boat and cares for you. What can a person or anything else do to you? Nothing! Absolutely nothing!

When we fear God in the right way, when we make Him the ultimate fear object of our life, we discover the fear that will cast out all other fears.

> *"There is no fear in love, but perfect love casts out fear" (1 John 4:18a ESV).*

MAKING THE GRACE CONNECTION

Pray as follows and then spend some time considering the questions as the Holy Spirit guides you.

Loving Father,

Thank You that You are always present with me and that You are all powerful. Thank You that You are in my boat and that You care for me. Thank You that You have adopted me and that Your Spirit leads me to cry, "Abba, Father." Help me to see You more and more as the loving Father that You are, and to know You more and more.

Thank You for your Holy Spirit who leads me out of slavery to fear. I pray that You will guide me and speak to me clearly in this time. I take my stand against the enemy and declare that he is not to interfere in any way.

In the name of Jesus.

Amen.

What are the top three fears that you face?

What difference would it make in your life if you were able to overcome them?

We have seen that behind every unhealthy fear is a lie, something that does not line up with what God says in His Word, the Bible.

What is the lie behind each of your fears? What truths from God's Word can you find to counteract each lie?

CHAPTER 6

CALM!

This book is one element of "The Grace & Freedom Project," which, it would be fair to say, has occupied the majority of my time over the last two to three years.

The main element of the project is a brand-new version of *The Grace Course*. I was involved in writing the course, selecting and coaching the presenters, working to find the best people to film it, identifying the filming location, and was there at the filming to direct proceedings.

This is one of the works that God prepared in advance for me to have the privilege of doing. It feels like a huge and important project that many people have invested a lot in.

Throughout the long development process, I have sensed God saying to me, "You have to live the message." I've taken this to mean that what I teach must be true not only in theory but in my own experience. And not just in my experience sometime in the past, but in my day to day experience now. Otherwise it's simply not authentic or honest. This helps me understand why James wrote this:

Not many of you should become teachers, my fellow believers, because you know that we who teach will be judged more strictly. (James 3:1)

When you have the privilege of spending many of your working hours grappling with the great Biblical truths of grace, and dare to teach them to others, it is only reasonable that God would expect integrity and honesty. Those of us who are called to teach do indeed have to live the message.

After many months of preparation, the presenters of *The Grace Course* flew to the South of England from all across the world, and we spent three days together rehearsing and praying. Finally, the big day arrived. We drove nervously to the filming location, met the film director and his crew, and started setting up to film. We came across many hitches and unforeseen issues. It was not until lunchtime that we were actually ready to film the first session. That was later than scheduled, so the pressure would be on to make up some time in order to keep to time.

Before plunging into the filming, we stopped for a brief lunch. Over lunch, I looked at my phone and read a message from my daughter which said simply, "Please pray for Eliza. We're in A&E [the ER] with her and they're helping her to breathe." A little later this was followed up by, "They're transferring her to ICU at a specialist children's hospital unfortunately. She'll need to be on a ventilator."

Eliza was our new granddaughter born just four weeks earlier, two-and-a-half weeks ahead of her due date. She had developed a bit of a cough that her doctor thought would simply pass. That day at lunchtime my daughter noticed that she was gasping for air and had started to turn blue. Her oxygen level had fallen to 73% —anything below 92% is a cause for concern.

Zoë (my wife) left the filming immediately in order to help out with Eliza's older sister.

I remained at the filming and tried my best to take charge of the first session as we began to film. "You have to live the message" was going round and round in my mind.

This filming was the culmination of years of hard work. It was a very expensive exercise. And as the executive producer, I was the one who knew exactly how it should look. Surely it couldn't work without me.

"You have to live the message."

In a moment of clarity, I understood that actually God was the executive producer and that He is the only One who really knows how this project needs to turn out. Furthermore, He was entirely capable of making it happen without me. And I realized that my place was with my family.

So after the first session, I handed the project over to my team and left to join my family. It took some time to prepare Eliza for the transfer by ambulance to the children's hospital, and I arrived at my daughter's home at the same time she and my son-in-law returned briefly to pack a bag. Zoë and I were able to pray with them briefly before they set off to catch up with Eliza at the children's hospital.

We then spent the next three days living in their home looking after our other granddaughter while they stayed with Eliza in the ICU.

During those three days, we constantly reminded ourselves that God is in our boat and that He loves us. We reminded ourselves that Eliza and *The Grace Course* are His, not ours, and constantly handed our granddaughter and the filming over to Him.

In short we found ourselves here:

> *Humble yourselves, therefore, under God's mighty hand, that he may lift you up in due time. Cast all your anxiety on him because he cares for you. (1 Peter 5:6-7).*

We experienced afresh that God does indeed have a mighty hand. Eliza made a full recovery, and it turns out, I'm not indispensable after all. My team did a great job without me, and the videos in *The Grace Course* have exceeded my expectations. They're just great.

We experienced afresh that God really cares for us. And I'm so grateful for the promise when we are going through tough times that He will lift us up in due time.

In this chapter, let's consider how we can stop being driven by anxiety, another of those "false motivators," and instead learn to live out of rest in God no matter what life throws at us.

A SPIRITUAL DANGER

The verses quoted above were written by Peter to Christians in modern day Turkey who were facing "various trials" that caused them to be anxious. Let's look at his advice to them again, and this time include the verse that follows them to add some context that may surprise you:

> Humble yourselves, therefore, under God's mighty hand, that he may lift you up in due time. Cast all your anxiety on him because he cares for you.
>
> Be alert and of sober mind. Your enemy the devil prowls around like a roaring lion looking for someone to devour. Resist him, standing firm in the faith, because you know that the family of believers throughout the world is undergoing the same kind of sufferings. (1 Peter 5:6-9)

Peter quite clearly links not casting your anxieties onto God with the reality that Satan is prowling around looking for someone to devour. Anxiety is a strategy that the enemy is highly likely to try to use against you. Because, if he can tempt you into anxiety, he can severely blunt your effectiveness as a disciple of Jesus.

It's imperative that we learn to recognize our anxiety and choose to resolve it. Note that I said "choose." It may feel that we are helpless in the face of circumstances that cause us anxiety, but Jesus said clearly, "Do not be anxious about tomorrow" (Matthew 6:34 ESV), and Paul says bluntly, "Do not be anxious about anything" (Philippians 4:6). Would God command us to do something we could not do? Of course not. It must, therefore, definitely be possible for every child of God to resolve anxiety. No matter what storms are raging around us.

WHAT IS ANXIETY?

Fear and anxiety are similar. The key difference between them is that fear has a definite object—we are frightened of something *specific* like snakes, heights, or death—but anxiety does not. It arises from a general uncertainty about the future. It is a vague unease that gnaws away at us caused by not knowing what is going to happen tomorrow.

My preferred definition of anxiety comes from our *Freed To Lead* course: "a disturbing unease or apprehension that comes from inappropriate concern about something uncertain."

Note that it comes from *inappropriate* concern. It's normal and appropriate to be nervous about an exam you're about to take or a plane you're about to catch. That anxiety arises from a particular situation, but it fades away when it's over. That's not what we're looking at here. Our focus is on the occasions we feel anxious when we don't need to, when our anxiety is inappropriate.

I don't want to be over-simplistic about the causes of anxiety. For the first couple of nights on my recent trip to Uganda, I felt really anxious and struggled to get to sleep. Yet there was nothing especially to worry about in my circumstances. It finally occurred to me to read the leaflet that accompanied my anti-malarial medication, which informed me that 10% of people who take it report side-effects of sleep problems and anxiety. That put my mind at rest, making it easier for me simply to ignore those feelings. On that occasion, my anxiety was chemically induced. Feelings of anxiety can also arise from biochemical reasons or as a result of stress or past trauma. We don't have the scope to look at those things here but instead will focus on that habitual anxiety that can so easily drive our lives if we allow it to.

LIVING IN AN ANXIOUS WORLD

A major challenge we face is that anxiety has become entirely normalized in our society and is present everywhere you look. It's implicated in a whole host of health issues, particularly those affecting the heart, bowels, and skin.

Look at any political debate and how issues assume enormous significance in people's minds. People are too anxious to have a rational argument and a lot of political "debate" sounds more like hysteria.

Look at the aftermath of the Covid pandemic and the increased anxiety about our health it has left us with.

Look at our news media and how they seize an issue, talking at length about the negative possibilities and dangers we might face.

I suspect that most people who know me wouldn't see me as an anxious person, and I tend not to view myself as an anxious person. However, God has shown me clearly that I have some deeply ingrained ways of thinking that are actually based on anxiety and, if I allow them to, prevent me from living out of His grace.

My natural tendency is to want to control the circumstances of my life, so my mind tends to go into overdrive considering all the different possibilities and how best to navigate them. Often, I find myself dwelling on the worst possible scenario, almost convincing myself that is what is actually going to happen. If I'm not very careful to guard my mind, I can easily live in a constant state of anxiety which, for me, tends to translate into busyness— because I feel that the only way to control life is to make sure I'm anticipating every possible issue and doing everything I can to sort them out.

But it's mentally exhausting. And it leaves God out of the picture. Life is so much more pleasant when I break out of that and come back to resting in the arms of my loving Heavenly Father.

HUMBLE YOURSELF

Peter specifies two things to do in order to deal with anxiety:

1. Humble yourself under God's mighty hand;
2. Cast all your anxieties onto the God who cares for you.

Do you find it somewhat counterintuitive that Peter's first piece of advice to those who are feeling anxious because of difficult circumstances is to humble themselves, the implication being that they need to stop acting pridefully?

King David wrote a lovely psalm with just three verses, Psalm 131, that has helped me understand the strong link between anxiety and pride:

> *My heart is not proud, O LORD, my eyes are not haughty; I do not concern myself with great matters or things too wonderful for me.*
>
> *But I have stilled and quietened my soul; like a weaned child with its mother, like a weaned child is my soul within me.*
>
> *O Israel, put your hope in the LORD both now and for evermore.*

This is King David writing. Who's he kidding that he doesn't concern himself with great matters? He has to deal with life and death decisions every day! What does he mean then? It's not that he doesn't do these things. He just recognizes that if he thought he could do them in his own strength, it would be pride.

When I fall back into living in anxiety, it takes me a while to realize it. But when the Holy Spirit finally gets through to me, I realize that the issue is essentially pride. It's not the circumstances I face that make me anxious so much as my lack of trust in the God who is in my boat and who loves me.

When I don't trust God with the details of my life and try to manage them myself, I get anxious and over busy. I may have the illusion of getting lots of things done, but in reality, since it is God who "builds the house" not me, I don't actually make a great deal of progress in the things that really matter. I burn up a lot of nervous energy essentially chasing my tail. And all the time, I'm totally unaware of it.

At the root of it is an unconscious choice to trust my own judgment rather than His, to think that I know best how to handle things. It can take me a while to realize what is happening and then to come back to the point where I still and quieten my anxious soul so that it rests like a contented baby in the loving arms of the mother who will provide for its every need.

The big question is this: are we going to believe what God tells us is true or are we going to trust our own judgment that has been shaped by our experiences and this fallen world?

Let's consider three areas of our lives where we need to learn to humble ourselves and trust God rather than our own judgment.

HUMBLING OURSELVES TO GOD'S GOAL FOR OUR LIVES

What are you hoping to achieve someday? Career success? Getting married and having children? Seeing your children achieve certain things? Having a successful Christian ministry?

Those can be good things. But you can never be sure that they are going to happen. You cannot make your boss promote you or determine how well the organization you work for does. You cannot guarantee that you will marry or have children. If you do have children, they will ultimately make their own choices, which may not be the ones you would have made for them. And God has a way of turning our concept of a "successful" ministry on its head.

In other words, all of these life-goals are in some way dependent on the cooperation of other people or on favorable circumstances that are not under your direct control. You do not know if they will work out because you do not know what will happen tomorrow.

That means that these life-goals will always feel uncertain. And that sets you up for anxiety. In fact, feeling continually anxious is a strong indication that you may be working towards a life-goal that feels uncertain, one whose fulfillment depends on people or circumstances that are not within your power to control.

Would God ever say, "I have a goal for you. I know you may not be able to fulfill it, but try anyway"? No. He would never ask you to do the impossible. Any life-goal that really is from God will have no uncertainty whatsoever attached to it.

So if we don't want to be constantly anxious, we have to let go of any goal that can be blocked by other people or circumstances we have no right or ability to control.

It's not wrong to aim for outcomes such as the examples I've given. I'm not saying we should stop working towards things that are clearly good like having children or a successful ministry. It's just a question of downgrading the significance of those things in our thinking, so that they are no longer *life-goals* upon which our whole sense of who we are depends but are simply *desires*, things we would love to see happen. If they don't happen, although we'll be disappointed, it's OK.

So what is the life-goal that God has for us that has no uncertainty attached to it?

As we've seen, above everything else, God wants you to become more and more like Jesus in character. He is concerned about what you *do* but He is *primarily* concerned about what you are *like*. Because what you do comes from what you are like. He is concerned about what He can do *through* you, but He is more concerned about what He can do *in* you.

If you get up every morning and head into your day with just one aim—of becoming more and more like Jesus in character—

no circumstance you face and no person you come across can prevent it from happening.

What if a difficult person attacks me unfairly or gets in my way? Or what if I get a really bad health issue? Or my business fails? None of those things can stop you from becoming more and more like Jesus. In fact, if you rely on God and persevere through those difficulties, they will actually *help* you become more and more like Jesus. So there's no uncertainty and therefore no anxiety.

If you think about it, the only person who can block God's goal for your life is... you!

Pause for a moment. Ask the Holy Spirit to show you the life-goals you have been unconsciously working towards. Do they depend on circumstances or people you cannot control? Do you need to let them go and downgrade them to a simple desire? Will you choose instead to adopt God's goal for your life, to become more and more like Jesus in character?

HUMBLING OURSELVES TO OUR GOD-GIVEN RESPONSIBILITIES

In His Word, God sets out clearly who is responsible for what. Some things are His responsibility, and some things are my responsibility. God will not do for me the things that He has said are for me to do.

Unfortunately, we tend to get this the wrong way around. We want to do the things that are His responsibility, and we want Him to do the things that are our responsibility.

Whose responsibility is it, for example, to ensure we have enough money? Whatever your answer to that question, an impartial observer looking at the way we live might well conclude that we believe that it is our responsibility. Biblically, it is not. The biblical principle is this:

So do not worry, saying, 'What shall we eat?' or 'What shall we drink?' or 'What shall we wear?' For the pagans run after all these things, and your heavenly Father knows that you need them. But seek first his kingdom and his righteousness, and all these things will be given to you as well. (Matthew 6:31-33)

Our responsibility is to seek God's Kingdom and His righteousness, in other words, to do what is right. Then we can expect God to do the part that is His responsibility—to provide everything we need so that we don't have to busy ourselves with that.

Paul commends the Philippian Christians for abiding by this principle. He praises them for sending financial gifts and says, "They are a fragrant offering, an acceptable sacrifice, pleasing to God. And my God will meet all your needs according to the riches of his glory in Christ Jesus" (Philippians 4:18b–19).

Often just the last sentence of this passage is quoted, as if God will always meet all our needs, regardless of our actions. In fact, this promise is made in the context of us first fulfilling our responsibility—in this case, giving.

So, we have a responsibility to live righteously, which includes working if we are able (see Ephesians 4:28) and giving away a portion of what God gives us.

Once we have done what God tells us is our responsibility to do, we can sit back free of anxiety because it is then 100% God's responsibility to meet our needs—and, of course, He will.

The Apostle John says, "Dear children, keep yourselves from idols" (1 John 5:21). An idol is anything that has become more important to us than God Himself—for example, material possessions, money, good health, social media status, or relationships.

When these things take on too much significance, we become anxious because we don't know what's going to happen tomorrow and we're scared of not ever obtaining what we want or of losing what we have.

God's Word helps us understand the truth that some day, we will in fact lose everything we own except one thing: our relationship with Jesus.

Do you need to come before God and humble yourself? To confess that other things have been more important to you? And to commit yourself to His purpose for you, to become more and more like Jesus? God gives you the responsibility to keep yourself from idols so you can be absolutely sure that that is entirely possible.

Let's try another example. Whose responsibility is it to make things happen in the area of service that God has given you? If, for example, you are in some kind of leadership role in your church, whose responsibility is it to ensure that the church grows and flourishes? Here is the biblical principle: "Unless the Lord builds the house, the builders labor in vain" (Psalm 127:1).

If you are a leader of a ministry or working in your own personal ministry, it's difficult to let God build it. If we know what needs to be done, we are tempted simply to try to do it ourselves. But even if we succeed in building something that seems great to us, if it was done in our own strength, it's not going to last.

Often we can find ourselves trying and trying to build something but we get nowhere and it feels like we're banging our heads against a brick wall. Finally we step back exhausted and He steps in and builds something amazing while we lie in a crumpled heap. Sometimes, however, He has to wait a long time for us to come to the end of our own resources.

Our responsibility is to be still before Him and wait patiently for Him (Psalm 37:7), pray, and then simply do what He tells us to do, leaving the outcome to Him.

HUMBLING OURSELVES TO GOD'S WORD

God has revealed in the Bible what He's like, how He's set up the world, and our part in His plans.

And that's why much of Satan's attack is directed at how people see the Bible. He wants you not to take it seriously, not to read it for yourself, not to spend that time with God each day where you humble yourself before Him and His Word.

Have you heard people say things like, "I only trust the red text in the Bible," or "I don't get the Old Testament, so I just skip it"?

Paul told Timothy, "The Spirit clearly says that in later times [which is now!] some will abandon the faith and follow deceiving spirits and things taught by demons" (1 Timothy 4:1).

He's talking about people who claim to be Christians following the teaching of demons. So don't be surprised if you hear Christian teachers implying that the Bible doesn't say what it plainly does say.

History is full of examples of people being led astray by fraudulent arguments and shady theology. But that does not make the Bible an unreliable guide. Not at all. It's totally consistent in what it says. And God promises to guide you into all truth by His Spirit. If you approach His Word with a humble, teachable spirit, you will understand what He has to say to you.

When Satan tempted Jesus in the wilderness, he used the phrase, "Did God *really* say?" And he uses that line with us too. Satan even quoted Bible verses and twisted their meaning.

Dealing with inappropriate anxiety can sometimes be as simple as making a decision to take God at His word. If you doubt that the Bible is God's message to us, then you simply won't be able to do that and you will be thrown back onto your own devices to deal with your anxiety. You will, in effect, be pridefully making up your own rules rather than trusting the way He has set things up.

It's so important that you don't just read Christian books and Bible study notes or just listen to people talking about the Bible. It's critical that you read the Bible for yourself and take what it says seriously. You can base your life decisions on God's promises. Don't think they apply to other people but your problems are different or too big. That's also a form of pride.

Don't come to it with a preconceived idea of what you want it to say, even if your intentions seem good. Focus on what it *actually* says.

I've watched countless Christians read in the Bible that they are holy ones, but totally miss the point that that's who they actually are! Because they've always heard they're sinners. They filter what is written plainly in the Bible through the theology they've been taught. It should be the other way around. Always judge what you've been taught according to the Bible.

And if a passage doesn't make immediate sense, don't gloss over it. Persevere, ask, research, and listen until you understand why the God who is love included it. Try to understand the culture it was written for and don't try to make it say anything that the original hearers could not have understood from it.

James describes someone who, in the face of uncertainty and anxiety-causing circumstances, asks God for wisdom but then, instead of persevering through the difficult situations, doubts God and falls back on their own resources. He says, "Such a person is double-minded and unstable in all they do" (James 1:8).

The Greek word for "anxiety" in the New Testament is a combination of two words meaning "divide" and "mind." Anxiety literally meant being in two minds—constantly going back and forth between one thing and another. Being double-minded.

Unless you have made that definite choice to trust God and follow His ways, you'll always be in two minds, sometimes believing Him and trusting Him and sometimes falling back on your own way of thinking. And that means you'll be unstable and anxious.

We are anxious because we do not know what is going to happen tomorrow, and we feel that we have to do everything we can to make sure that what happens is what we would ideally like to happen.

But although we don't know exactly what is going to happen tomorrow, if we humble ourselves to trust that the Bible is the very Word of God, actually we know exactly what's going to happen in the grand scheme of things. You may like to pause and take a look at 2 Corinthians 12:9-10 and Philippians 4:13 for example.

You'll see written clearly in black and white by God Himself that tomorrow God will still be your loving, protective Father. Whenever you feel weak, He will be strong. And you will always be able to do whatever He asks of you because Jesus will give you strength. That's what's going to happen tomorrow. And I'm looking forward to it!

CASTING OUR ANXIETY ONTO CHRIST

Towards the end of this book, you will find The Steps To Experiencing God's Grace. This is a gentle time between you and the God of grace where you're invited to ask the Holy Spirit to show you the things that are getting in the way of experiencing God's grace. You will then submit to God by dealing with those things through repentance and resist the devil who will have no choice but to flee from you (James 4:7).

The process contains seven steps, the sixth of which is called "Exchanging Anxiety For God's Peace." It's a very practical way to "cast all your anxiety on him because he cares for you" when you are facing circumstances that make you anxious because of the uncertainty of what will happen tomorrow.

Let's look at the Biblical principles behind casting our anxiety on Him. Once you know them, you can use them whenever you realize that anxiety has begun to take hold of you.

1. Pray

Philippians 4:6 (NASB) says: "Be anxious for nothing, but in everything by prayer and supplication with thanksgiving let your requests be made known to God."

Start with prayer. Prayer focuses our mind on God, His character, and His love. Prayer takes our focus off our anxiety and puts our attention on the One who cares for us.

Note that the reason you can cast your anxiety onto God and leave it with Him is "because he cares for you." So as you come to pray, remind yourself of just who God is, especially His unimaginably great power and His limitless, unconditional love for you.

Paul reminds us to include thanksgiving as part of our prayers. Thanksgiving focuses our attention on what God has done in the past, and what He's already doing in our current situation.

I was fascinated to learn recently that the part of our brain that produces anxiety is the same part that is engaged when we give thanks. Apparently, this means that we are unable to feel thankful and anxious at the same time. 2,000 years on science has caught up with Philippians 4!

2. State The Problem

When we're anxious, we struggle to put things into perspective. It's possible to find tremendous relief simply by clarifying the issue.

A problem well stated is half solved. So take some time simply to write down what the issue is as simply and as clearly as possible. Stick to the facts of the situation

Something I find helpful at this point is to ask myself: In the light of eternity, how important is this particular issue?

3. Focus On Facts and Reject Assumptions

In stating the problem, stick to the facts of the situation.

We're anxious because we don't know what is going to happen. And because we don't know, we tend to make assumptions. For many of us, our minds leap to the worst possible outcome, and, before we know it, we've convinced ourselves that's what's going to happen!

In many cases the toll exacted by continual worry can be greater than if our worst-case scenario actually came to pass.

A fact might be something like "I have found a strange lump." An assumption would be, "I have cancer, and I am going to die!"

A fact might be, "I do not have enough money to pay my bills." An assumption would be, "I am going to be thrown out of my house."

A fact might be, "My employer is planning to lay off some people." An assumption would be, "I am going to lose my job."

In the vast majority of cases, of course, the worst doesn't happen. And even if it does, we have all the resources of Heaven to call on.

4. Determine Your Responsibilities

Work out prayerfully before God in the situation that is causing your anxiety:

- What is *your* responsibility?
- What is *God's* responsibility?
- And what is *someone else's* responsibility?

The key principle is that you are responsible only for the things that you have both the *right* and *ability* to control. You are not responsible for anything else. Generally speaking, the things God has given you the right and ability to control will boil down to things in your own life. And, by the way, if you aren't choosing to live a responsible life, then you probably should feel anxious!

You can't do anything about the fact that you have found a lump. But you can control what you choose to think, believe, and do.

It would be sensible, for example, in the case of a possible medical issue to see a doctor. Another sensible thing would be to go through *The Steps To Freedom In Christ* or *The Steps To Experiencing God's Grace* to check that there is no spiritual issue at the root of this.

Once you've clarified what you're responsible for, then fulfill your responsibilities. Don't just pray about them.

You can cast your anxieties onto Jesus, but if you try casting your responsibilities on Him, He will cast them right back at you!

You might need to forgive someone. You might need to pay a debt or put some other thing right. He won't do that for you.

Once you have fulfilled your responsibility, you can confidently say, "Now it's up to You, God," and leave everything else with Him. You can be sure that He will play His part. So leave it with Him. Don't pick it up again.

BE ALERT

Be alert and of sober mind. Your enemy the devil prowls around like a roaring lion looking for someone to devour. Resist him, standing firm in the faith, because you know that the family of believers throughout the world is undergoing the same kind of sufferings. (1 Peter 5:8-9)

We've already noted that Peter is very clear about anxiety: it can put us in spiritual danger. He exhorts us to be alert, keep our minds clear, and resist Satan by standing firm in the truth.

"You have to live the message."

When I finished my first draft of Chapter 5 of this book and came to this chapter, I sensed that God was telling me to set it aside for the moment and come back to it later. That seemed a bit strange, but I went with it and wrote Chapters 7 and 8 before coming back to this one.

Each chapter took three or four weeks to write, and God chose to work on me during that period of six or seven weeks. He showed me that I had let down my guard and was allowing the enemy to hold me back because I had slipped back into anxiety.

It started with a niggly cough that just wouldn't go away—slightly annoying but otherwise I felt fine. It was a little worse by the time we set off to enjoy a week's vacation with our family. I woke up on our second morning, coughed, and found I could not breathe. The cough seemed to have dislodged some mucus that clogged up my airways, and I couldn't dislodge it. My body's natural reaction was to keep gasping for air in an increasingly panicky way. It went on a long time which makes me realize I must have been getting at least some oxygen, even if it felt like I wasn't, and eventually a good slap on the back from Zoë dislodged it and enabled me to breathe normally again.

It was a scary moment. Then it happened again, and again, always at night. I sought medical help and the major "nasty" causes were ruled out which was a relief. But day after day it got steadily worse until I was having four or so of these breathing attacks during a night, each one of them quite scary because I did not seem to be able to breathe during them.

As I write, these scary episodes have been going on for three weeks. I have had a number of tests but it's not yet clear what the medical issue is. Medication seems to have helped somewhat but has not solved it. I now get some of these attacks during the day as well as the night. I have been able to resolve all of them eventually and logically I realize that they are not life-threatening. But I can tell you that waking up three or four times in the night unable to breathe is nevertheless really scary. And if I'm not careful, anxiety grips me, and my mind goes into overdrive wondering if in fact there will be an episode that I won't be able to get through. So going to bed at night is not a nice prospect.

"You have to live the message."

It's not lost on me that I started this chapter with the description of our granddaughter's breathing difficulties, and I'm ending it with a description of my own.

During this time, God has gently reminded me of Psalm 131 and shown me how my soul has definitely not been like a "weaned child with its mother" but how I have been racing around trying to manage things on my own. In short, I have slipped back into old patterns of living, and in this area, I have not been living the message. Even though I have learned these lessons many times before, they had become "theory" rather than "real" to me. I now understand why I had to wait to write this chapter—there is no way I could have written it with integrity six weeks ago.

In His mercy, God has given me a huge wake-up call and a spur to do life radically differently. I see this time as God's loving, gentle discipline for me.

The devil is prowling around looking for someone to devour. Frustratingly for him, he has no power to march into our lives and do damage to us—in the spiritual realm, we are seated with Christ far above Satan and every demonic power. All he can do is tempt us, accuse us, and deceive us. But he's very good at those things. He knows our vulnerabilities and prods at them relentlessly.

Recently I've fallen for the enemy's lies that I can control the events of my life and have been desperately scurrying around trying to do that. My mind is filled with a million things to do, and I'm always on some kind of mission to "achieve" something. These things are good and are things God has prepared in advance for me to do. But I have neglected rest, seeking God, and spending proper quality time with my wife. I have allowed anxiety back into my life.

It's become equally clear to me that this comes from pride—thinking that I can do things in my own strength, being too busy "doing important things for God" to spend much time actually speaking with or waiting on God.

I want to keep humbling myself before God and responding to what He is saying. The last couple of weeks has brought me much more in touch with Him, and I'm loving it.

Yesterday evening, I felt apprehensive about the coming night with potential breathing attacks, and I went for a walk along the river near where we live. I stopped for some time and prayed through it. It was so good to encounter the God of grace who simply loves me and is, I think, delighted that I am finally responding and waking up to my sin.

My outward walk had been quick and purposeful and as I turned over in my mind again the prospect of the coming night, I barely noticed the beautiful river and countryside around me. On the way back, however, my soul was peaceful. I knew God was by my side for the coming night. I knew I was forgiven and loved. I knew God was only too happy for me to pick myself up, dust myself down, and continue my walk with Him. I knew there was no condemnation whatsoever. And I found myself walking much more slowly and stopping to admire the wonder and beauty of God's creation. The sunset that evening was amazing. The river was full of life and beauty. All was well.

This is not the first time that God has brought me back from living in prideful anxiety. Or even the second. Or the third. It's a vulnerability I will always have, but there is nothing inevitable about falling back into it. I need to be alert and remain on my guard against the tempting thoughts the enemy throws my way.

As I expressed my concern to God about the ways anxiety runs deep in me I sensed Him reminding me of the amazing words of Jesus in Matthew 6:33: "But seek first his kingdom and his righteousness, and all these things will be given to you as well." I simply need to focus on seeking Him and His ways first. Everything else will then fall into place. It's as simple as that. So each day that is my focus, and I am confident that as long as I keep seeking Him, I can walk forward in a state of internal rest, trust and humility.

In all this, God has taken great pains to show me that He is there with me and that I do not need to fear. When I returned from my walk and bedtime was drawing near, I put my worship playlist on in shuffle mode and the first song Spotify selected for me was "This is the air I breathe" by Marie Barnett:

> This is the air I breathe
> This is the air I breathe
> Your holy presence
> Living in me
>
> This is my daily bread
> This is my daily bread
> Your very word
> Spoken to me
>
> And I... I'm desperate for you
>
> And I... I'm lost without you[1]

There is nothing more fundamental to life than being able to take a breath. On the 20 or 30 occasions in the last few weeks when I have not been able to breathe, there's a desperate struggle to do anything to get some oxygen. God wants me to have that same desperation when it comes to seeking Him and knowing Him. So that I will do whatever it takes to seek Him and His Kingdom first.

As I write this, I am still getting the breathing attacks, and they are horrible. But I have the assurance that nothing can separate me from the love of God, and nothing can take me out of His hand.

THE GOD OF ALL GRACE WILL LIFT YOU UP

Let's come back to our core passage and add two more verses:

---

1. Breathe by Marie Barnett. © 1995 Mercy Vineyard Publishing (ASCAP) (adm at IntegratedRights.com). All rights reserved. Used by permission.

Humble yourselves, therefore, under God's mighty hand, that he may lift you up in due time. Cast all your anxiety on him because he cares for you.

Be alert and of sober mind. Your enemy the devil prowls around like a roaring lion looking for someone to devour. Resist him, standing firm in the faith, because you know that the family of believers throughout the world is undergoing the same kind of sufferings.

And the God of all grace, who called you to his eternal glory in Christ, after you have suffered a little while, will himself restore you and make you strong, firm and steadfast. To him be the power for ever and ever. Amen. (1 Peter 5:6-11)

The promise in these great verses is that the God of all grace will lift us up in due time. Tough times don't last forever. When trials and tribulations come and tempt us to anxiety, God will use them to build spiritual muscle in us and prepare us for the works He has prepared in advance for us to do—if we let Him.

Jesus is not surprised that we get anxious. He's certainly not surprised that I fell back into old unhelpful patterns. And He's always ready to help us resolve our anxiety and move forward towards the destiny He has for us.

As we conclude this chapter, I can't think of anything better than to read slowly and prayerfully His beautiful words to us about anxiety that show us just how well He understands us and how humbly trusting Him is the ultimate antidote:

"Therefore I tell you, do not worry about your life, what you will eat or drink; or about your body, what you will wear. Is not life more than food, and the body more than clothes?

Look at the birds of the air; they do not sow or reap or store away in barns, and yet your heavenly

Father feeds them. Are you not much more valuable than they?

Can any one of you by worrying add a single hour to your life?

And why do you worry about clothes? See how the flowers of the field grow. They do not labor or spin. Yet I tell you that not even Solomon in all his splendor was dressed like one of these. If that is how God clothes the grass of the field, which is here today and tomorrow is thrown into the fire, will he not much more clothe you—you of little faith?

So do not worry, saying, 'What shall we eat?' or 'What shall we drink?' or 'What shall we wear?' For the pagans run after all these things, and your heavenly Father knows that you need them.

But seek first his kingdom and his righteousness, and all these things will be given to you as well.

Therefore do not worry about tomorrow, for tomorrow will worry about itself. Each day has enough trouble of its own."
(Matthew 6:25-34)

Does God care for you? Yes! He is love. He is the God of all grace. He has good plans for you. Humble yourself before Him, cast your anxiety upon Him, be alert to Satan's lies, and He will lift you up in due time.

So let me say to you, as Jesus said to the stormy sea, "Hush, be still." You can cast your anxiety onto the God who is present and powerful, and leave it with Him because He does care for you. You can be calm, even in the middle of the storms that you will inevitably pass through.

In a society which has anxiety woven into its very fabric, what a fantastic opportunity we have as children of God to model an entirely different way of living based on trust in the God of all grace.

MAKING THE GRACE CONNECTION

As we've seen, the reason you *can* cast your anxiety onto God is because He cares for you. He is the God of all grace. He *is* real, He *is* strong, and He *is* love.

But if you're not sure that He genuinely cares for you, you may bring a concern to Him and ask for His help, but chances are you'll pick it back up and try to solve it yourself.

If you want the truth to set you free, you have to *know* the truth. Jesus said, "I am the Truth." Truth is not just a concept. It's a *person*. And it is knowing Him that enables us to trust Him.

What makes it tricky is that the world and the devil paint caricatures of God that keep us from really knowing Him. And our experiences with our own parents and other authority figures can shape our view of our Heavenly Father.

Perhaps your experiences have led you to believe that God is unjust. Or that He's unkind or even cruel. Maybe you feel God is hard to please.

All of us need to unravel some distorted images if we are to know God as He really is and trust Him.

Dr. Neil Anderson produced a list of amazing Biblical truths called *My Father God* that many find especially helpful in identifying and dismantling faulty ideas about God that we have unconsciously developed over the years.

It contains eleven statements in which you are invited to reject common lies about God and affirm your choice to believe what God says is actually true instead.

When you truly know this all-powerful God and His astonishingly gracious disposition towards you, why on earth would you be anxious? Why on earth would you think that you know better than He does?

To start, read the whole list out loud. Take note of any statement that seems to stick in your throat or just doesn't ring true to you.

You will then find each statement repeated together with a few thoughts to help you engage with it and uncover any faulty understanding of God you may have.

This is potentially life-changing. There's no need to rush—please take as much time as it takes to go through the statements and notes. If you take a day or even a week on each statement, it will be a very good investment in your future fruitfulness.

My Father God

- I reject the lie that You, Father God, are distant and uninterested in me.

  I choose to believe the truth that You, Father God, are always personally present with me, have plans to give me a hope and a future, and have prepared works in advance specifically for me to do.

  (PSALM 139:1-18; MATTHEW 28:20, JEREMIAH 29:11, EPHESIANS 2:10)

- I reject the lie that You, Father God, are insensitive and don't know me or care for me.

  I choose to believe the truth that You, Father God, are kind and compassionate and know every single thing about me.

  (PSALM 103:8-14; 1 JOHN 3:1-3; HEBREWS 4:12-13)

- I reject the lie that You, Father God, are stern and have placed unrealistic expectations on me.

  I choose to believe the truth that You, Father God, have accepted me and are joyfully supportive of me.

  (ROMANS 5:8–11; 15:17)

- I reject the lie that You, Father God, are passive and cold towards me.

  I choose to believe the truth that You, Father God, are warm and affectionate towards me.

  (ISAIAH 40:11; HOSEA 11:3–4)

- I reject the lie that You, Father God, are absent or too busy for me.

  I choose to believe the truth that You, Father God, are always present and eager to be with me and enable me to be all that You created me to be.

  (PHILIPPIANS 1:6; HEBREWS 13:5)

- I reject the lie that You, Father God, are impatient or angry with me, or have rejected me.

  I choose to believe the truth that You, Father God, are patient and slow to anger, and that when You discipline me, it is a proof of Your love, and not rejection.

  (EXODUS 34:6; ROMANS 2:4; HEBREWS 12:5–11)

- I reject the lie that You, Father God, have been mean, cruel, or abusive to me.

  I choose to believe the truth that Satan is mean, cruel, and abusive, but You, Father God, are loving, gentle, and protective.

  (PSALM 18:2; MATTHEW 11:28–30;
  EPHESIANS 6:10–18)

- I reject the lie that You, Father God, are denying me the pleasures of life.

  I choose to believe the truth that You, Father God, are the author of life and will lead me into love, joy, and peace when I choose to be filled with Your Spirit.

  (LAMENTATIONS 3:22–23; GALATIANS 5: 22–24)

- I reject the lie that You, Father God, are trying to control and manipulate me.

  I choose to believe the truth that You, Father God, have set me free, and give me the freedom to make choices and grow in Your grace.

  (GALATIANS 5:1; HEBREWS 4:15–16)

- I reject the lie that You, Father God, have condemned me, and no longer forgive me.

  I choose to believe the truth that You, Father God, have forgiven all my sins and will never use them against me in the future.

  (JEREMIAH 31:31–34; ROMANS 8:1)

- I reject the lie that You, Father God, reject me when I fail to live a perfect or sinless life.

  I choose to believe the truth that You, Father God, are patient towards me and cleanse me when I fail.

  (PROVERBS 24:16; 1 JOHN 1:7–2:2)

- I am the apple of Your eye!

  (DEUTERONOMY 32:9–10)

Connecting With The Truth About Our Father God

I am indebted to Dan Studt, President of Freedom In Christ Ministries USA, for allowing me to base much of what follows on his excellent devotional series on these truths (available at www.ficm.org).

As you consider each statement, ask the Holy Spirit to lead you into all truth. Read the statement out loud. Then read through the notes slowly at least once. Finally read the statement out loud again, declaring to the heavenly realms that this is true because God has said it is true.

You may like to select one or more statements that you particularly need to connect with in a deeper way, in your heart not just your head. For these, declare them every day until you know that something has changed in you.

STATEMENT #1

I reject the lie that You, Father God, are distant and uninterested in me. **I choose to believe the truth that You, Father God, are always personally present with me, have plans to give me a hope and a future, and have prepared works in advance specifically for me to do.**

O LORD, You have searched me and known me... You understand my thoughts... And are intimately acquainted with all my ways. (Psalm 139:1-3 CSB and NASB)

If I take the wings of the dawn, if I dwell in the remotest part of the sea, even there Your hand will lead me, and Your right hand will lay hold of me. (Psalm 139:9-10 NASB)

For You formed my inward parts; You wove me in my mother's womb... skillfully wrought..." (Psalm 139:13 & 15c NASB)

All my days were written in Your book and planned before a single one of them began." (Psalm 139:16 CSB)

Your loving heavenly Father is not distant or uninterested in you. He knows you, understands you, and is intimately familiar with all your ways.

He knows you so well because He is the one who formed you, and He is always with you.

He has carefully crafted you to fulfill a glorious purpose as you walk with Him. He has things that He has specifically prepared with you in mind.

STATEMENT #2

I reject the lie that You, Father God, are insensitive and don't know me or care for me. **I choose to believe the truth that You, Father God, are kind and compassionate and know every single thing about me.**

For the word of God is living and active and sharper than any two-edged sword, and piercing as far as the division of soul and spirit, of both joints and marrow, and able to judge the thoughts and intentions of the heart. (Hebrews 4:12-13 NASB)

Our heavenly Father knows every single thing about us, including the things we perhaps wish He didn't know! And yet:

The Lord is compassionate and merciful, slow to get angry and filled with unfailing love. He will not

*constantly accuse us, nor remain angry forever. He
does not punish us for all our sins; he does not deal
harshly with us, as we deserve. For his unfailing love
toward those who fear him is as great as the height
of the heavens above the earth. He has removed
our sins as far from us as the east is from the west.
The Lord is like a father to his children, tender and
compassionate to those who fear him. For he knows
how weak we are; he remembers we are only dust.
(Psalm 103:8-14 NLT)*

Consider that these verses were written to the entire nation of
Israel regarding their history as a people. If the LORD is able to
be compassionate, gracious, patient, and full of faithful love to
millions of people over hundreds of years, then our short lifetime
and finite amount of sin cannot diminish God's ability to be
gracious, patient and loving toward each of us as individuals.

*See what great love the Father has lavished on us,
that we should be called children of God!... All who
have this hope in him purify themselves, just as he
is pure. (1 John 3:1&3)*

When we believe our Father is insensitive and uncaring and
therefore unwilling to help us, our only option is self-effort and
independent striving. Self-reliance only leads to further defeat.
But when we approach our Father as One who is sensitive and
caring—trusting in what He has done through Jesus on our
behalf—we find grace to help us in our time of need.

STATEMENT #3

I reject the lie that You, Father God, are stern and have
placed unrealistic expectations on me. **I choose to
believe the truth that You, Father God, have accepted
me and are joyfully supportive of me.**

When you picture God looking at you, what expression is on His face?

Many of us imagine that God's face toward us is one of disappointment, disgust, or even disdain. We feel we simply don't live up to His expectations and never will.

But that's a picture based on our performance. We need to replace it with one that is based on Father God's character and steadfastness:

> But God proves his own love for us in that while we were still sinners, Christ died for us. How much more then, since we have now been justified by his blood, will we be saved through him from wrath. For if, while we were enemies, we were reconciled to God through the death of his Son, then how much more, having been reconciled, will we be saved by his life. And not only that, but we also boast in God through our Lord Jesus Christ, through whom we have now received this reconciliation. (Romans 5:8-11 CSB)

> The LORD your God is in your midst, a mighty one who will save; he will rejoice over you with gladness; he will quiet you by his love; he will exult over you with loud singing. (Zephaniah 3:17 ESV)

Your Father God makes a joyful noise when He looks at you! His face lights up to see you! Can you picture Father God smiling upon you? Can you picture His face lighting up when He looks at you?

This has nothing to do with your performance on any particular day. Rather, it is based simply on His gracious, loving character and on what Jesus has done to make you a holy one.

STATEMENT #4

I reject the lie that You, Father God, are passive and cold towards me. **I choose to believe the truth that You, Father God, are warm and affectionate towards me.**

Most parents do the very best they can, but no human parent gets it right all the time.

Did you have a parent who seemed to keep their distance from you? Who disciplined you somewhat more harshly than was helpful? Who seemed to turn their back on you?

It's easy to project that same attitude onto our heavenly Father. We can think that He is constantly frustrated with us or keeping His distance from us.

But the truth is no matter how far we have fallen, He is patiently watching for us to return, just like the father in Jesus' story:

> *"But while he was still a long way off, his father saw him and was filled with compassion for him; he ran to his son, threw his arms around him and kissed him. The son said to him, 'Father, I have sinned against heaven and against you. I am no longer worthy to be called your son.' But the father said to his servants, 'Quick! Bring the best robe and put it on him. Put a ring on his finger and sandals on his feet. Bring the fattened calf and kill it. Let's have a feast and celebrate. For this son of mine was dead and is alive again; he was lost and is found.' So they began to celebrate." (Luke 15:20-24)*

Our Heavenly Father is warm and affectionate toward us. He protects us in His mighty hands:

> *See, the Lord God comes with strength, and His power establishes His rule. His reward is with Him, and His gifts accompany Him. He protects His flock like a shepherd; He gathers the lambs in His arms*

and carries them in the fold of His garment. He gently leads those that are nursing. (Isaiah 40:10-11 CSB)

"I am the good shepherd. I know My own sheep, and they know Me, as the Father knows Me, and I know the Father. I lay down my life for the sheep... I give them eternal life, and they will never perish—ever! No one will snatch them out of My hand. My Father, who has given them to Me, is greater than all. No one is able to snatch them out of the Father's hand. The Father and I are one."
(John 10:14-15, 28-30 CSB)

STATEMENT #5

I reject the lie that You, Father God, are absent or too busy for me. **I choose to believe the truth that You, Father God, are always present and eager to be with me and enable me to be all that You created me to be.**

Our earthly parents could only do so much. They were human. Finite. Limited.

This is not the case with our heavenly Father. His power and presence have no limits. His love is greater than we can imagine. And His ability to be with every person on the planet, in every moment, is beyond our comprehension.

No matter our circumstances, we can count on our Father's presence: "For he himself has said, I will never leave you or abandon you. Therefore, we may boldly say, The Lord is my helper" (Hebrews 13:5b-6a, CSB).

Unlike earthly parents who are overwhelmed by busyness, abandoned us, or were simply not good at relating to us, God is always accessible and delighted to be with you.

STATEMENT #6

I reject the lie that You, Father God, are impatient or angry with me, or have rejected me. **I choose to believe the truth that You, Father God, are patient and slow to anger, and that when You discipline me, it is a proof of Your love, and not rejection.**

You may have had earthly parents who appeared to punish you for doing wrong. Punishment looks back to the past and exacts the cost of bad behavior from a person. It's about releasing anger toward the person.

> *But he was pierced for our transgressions,*
> *he was crushed for our iniquities;*
> *the punishment that brought us peace was on him,*
> *and by his wounds we are healed. (Isaiah 53:5)*

All your punishment fell on Jesus at the Cross. God will never, ever punish you.

> *And have you forgotten the exhortation that addresses you as sons? 'My son, do not regard lightly the discipline of the Lord, nor be weary when reproved by him. For the Lord disciplines the one he loves, and chastises every son whom he receives.' It is for discipline that you have to endure. God is treating you as sons. For what son is there whom his father does not discipline? If you are left without discipline, in which all have participated, then you are illegitimate children and not sons. Besides this, we have had earthly fathers who disciplined us and we respected them. Shall we not much more be subject to the Father of spirits and live? For they disciplined us for a short time as it seemed best to them, but he disciplines us for our good, that we may share his holiness. For the moment all discipline seems painful rather than pleasant, but later it yields*

the peaceful fruit of righteousness to those who have been trained by it. (Hebrews 12:5-11 ESV)

God will, however, discipline us from time to time. Discipline is forward-looking. It seeks to make use of the incident or behavior to teach and mold the child into the character of Christ. Discipline is focused on your best interests and long-term development. His will is that we would grow in Christ-like character, and He desires to use every person and incident in our lives toward that purpose.

And we know that in all things God works for the good of those who love him, who have been called according to His purpose... to be conformed to the image of His Son. (Romans 8:28, 29b)

Are these things sometimes painful? Yes. Are they for our good? Yes. Does God ever have mixed motives? Never.

STATEMENT #7

I reject the lie that You, Father God, have been mean, cruel, or abusive to me. **I choose to believe the truth that Satan is mean, cruel, and abusive, but You, Father God, are loving, gentle, and protective.**

The Lord is my rock and my fortress and my deliverer, my God, my rock, in whom I take refuge, my shield, and the horn of my salvation, my stronghold. (Psalm 18:2 ESV)

A bruised reed he will not break, and a faintly burning wick he will not quench; he will faithfully bring forth justice. (Isaiah 42:3 ESV)

I have loved you with an everlasting love. (Jeremiah 31:3 ESV)

Our Father God cares for us. He is looking out for us. He is our stronghold.

He would never abuse us but only ever does things that are in our best interest.

"The thief comes only to steal and kill and destroy; I have come that they may have life, and have it to the full." (John 10:10)

God is not mean, cruel, or abusive. He is loving, gentle, and protective. If you struggle to understand why God allowed a certain situation to happen, do not overlook the fact that we live in a fallen world, whose prince is a cruel, evil tyrant.

And do not overlook the part that other people, under the influence of Satan and their own selfish desires, can play in doing us harm.

At the Cross Jesus completely disarmed Satan (Colossians 2:15) and Ephesians 1:19-22 says that Jesus is seated at God's right hand, the ultimate seat of power and authority, "far above all rule and authority, power and dominion." God has placed all things under His feet, and we are told that He is now "head over everything." That's a great position of power!

What is our position? Ephesians 2:6 says "And God raised us up with Christ and seated us with Him in the heavenly realms in Christ Jesus." We are seated with Jesus, far above Satan and all demonic powers!

Why not ask Him to reveal to you where He was at the times of your life that were most difficult? Wait for Him to show you.

STATEMENT #8

I reject the lie that You, Father God, are denying me the pleasures of life. **I choose to believe the truth that You, Father God, are the author of life and will lead me into love, joy, and peace when I choose to be filled with Your Spirit.**

"I am the man who has seen affliction by the rod of the LORD'S wrath..." (Lamentations 3:1). This is the prophet Jeremiah's description of his circumstances. He went on to use words and phrases like besieged and surrounded with bitterness and hardship... weighed me down with chains... he mangled me and left me without help... pierced my heart.

Jeremiah felt like God had stolen all the joy of life.

Not only that, but Jeremiah felt that God, the Author of life, was beating him down to the point of giving up.

That's how he felt. But eventually, he realized that he had it all wrong:

> I will never forget this awful time, as I grieve over my loss. Yet I still dare to hope when I call this to mind: The unfailing love of the LORD never ends! By his mercies we have been kept from complete destruction. Great is his faithfulness; his mercies begin afresh each day. I say to myself, "The LORD is my inheritance therefore, I will hope in him!" (Lamentations 3:20-24 NLT & CSB)

Getting his thinking straight totally transformed him.

God wants only the best for you. But He knows far better than we do what that looks like.

Don't buy the lies of the world, the flesh, and the devil that the pleasures of this life are paramount.

As we submit to the One who is Life, we will experience true life in Him and exhibit the fruit of the Spirit: love, joy, peace, patience, kindness, goodness, faithfulness, gentleness, and self-control (see Galatians 5:22-23).

STATEMENT #9

I reject the lie that You, Father God, are trying to control and manipulate me. **I choose to believe the truth that You, Father God, have set me free, and give me the freedom to make choices and grow in Your grace.**

In his pride, Satan sought to usurp God's position as Sovereign. Adam and Eve were tempted by the desire to gain more power, "to be like God." Jacob controlled his father, Isaac, by tricking him into giving Jacob the blessing instead of his brother. Sarah wanted children, so she had Abram sleep with her servant. In all these examples, we see people attempting to exert power over others as a means of control. Whether that control comes in the form of physical force, like slavery or abuse, or in a more subtle form, like false teaching or manipulation, the impact is the same: a return to slavery.

God's Sovereignty means that He has supreme authority over all things. Every inch of creation lies under His Lordship. Psalm 103:19 (ESV) says, "The LORD has established his throne in the heavens, and his kingdom rules over all."

But even though our Father God is Sovereign, He is not controlling. In His infinite love and kindness, He designed creation in such a way that He provided us with freedom and personal responsibility.

He does not make us obey Him or submit to Him. It's our choice. But every choice has consequences.

> *It is for freedom that Christ has set us free. Stand firm, then, and do not let yourselves be burdened again by a yoke of slavery. (Galatians 5:1)*

STATEMENT #10

I reject the lie that You, Father God, have condemned me, and no longer forgive me. **I choose to believe the truth that You, Father God, have forgiven all my sins and will never use them against me in the future.**

Over 500 years before Jesus was born, our loving heavenly Father told us through the prophet Jeremiah that He would make a new covenant that was not based upon our performance. He said it is "not like the covenant that I made... I will put my law within them, and I will write it on their hearts. And I will be their God, and they shall be my people... for they shall all know me... For I will forgive their iniquity, and I will remember their sin no more" (Jeremiah 31:32-34, ESV).

Condemnation is related to judgment. All judgment for our sin was placed on Jesus when he hung on the cross. There is no more payment needed to deal with our sin before God.

> There is therefore now no condemnation for those who are in Christ Jesus. (Romans 8:1 ESV)

Remember, now means *now* and no means *no*!

When we confess our sins (which simply means to agree with God that what we've done is wrong), "He is faithful and righteous to forgive us our sins and to cleanse us from all unrighteousness" (1 John 1:9 CSB).

STATEMENT #11

I reject the lie that You, Father God, reject me when I fail to live a perfect or sinless life. **I choose to believe the truth that You, Father God, are patient towards me and cleanse me when I fail. I am the apple of Your eye!**

For all have sinned and fall short of the glory of God, and all are justified freely by his grace through the redemption that came by Christ Jesus. (Romans 3:23-24)

It's easy to fall for Satan's lie that you have done something that would absolutely disqualify you from belonging to God. We have thoughts such as, "You're the only one like this! Do you think anyone else is struggling with that? God would never want you!"

Well, *everyone* has sinned and fallen short of God's standards. We've *all* missed the mark. You are not alone.

Our heavenly Father is "compassionate and gracious, slow to anger and abounding in faithful love" (Psalm 103:8 CSB). God is not surprised when we fail. But He lavished His grace upon us anyway because of who He is—not because of what we have or have not done.

We have no need to pretend, or to try to be something we are not. God does not place unrealistic expectations on us. Why do we put them on ourselves?

You really are the apple of God's eye!

CHAPTER 7

FRUITFUL!

Let's take stock. Paul says, "For Christ's love compels us" (2 Corinthians 5:14) and John tells us, "We love because he first loved us" (1 John 4:19). God wants our motivation to be love and nothing but love. That's what I want for my life too. And I'm pretty sure you do as well.

We've considered four "false motivators": guilt, shame, fear, and anxiety. In this chapter and the next one, we will look at a fifth hindrance to being compelled by love alone: pride.

Pride is like bad breath. Everyone knows you've got it except you! In this chapter, we'll see how it can prevent us from making a real difference for eternity. In the next chapter, we'll see how it prevents us from being the answer to the only prayer Jesus is recorded as praying for those of us who come after His original disciples.

HOW CAN WE BEAR FRUIT?

One time I was approached after a conference by someone who clearly wanted his life to glorify God and be as fruitful as possible.

He said he felt God wanted him to start a Christian ministry, and he had been looking at how Freedom In Christ Ministries had grown so quickly. He said, "How did you do it?"

I said, "I don't really know. It just kind of happened. If God wants you to do something similar, He will do it—just stay close to Him and cooperate with Him."

That clearly didn't satisfy him because after the conference he sent me an e-mail asking me again to tell him step by step how to create a ministry like Freedom In Christ.

I honestly did think hard about how I could help him. Clearly, I could have said some practical things like, "Get a board of godly people together," or "Put a basic strategy together." We all naturally think that it comes down to our own efforts. And we therefore risk burning out or being overwhelmed. Most of us learn this the hard way as God will often allow us to struggle under the burden of trying to do it ourselves.

I sent him an email back saying much the same thing as I'd said when we met, adding that it's when we persevere through difficulties that God really seems to prepare us for future ministry.

I've not heard from him since but I suspect that he had heard God correctly about starting a ministry. I also suspect that he is now in fruitful ministry, but that it was nowhere near as straightforward as he imagined, with many difficulties along the way, every one of which God will have used to keep chiseling away at His work of art.

His question is the same question many of us audibly or inaudibly ask at one point or other: how can I produce and maintain fruitfulness? How can I ensure that the rest of my life makes a real difference for eternity?

APART FROM JESUS WE CAN DO *NOTHING*

So how can we bear fruit for Jesus? Some of His most important words, coming near the end of His earthly life, shed light on this:

"I am the true vine, and my Father is the gardener. He cuts off every branch in me that bears no fruit, while every branch that does bear fruit he prunes so that it will be even more fruitful. You are already clean because of the word I have spoken to you. Remain in me, as I also remain in you. No branch can bear fruit by itself; it must remain in the vine. Neither can you bear fruit unless you remain in me. I am the vine; you are the branches. If you remain in me and I in you, you will bear much fruit; apart from me you can do nothing." (John 15:1-5)

Jesus didn't say, "Apart from Me you can't do very much." He said, "Apart from Me you can do *nothing*."

Now, you can get out of bed, eat breakfast, brush your teeth, get dressed, go to work, make a living, raise a family, grow old, retire and die without Jesus. Millions do that every day. So what did Jesus mean when He said, "apart from Me you can do nothing"? Simply that you can do nothing of eternal value unless you depend completely on Him, unless it is from a position of resting in His ability and staying connected to Him.

OUR ONE RESPONSIBILITY

If you ever venture into a vineyard, I can assure you that there is one thing you will never hear. You will never hear the sound of branches grunting and groaning, straining to get grapes to pop out on them. And there is something I guarantee you will not see: branches disconnected from the vine with healthy fruit growing on them.

Branches don't bear fruit because they try really hard. And neither do we. Branches that are not attached to the vine do not and cannot bear fruit. These are two inviolable laws of the vineyard.

What is the branch's one responsibility? Our natural reaction would be to say, "To bear fruit!" Nope. It is to abide in, stay close to, remain with, be at home in the vine. The gardener knows that if he makes sure the plant is healthy with the branches firmly connected to the vine, it will bear fruit.

Here's a key principle: Christians who focus on their need to bear fruit put themselves into a law-based system of fearful, anxious performance...with the resulting guilt and shame if they fail, and pride if they appear to succeed.

But Christians who focus on simply abiding in Jesus enter into a life of "grace-rest" where, paradoxically, they bear much fruit.

There is a progression we need to go through in our understanding of who Jesus is. It is not enough to know Jesus as Savior, though that is the essential starting place for all of us. It is not even enough to know Him as Lord, though we do need to come to that place of submission. We need to understand the truth that He is our very Life (Colossians 3:3).

Then we simply need to stay connected to Him.

Jesus Himself modeled this for us. He is the Son of God. Everything that has been created was created through Him. Yet when he chose to give up all the glory of Heaven and came to this earth, he took an attitude that is shocking:

> *"Truly, truly, I say to you, the Son can do nothing of his own accord, but only what he sees the Father doing." (John 5:19 ESV)*

In verse 30 of the same chapter, He added "I can do nothing on my own."

Even though He was God, numerous times Jesus made it clear that He was not operating out of His "God-ness." He was modeling how God wants us to live too—we can do absolutely nothing apart from Him.

Did you know that Martin Luther once wrote that he had so much to do that he had to get up three hours earlier than usual to pray? How does that make you feel? Guilty probably! Perhaps you've tried to emulate him or something similar you've heard about.

Are you still doing it? If you're anything like me, you tried hard for a few days or weeks but couldn't keep it up and walked away feeling like a failure.

How did Jesus approach prayer? Prayer was a lifestyle for Jesus. He too was usually up early, walking the mountains and talking to His Father. This is not a formal, dutiful prayer life. I imagine there were long times of silence as you often get between people who know each other well—a comfortable silence.

God probably isn't asking you to get up three hours earlier to pray right now. But He would be so delighted if you came to Him just because you want to—with no agenda—even for 10 minutes. As you do that more and more, you will probably get hold of the truth, like Jesus did and Luther did, that without God you can do nothing whatsoever of any lasting value.

And you may well end up getting up early to pray—not out of guilt or the need to check some kind of spiritual performance box but out of a real understanding of truth and because you just love spending time with God. You will not be focusing on the fruit— how many hours of prayer you can do—but on the One who is the True Vine. And paradoxically you will bear fruit!

REST IN HIM

Jesus made an offer, specifically to people who felt overwhelmed by the demands of trying to live up to a certain set of expectations. And it was this:

> *"Come to me, all who labor and are heavy laden, and I will give you rest. Take my yoke upon you, and learn from me, for I am gentle and lowly in heart, and you will find rest for your souls. For my yoke is easy, and my burden is light." (Matthew 11:28-30 ESV)*

What an amazing statement of grace! Can you imagine a god from any other religion making that kind of offer? God doesn't want us to labor and be laden down. He wants us to rest. He genuinely offers us a yoke that is easy and a burden that is light. As we've seen, there is nothing that God demands we do. Absolutely nothing.

Interestingly the picture Jesus gives us when He offers us rest is that of two oxen plowing a field. That looks more like hard work than rest, doesn't it?

I don't want to give you the impression that the Christian life is supposed to be something where you just float along singing lovely songs and hearing God's voice all the time. The rest we're talking about doesn't mean lying around doing nothing. It's an *internal* rest that is based on faith and dependence upon God. Our focus is not on bearing fruit but on remaining in the Vine, on our relationship with Jesus. There's a sense that we rest from our works, but the works still get done.

God has always wanted His people to understand that rest is key. When God made the world, He worked for six days and then rested on the seventh. God didn't go off for a nap—that's not the sense of the original Hebrew word at all. God "rested" because His all-powerful reign over the universe began and all was as it should be.

But what about Adam? Just the opposite. He was created on day six, so the first full day of Adam's life was the seventh day when God rested. Everything was already done. Everything he needed was on hand. There was nothing whatsoever to worry about. The first full day of his life was that day of rest, a day of *connecting* with God, *knowing* that God was in charge, and *actively trusting* Him.

So he rested first, and then God put him to work. And that's the principle God wants us to embody. We rest, then we work. It's not meant to be that we work hard and then rest to recover. It's the other way around. Out of rest comes fruitful ministry.

First, we rest in God's reality and provision, and then we work. We learn to trust God, then we bear fruit.

And yet so much of our lives are spent the other way around—we wear ourselves out, and then we rest to recover. If you're anything like me, I can find myself working harder and harder, and in desperation praying, "Oh Lord, bless the work of my hands and I'll trust you more!"

When all along, it's supposed to be the other way around. Trust God, then bear fruit. If you want to bear fruit that will remain; if you want to have an impact on this planet that lasts into eternity; if you want to come into alignment with God's kingdom purposes for your life, your family and your world; then it has to start with resting in the true Vine, Jesus Christ, who is our very Life.

How can we tell if we are relying on our own strength to bear fruit? Essentially when we realize that we are trying to control events or people.

The guy who was desperately trying to start a ministry was perhaps trying to control *events*. He had probably heard accurately from God, but his role was then primarily to remain in the Vine and let God make it happen, not to try and bring it about himself. It's taken me a long time to realize that when I sense God wants to do something, my role is to pray and wait, and then walk through the door that He unfailingly opens.

Sometimes we can also try to control *people*. The Pharisees were zealous for God and were trying to win favor with Him by imposing their strict interpretations of the law on everyone, even to the extent that some of them were sneaking around trying to catch people in the act of adultery. The elder brother reminded his father of all the good works he was slaving away at, but he was effectively trying to control the father by using his good works to make the father bless him.

I've lost count of the number of people I've invited to join us in Freedom In Christ, usually because I have a sense that God is calling them. I'm really careful not to put any pressure on them whatsoever. Sometimes they say, "I'm not sure God is calling me to join you," to which my response is always along the lines of,

"Well, we only want you if God is definitely calling you so please don't feel any pressure whatsoever. Take your time and make sure you've heard from Him." When I sense I should ask someone to take on a particular task, I usually end by saying something like, "No pressure whatsoever," and I really mean it. Interestingly, nearly everyone I sense I should ask to join us or to take on a task senses the same nudge from God and ends up being a blessing to the ministry.

Those who realize that apart from God they can do nothing do not need to try to control either events or people. They rest in the knowledge that their Father God can be trusted to take care of people and events outside of their realm of control. They know that He really does work all things together for their good (Romans 8:28).

● THE GATEWAY OF BROKENNESS

So how do you enter this grace-rest life?

It isn't easy. Because we have a natural inclination not to abide in the vine and rely completely on Jesus but to rely instead on our own strength and abilities.

We have seen that King David's antidote to pride in Psalm 131 was to "still and quieten" his soul. David recognizes that deep inside there's a part of him that cries out constantly like a child still on breast milk. Our souls are always crying out—from guilt, shame, fear or anxiety, or because they want to give in to the fleshly urges that come with the subtle voice of temptation. Or because they want to control people or events. There's a restlessness.

So how did David learn to still and quieten his soul? He was anointed to be king when he was still a young man. But it was years before it actually happened, and he found himself thrown into a nightmare scenario where he spent years in the wilderness in fear of his life as King Saul tried to hunt him down. He learned that God is real and can be trusted to keep His word. He learned that God is good and had plans to give him a hope and a future. He learned that God would bring about those plans in His own time when David was ready.

Like David we need to learn to still and quiet our soul, to come to the point of complete dependence on God. When we feel guilty, to lay it at the foot of the cross and walk away. When we feel ashamed, to recognize that we are new people with a new name. When the fleshly urges come, to know that they only bring bondage, and we can choose not to give in to them. When fear comes, to know that only God has the right to be feared and He is for us. When anxiety grips us, to cast it onto Jesus and leave it with Him. And when we are tempted to pride, to know that we can do absolutely nothing apart from Him.

God is actively looking to help us deal with the pride and control that holds us back and help us enter into a life of grace-filled rest. How? I wish I had good news for you! Well, actually it really is good news. It just isn't easy news.

His cure is to bring us to a point of brokenness in order to teach us how absolutely dependent we are on Him. Being completely dependent on someone else is a nightmare scenario for most of us—think about growing old or sick for example—yet Jesus wants us to learn to be dependent on Him. In His grace, He works on us as gently as He can.

There is a process of cutting and hacking away at fleshly self-centeredness and self-reliance that all of God's people—no exceptions—must go through in order to enter God's rest. Jesus called it "pruning." Hebrews 12 calls it "discipline." And the writer of the letter tells us to be diligent to enter into God's rest. It's not easy. And it's definitely not fun. In fact, it's downright painful, which is why it requires diligence and endurance, otherwise known as "hanging in there." But it is the gateway into the grace-rest life. And it is more than worth it.

Let's take a look at Hebrews 12:

> "My son, do not regard lightly the discipline of the Lord, nor be weary when reproved by him.

For the Lord disciplines the one he loves,
and chastises every son whom he receives."

For the moment all discipline seems painful rather
than pleasant, but later it yields the peaceful fruit of
righteousness to those who have been trained by it.
(Hebrews 12:5b,6,11 ESV)

I don't like words like "discipline" or "reproved." I'm guessing you don't either. The strongholds of self-sufficiency, self-reliance, self-satisfaction, and selfishness run very deep. They require strong measures to remove them. God's cure is to discipline us in love to bring us to the point of brokenness.

He wants us to see—and we really do need to see—how utterly futile our own efforts are and how absolutely dependent upon Him we really are. We need to learn, not just in our head but in our heart, that apart from Jesus we really can't do anything of eternal value. This is where we discover that Jesus is not just our Savior but our very Life.

It may come as a surprise to learn that even Jesus had to go through this: "Although he was a son, he learned obedience through what he suffered" (Hebrews 5:8 ESV). There is no shortcut. But when we understand that difficult situations are actually helping us grow and bear fruit, we can learn to embrace them even if we don't enjoy them.

I now know that pride has been a huge issue in my own life, but there was a time when I was blissfully unaware, when I thought I was doing fine in my Christian life; but in fact, there was precious little real fruit.

I was on the leadership team of a small church and another member of the team was really struggling because she felt that she had heard from God something that was very difficult to share. This is what I wrote in my journal at the time:

> Last night at the leaders meeting, Sandra came.
> Turns out she has had a very specific word from
> God that has caused her real agony and upset

> since Sunday. The main point was that God is grieving over our church because we are hard hearted.
>
> She then had very specific things for each of us. Mine was having a "holier than thou" attitude, not being vulnerable, making people think they cannot be as holy as me—apparently this is causing discouragement to Christians and putting non-Christians off.

I remember being quite shocked and mumbling something like, "Thank you for that, Sandra, I can't quite see it myself but will certainly go and pray about it." I then looked around the room at the other leaders, certain, I think, that they would back me up and reassure me that that's not what I was like at all. But they all studiously avoided meeting my gaze! No one felt the need to jump in and correct or even slightly modify what Sandra had said!

Let me read a little more from my journal:

> Zoë and I talked this evening and concluded that basically we have been brought up to believe that we can "handle" things—and indeed in one sense we can. As capable people we tend to rely on our own resources. As a result we hardly ever ask for help because we don't think we need any; we don't let people get close because we don't think we have any needs; I am ready to offer advice and "wisdom" but don't seem to need any myself....
>
> I don't think we yet realize what an offense this attitude is to God. Tonight we repented and prayed that God would smash the strongholds of pride, independence, and self-sufficiency in us.

I remember that led to a period of some weeks where I just became increasingly aware and increasingly horrified of how proud I had been. I spent hours in prayer just saying sorry to God. Often, I would just end up lying flat out on the floor before Him.

Here's one final entry from my journal from that period:

> I have realized that my relationship with Jesus
> is very weak and that much of my Christianity
> has been about making me feel good—building
> myself up in the eyes of others etc. I feel totally
> weak and helpless and happy and excited.

It's strange but when you get to the point of realizing your weakness and helplessness and throw yourself onto God's mercy, it somehow feels like the place you were always meant to be—like the younger brother when he returned and fell into his father's arms.

It's scary to read that God opposes the proud (James 4:6). In His love for us, He unleashes events in our lives that overwhelm us, that take us out of our depth and into realms where we find ourselves beyond our ability to cope. Pride literally does come before a fall. But we never get to experience the power of God in our lives, unless we are brought to "an end of ourselves."

Whatever breaking instrument God uses in our lives—loss of reputation, misunderstanding, injustice, health issues or financial difficulties—it will be tailor-made to get down to the issues of pride and control in our lives. God's goal is to strip away those things that we have made to be substitutes for God. In His relentless love for us, He sets out to woo us back to himself. He wants to rescue us from all other attachments and restore the intimacy of our relationship with Him.

The apostle Paul had been given amazing insights into the truths of God that could easily have made him proud. Yet he found a depth of the grace-rest life that few have attained. He tells us how:

> So to keep me from becoming conceited because of
> the surpassing greatness of the revelations, a thorn
> was given me in the flesh, a messenger of Satan to
> harass me, to keep me from becoming conceited.
> Three times I pleaded with the Lord about this, that
> it should leave me. But he said to me, "My grace
> is sufficient for you, for my power is made perfect

*in weakness." Therefore I will boast all the more
gladly of my weaknesses, so that the power of Christ
may rest upon me. For the sake of Christ, then, I
am content with weaknesses, insults, hardships,
persecutions, and calamities. For when I am weak,
then I am strong. (2 Corinthians 12:7-10 ESV)*

God isn't the cause of every difficulty we encounter. But He will use every difficulty for our good. He never wastes any experience.

No one is saying that we should enjoy difficulties. But they aren't always things to be prayed out of the way. Tough times are where we learn to trust Him. His grace is enough even if it doesn't feel like it.

If you want to be proud of anything, be proud of your weaknesses! That's when Christ's power can really work in you.

Eagles are huge birds. They can have a wing span of 9 feet and can weigh over 25 pounds. That's about the same as a medium-sized dog such as a cocker spaniel (the weight, not the wing span!). If you've ever seen an eagle, you know that they fly to a great height—imagine how much energy is required to get a bird that big so high. You'd think it would be a huge amount.

In fact, all an eagle does is jump off a high place, find some rising warm air and circle in it. They have a mechanism that means they can simply lock their wings in place so there is practically no energy required to get them to those amazing heights. It's all done by the warm air.

*Even youths shall faint and be weary,
and young men shall fall exhausted;
but they who wait for the LORD
shall renew their strength;
they shall mount up with wings like eagles;
they shall run and not be weary;
they shall walk and not faint.
(Isaiah 40:30-31 ESV)*

Part of resting is waiting for God, looking for the warm air if you like. The idea behind the Hebrew word translated here as "wait" is something like "to gather together" much as strands in a rope are bound together to make something much stronger. There's a sense that as we wait on God, we are bound together with Him and become strong in His strength.

As we lock our wings and rest in Him, He renews our strength, and we rise up.

One very simple practical way in which we can wait for God rather than rush ahead in our own understanding is to build some space into our decision-making process to allow God to have the lead. Do you have a decision to make? If you can, why not try delaying it for a few days—maybe a week—to invite God to put His plan in place, if it should contradict yours?

I am wired to do. I love having loads of things to do and can quite easily run on pure adrenaline. At those times, I am likely to charge ahead in my own strength with the result that I get stressed and overloaded. Yet if I don't have enough to do, my soul shouts out and I feel aimless and unsettled. This is not a good way to live and really gets in the way of entering God's rest. God blessed me with a really difficult period, the most difficult period of my life so far, to help me grow in this. It lasted two years or so.

Zoë, my wife, collapsed in the middle of the night with no warning. She couldn't get up. I thought she had died at one point. I called an ambulance that took her to hospital. She recovered to a certain extent, and then we embarked on a variety of different tests to try to figure out what had happened and what might be wrong with her.

One by one, every obvious serious medical issue was ruled out which was a relief. But she didn't regain her usual strength and at various points when she did a little too much, she would relapse. She was very tired. She felt ill. She had headaches. Each time she relapsed, she got worse until she was at a point where she couldn't really leave the house. Once every two or three days she could perhaps shuffle the 50 yards or so to the postbox and that was it. Finally, she got a diagnosis of Chronic Fatigue Syndrome.

Not a great comfort—it's an extremely debilitating illness, and the doctors have very little success with it.

I had to keep the home and the family going. It became quite stressful but in a way, I thrived on all the doing. I became adept at cooking lots of meals at once and freezing them and that seemed to give me a great sense of accomplishment. But I had to ease off on my ministry commitments. I accepted hardly any speaking engagements. I cut back a lot on my time in the office. Guess what? I found that God was well able to keep everything going—and not just going but growing—without my assistance.

During this period, one of our intercessors tentatively sent me a word that she felt God wanted to say to me:

> Am I not your hope? If there were no ministry, would I not still be your hope? Your joy? If everything was stripped away, would I be enough? This is a hard question for my beloved. So many believe they need to be My slaves in order to please Me, when it is their hearts I brood over.

It is indeed a hard question! If everything were stripped away, would Jesus be enough?

Shortly after that, and during this two-year period of Zoë's illness, I did accept a ministry engagement. I went out to Portugal to meet Samuel Paolo, a pastor who was interested in getting Freedom In Christ started there. I could see he was an incredibly busy man involved in running a busy church, coordinating evangelicals across Portugal and leading projects to feed the poor locally and help children in Africa. On the way back to the airport at the end of the trip, I did my usual "no pressure" thing and said, "Please don't feel you have to start Freedom In Christ here just because we've met. Only do it if you feel called to it." He replied, "Don't worry, I won't," and told me his story.

He told me how he had once been so driven to keep "doing" that his marriage and ministry were at the point of meltdown. He finally got alone with God and felt Jesus saying, "If you didn't have any of this ministry, would I be enough?" At which point the hairs on the back of my neck stood up as I recalled the word I had just received from our intercessor! He was honest enough to tell me that his answer to the question was, "Not really, Lord, no." And I knew straightaway that my honest answer would be exactly the same.

He worked through it to the point where now he could say, "Yes, Jesus, you are enough." He is still an incredibly busy guy with lots going on but internally he is now at rest. He is doing only what the Father is telling him to do and I'm so glad the Father did—a couple of years later—tell him to start Freedom In Christ in Portugal. He has seen great fruit in a difficult place.

On my first visit, he showed me a plot of land and shared his dream to build a church on it. At that time, his church was meeting in a mechanic's workshop and had little money. Today there is a thriving church in a wonderful building on that plot of land. Fruit comes from remaining in the vine and nothing else.

Zoë was ill for two years but made a complete recovery. In that time, both of us learned a deeper level of dependence on God. We have often debated whether, if we could, we would go back and change the past so that we not have to endure that difficult time. We have concluded that we gained so much from it that we wouldn't change a thing.

The proof of the pudding is in the eating, of course, and I know I would find it really hard if the ministry were taken away from me. But the bottom line is, yes, Jesus, you are enough.

> Through many dangers, toils and snares,
> I have already come;
>
> 'Tis grace has brought me safe thus far,
> And grace will lead me home.

Freedom In Christ Ministries has expanded into 40 or so countries, and the Freedom In Christ Course has been translated into 40 or so languages and reached millions of people. I love the fact that all of this has so clearly been God's doing. I could never have done it. Right now, I sense that God is saying that He has a lot more He wants to do through the ministry. Having seen how He has worked so far, I know that I don't need to try to make things happen. I simply need to put one foot in front of the other and wait for Him to open the doors and provide what we need.

I also know that the sky is the limit regarding personal fruitfulness because it doesn't depend on me but on God Almighty Himself. There's a wonderful corresponding truth to "I can do nothing on my own":

> *I can do all things through him who strengthens me.*
> *(Philippians 4:13 ESV)*

What is the fruit that God wants to see in your life? Remember that God is primarily concerned with what you are *like* rather than what you *do*. He looks at the heart. The fruit of the Spirit is not external ministry, it's love, joy, peace, gentleness, self-control. All of those are character attributes. Yet as we develop those character attributes, they will flow over into the things we do.

And there are indeed works that God has prepared just for you to do since before the creation of the world. You don't know what they all are yet. No matter how huge they may be, they are all completely possible.

COUNTING THE COST

In Matthew 16, we see a crucial moment in Jesus' ministry where God reveals to Simon Peter exactly who Jesus is.

> *From that time on Jesus began to explain to his*
> *disciples that he must go to Jerusalem and suffer*
> *many things at the hands of the elders, the chief*
> *priests and the teachers of the law, and that he*
> *must be killed and on the third day be raised to life.*
> *(Matthew 16:21)*

But Peter interrupts Him, and tells Him that He can't possibly be right: "Never, Lord! This shall never happen to you!"

Think about that. Peter has just realized that he's face-to-face with God Himself. And his response is to tell the Creator of the Universe that He's got it all wrong. How arrogant can you get?

Adam's downfall came when Satan persuaded him that he too knew better than God. And all of us are prone to do exactly the same thing that Adam and Peter did.

God says, "As the heavens are higher than the earth, so are my ways higher than your ways and my thoughts than your thoughts" (Isaiah 55:9).

Our finite minds can never fully grasp who God is and how He works. That's why Augustine said "If you understand, it is not God," because He is so different from us. He breaks our paradigms at every turn.

Jesus rebukes Peter severely and continues with His train of thought. He has just told them that He will die. With that image of His own future death on the cross in His mind, He says:

> "Whoever wants to be my disciple must deny themselves and take up their cross and follow me. For whoever wants to save their life will lose it, but whoever loses their life for me will find it" (Matthew 16:24-25).

Dietrich Bonhoeffer coined the phrase "cheap grace" to describe someone who wants to enjoy all the benefits of the kingdom of God without any true heart discipleship—taking up our cross and following Christ. If someone has that mentality, they have not understood the grace of God.

Having read this book up to this point, do you still want to be an even more fruitful disciple of Jesus? Why not pause and give that question due consideration? And then tell Jesus what you are thinking.

From this time many of his disciples turned back and no longer followed him. "You do not want to leave too, do you?" Jesus asked the Twelve. Simon Peter answered him, "Lord, to whom shall we go? You have the words of eternal life. We have come to believe and to know that you are the Holy One of God." (John 6:66-69)

MAKING THE GRACE CONNECTION

Do you have a tendency to try to "make things happen" by trying to control events or people? If so, talk to God about it.

Read 2 Corinthians 12:7-10 again. Paul says that he is now content with "weaknesses, insults, hardships, persecutions, and calamities." Do you think he really means that?

Think about a time when you experienced brokenness. What fruit did it later produce in your character or in your life?

How do you feel about the possibility that God might take you through further hard times?

CHAPTER 8

PEACEMAKER!

We've looked at false motivators that keep us from being motivated by love alone. We've considered how we can make the rest of our lives count for eternity by bearing fruit that will last as disciples of Jesus. We've seen that God has prepared specific things for us to do as individuals.

The context of all of this, of course, is the incredible mission that God has given to all of His people:

> Then Jesus came to them and said, "All authority in heaven and on earth has been given to me. Therefore go and make disciples of all nations, baptizing them in the name of the Father and of the Son and of the Holy Spirit, and teaching them to obey everything I have commanded you. And surely I am with you always, to the very end of the age. (Matthew 28:18-20)

Because God would never ask us to do something that is impossible, any command that He gives us also functions, in effect, as a promise. If we have been given a command to disciple nations, we can fully expect to do just that.

In this chapter, we'll start to appreciate just how significant grace is in this mission.

JESUS DELEGATES SPIRITUAL AUTHORITY TO US

Let's notice first of all that Jesus doesn't just command us to go and make disciples. He starts by stating a crucial prerequisite: "All authority in heaven and on earth has been given to me." Only on that basis does He then go on to say: "*Therefore* go and make disciples of all nations..."

He is helping us understand that bringing people into His Kingdom takes place against the backdrop of the spiritual battle that is raging. At the cross Jesus "disarmed the powers and authorities, [and] he made a public spectacle of them" (Colossians 2:15). He is now seated at the right hand of the Father far above every demonic power and authority. And in this statement, He delegates that incredible spiritual authority to us, specifically so that we can disciple nations.

My Western worldview had led me to totally misunderstand the spiritual world. I knew it was real theologically, but to be honest, I had no idea how it worked practically. So I tended to ignore it. Even though I'd read those words of Jesus hundreds of time, I couldn't explain coherently why Jesus was talking about authority here. And I certainly would have had no idea how to exercise that authority.

Why do we need authority? Isn't it just a question of sharing the good news with the lost? Well, Jesus did tell His disciples that the harvest is plentiful and that they needed to pray for more workers to go and bring it in. So we certainly need people to go and share that good news.

Our Western worldview makes us think that if we tell somebody something in a fairly clear way, they will process the words we say and probably make a reasoned response. But Paul tells us that there's something else going on that makes that unlikely when it comes to sharing the Gospel: "The god of this age has blinded the minds of unbelievers, so that they cannot see the light of the gospel that displays the glory of Christ, who is the image of God" (2 Corinthians 4:4).

Think about that. If someone's mind has been blinded by Satan, just telling them the gospel message won't always work. If we want people to come into God's Kingdom and know the truth, we have to find a way to deal with the blindness in their minds. This is not primarily a question of intellectual understanding. It's a spiritual problem.

How can we counteract it? With the spiritual authority over Satan that Jesus has delegated to us.

How do we exercise that authority? We often overlook a clear but counterintuitive fact that Jesus tells us:

> *"By this all people will know that you are my disciples, **if you have love for one another.**"*
> *(John 13:35 ESV)*

The one thing Jesus chose to pray for us, who come after His original disciples, is that we would all be one, just as He and the Father are one. Why? "So that the world may believe that you have sent me" (John 17:21 ESV).

Psalm 133 affirms this when it tells us that it is in unity that "the Lord has commanded the blessing, life forevermore" (Psalm 133:3b ESV). When we love each other, we activate that spiritual blessing, that authority, that spiritual power. Satan cannot resist it, and people's minds are unblinded.

Loving each other is how we exercise that spiritual authority. Grace is the means God has given us to change the spiritual atmosphere in the communities we live in.

If you want to see this authority working in practice, look at the book of Acts. The early Church had no real resources, but they loved each other so much that they shared everything. And thousands of people at a time had their eyes opened to the light of the gospel and responded to it.

This vital ingredient—love—is how the world will know about Jesus, not just because they see it in action and are impressed by it, but because of the real spiritual power it unleashes.

I'm not saying that your evangelistic activities won't see any results at all if there is not unity across the Church in your area. I think we can, however, conclude that they will bear far greater fruit if there is unity. Where there is unity, there is real, tangible blessing.

I used to ask God a lot to send revival, and I'm not knocking that for a moment. But sometimes I feel that God would be justified in saying back to us, "I've done my bit. I sent Jesus to die and to defeat Satan. I've delegated spiritual authority to you and made it possible for you to disciple nations. Won't *you* please send revival? Exercise the authority I've given you by acting with grace towards each other, and then go and tell people about Jesus and you'll be amazed."

In Acts, no fewer than ten times, Luke used a particular word to describe unity. It's usually translated as "with one mind" but its literal sense is "with one passion."

When we begin to understand the crucial importance of loving one another in reaching this world for Christ, then true unity among God's people is something I can definitely be passionate about.

IT IS SOMETHING WE CAN ONLY DO TOGETHER

Given the significance of unity, it's no surprise that the New Testament continually urges us to be united. It also talks of us being "the Body of Christ." This is more than just a metaphor. We literally are the actual flesh and blood, the arms and legs, through whom God works in the world.

Together we, the Church, are God's chosen instrument to disciple the nations. There is no Plan B.

As individual Christians on our own, we're like a dismembered leg or a single eye—no use whatsoever without the rest of the body. You can't be fruitful on your own, even if you're listening to the best spiritual podcasts or reading the best Christian books.

So if you're not part of a local church fellowship, can I encourage you to join one, even if it's been a painful experience in the past?

And I'd recommend you don't set too many criteria as to what you want to see in a church. "Where do *You* want me to serve You, Lord?" is the question to ask. In my case, He's always put me in local churches that are not the ones I would have chosen myself. When I became a Christian, aged 13, the "happening" church (which also seemed to have most of the attractive young women!) was not the one that I felt He was telling me to join. I wrestled with it but eventually threw my lot in with what looked to me like a sleepy traditional church full of old people. But within a few years it was thriving and was exactly the right place for me to be—especially since it's there that I met one particularly attractive young woman who is now my wife!

He may well place you somewhere unexpected, but He knows where your unique contribution will work best.

Then find the place that God has for you in that church. When you know that God Himself has specifically called you to a unique role in a particular part of His Body, you are much more likely to persevere when it gets tough (as it will from time to time).

And if He hasn't made you the leader, follow those whom God has chosen to lead. All of us sometimes think that we know better than our leaders. But unless they're clearly overstepping the bounds of their authority or are in obvious sin, it's our job to encourage, support, and follow them—warts and all.

Being part of a church is not easy. But it is essential. Satan understands the power of our unity so we can expect the spiritual battle to be focused on that. He will relentlessly tempt us into disunity. So we'll always experience people who see things differently, make mistakes, attack us, offend us, or just really get up our nose. If you want to see demonic activity in your church, look at the number of people who fall out with each other, look at unforgiveness, look at the number of people who divide into factions or who complain about the leader whom God has put in place.

There's a great biblical principle: "If it is possible, as far as it depends on you, live at peace with everyone" (Romans 12:18).

We are to do what is in our power to do—the "as far as it depends on you" bit—and leave the rest to the other person and to God.

Learn to forgive, relentlessly. Yes, there is pain and cost when we forgive someone. But, although you let the person off your hook, they're not off God's hook. You can hand all of that pain, and those demands for justice and revenge, over to God, safe in the knowledge that He will ensure that justice will be done. In the meantime, you can walk free of it, and you can prevent Satan getting a foothold in your church fellowship.

Just as it takes two to tango, it also takes two to cause division. So resolutely refuse to have any part in division.

As far as it depends on us, let's do everything we can to unleash the spiritual power that unity brings in the place where God has put us.

Because we have been traveling a lot recently, last Sunday was the first time my wife and I were at our own local church in quite a while. We were serving as welcomers on the door and were both amazed at how many new faces we saw coming in, and how the congregation had grown in just a few weeks. People are just coming and wanting to know more about Jesus. There's no clear reason for this—there's been no unusual evangelistic activity, nothing obvious we can identify as the cause.

For the last couple of years, I've had the privilege of being on the leadership team, and we've had to address some really difficult doctrinal disputes. By God's grace, they have been handled really well. Not only did we not fall out with each other but through the course of many long meetings, we actually strengthened our love for one another as we listened carefully and sympathetically to different convictions and points of view and prized relationship above winning arguments. We still don't all agree on the theological questions, but we are more united than ever. We have also worked hard to foster unity with all the other Christian churches in our area and have tried to bless them as we are able.

As I have pondered the many new arrivals, I have sensed God affirm that they are part of the blessing that comes from unity. As we have loved each other, it has changed the spiritual atmosphere. It has overcome spiritual blindness. We have unwittingly exercised the authority that Jesus gave to us to make disciples.

Jesus said, "Blessed are the peacemakers, for they will be called children of God" (Matthew 5:9). Being a peacemaker and being a child of God are two inseparable sides of a coin. If you are a child of God living out of your identity in Christ, you will be a peacemaker.

And as peacemakers, we will be those who defuse issues in our church fellowship where Satan is attempting to stir up division. We will be those who do whatever we can to love our brothers and sisters in other parts of the Church.

A DISCIPLE IS DIFFERENT FROM A CONVERT

For decades, the Western Church has focused on seeing people come to Christ—on making *converts*. But the mission Jesus gave us was not just about bringing people into the Kingdom. It also includes helping them become growing, active, fruitful, effective *disciples* of Jesus.

Babies are cute. But if they continue to behave like babies as they grow up, they become a lot less attractive. Any Christian can become an old Christian—all it takes is time! Any Christian can become a mature, fruitful disciple—but many do not. Churches full of old Christians who have not matured are difficult places to be a leader. And they make a very limited impact.

Most leaders would agree that far too many of their congregation struggle to take hold of basic biblical truth and live it out. Even though we have more excellent resources than ever before in the Church, many Christians still take a painfully long time to mature. Some seem "stuck" in the past. Some go round and round in cycles of spiritual confusion and habitual sin. Others keep coming forward for help with the same issues time and time again.

So let's try to get to grips with what it means to be a real disciple.

A literal translation of the Greek word for "disciple" is "learner." But for people like me who have been conditioned by a Western worldview, the concept of learning is almost exclusively bound up with learning facts, learning about things, learning how to behave.

And indeed, the Western Church tends to see discipleship essentially as teaching Christians what to do or how to behave now that they have turned to Christ. It has, for example, taught them about the importance of daily devotions, the sacraments, baptism, worship and so on. There is, of course, a place for all of those things, but in my view, that is not the essence of discipleship.

If people get the impression that discipleship or growing as a Christian is all about "learning to behave in the right way" it tends to lead to joyless legalism where they try their best to perform well, to live up to expectations. Either they give up and walk away with a sense that they are letting God down or they feel smug that they are "good Christians."

So how do we disciple someone who has just turned to Jesus?

We don't start by telling them what's *wrong* with them: "Now, you need to stop that... and that... and that! And start to do this... and this... and this!" We need to tell them what's *right* with them! They need to know that they are now holy, that they are loved, and that Jesus calls them to incredible fruitfulness. In short, they need to understand the fullness of God's grace towards them.

Then they need to understand the reality of the spiritual battle that they are in and how to ensure that they keep walking in the victory Jesus has given them. This involves learning to submit to

God and resist the devil.

Finally, we need to teach them a lifestyle based on identifying lies they have believed and replacing them with the truth from God's Word. This is what the Bible calls renewing your mind and is the way we will be transformed (Romans 12:2).

This three-pronged approach is at the heart of all of the discipleship materials produced by Freedom In Christ Ministries —we characterize the three stages as "Truth, Turning, and Transformation." So far in this book, we've focused mainly on Truth. I'll talk more about Turning and Transformation in our final chapter.

Let's step back and ask a fundamental question. Why do we disciple people? What are we wanting to achieve?

In 1 Timothy 1:5 (NASB), Paul says, "The goal of our instruction is...". Before we look at how he completes that sentence, let me ask you a question: what word or phrase would you put there?

Maybe you would say, "Knowing more about Jesus," "understanding the Bible," "living as God wants us to live," or something similar.

What Paul actually says is, "The goal of our instruction is *love*" (1 Timothy 1:5 NASB).

Not learning facts, or doctrines, or how to behave. But becoming like God who is love.

This is a focus that we have lost sight of. You can graduate from most Bible colleges purely on the basis of what you know. You don't even have to answer all the questions correctly! The goal of our instruction is what? Knowledge? No, the goal of our instruction is supposed to be love.

When you put this in the context of what we have looked at so far in this chapter, doesn't that just make perfect sense? Our aim is to help people connect with God's love for them—in their heart not just their head—so that they will then love Him back and love others too. *So that the world may know.* So that everyone will see that we are disciples of Jesus. So that the mission He gave us will be fulfilled.

In Luke 6:40 Jesus said, "The student is not above the teacher, but everyone who is fully trained will be like their teacher." Again we see that God's focus is not primarily on what we *do* but on what we are *like*. It's about inner transformation. Remember, the fruit of the Spirit in Galatians 5:22-23—"love, joy, peace, forbearance, kindness, goodness, faithfulness, gentleness and self-control"— are all character qualities. Because what you do will then flow from what you are like—and you'll do those acts of love and sacrifice not because you feel you have to but because you want to, out of love for Jesus.

Here's my definition of a disciple: "A follower of Jesus who is learning to become more and more like Jesus in character, and to do the works that God has prepared for them in the strength that He supplies."

In Jesus' day, it was a prestigious thing to be a disciple of a distinguished teacher. The Apostle Paul, for example, tells us that he was "educated at the feet of Gamaliel" (Acts 22:3 ESV), who is described in Acts 5:34 as "a teacher of the law, who was honored by all the people." Even today, he has the reputation of being one of the greatest Jewish teachers of all time.

Now, you couldn't just choose to become a disciple of someone like Gamaliel. He had to choose you. And he didn't choose just anyone. He chose the best, the very very best. There would have been plenty of people who aspired to become a disciple of Gamaliel but few made the grade. You had to be absolutely outstanding.

Jesus did things differently. Far from calling the crème de la crème, Jesus called lowly fishermen, reviled tax collectors, even you and me!

The original disciples were all young men, probably aged mid-teens to early 20s. They had jobs such as fishermen precisely because they weren't the crème de la crème. No rabbi had come to them and said "Follow me." But then out of the blue, one did. It helps me understand why they immediately left everything and followed. You can imagine them saying, "Really? Do you mean it? I'd better go before He changes his mind... My mom will be so proud...."

Being one of Jesus' disciples was not like a university course where you learn facts from lectures and books. The aim was not just to know what the teacher knew. The aim was to become *like* the teacher. Discipleship was rooted in an intensely personal relationship. Jesus called them (and us) first and foremost to follow Him (see Matthew 4:19), to have intimate fellowship with Him (see 1 Corinthians 1:9) and to enjoy Him. It is through knowing the teacher that we begin to take on the characteristics of the teacher (see 2 Corinthians 3:18).

When Jesus called them, He was in effect saying, "You can be like me."

When Jesus called *you*, He was in effect saying, "You can be like me."

"But what about all those failures I've had? All that stuff in the past..."

"I am choosing *you*. You *can* be like me."

Wow! As you connect with God's love, you can have every expectation of becoming more and more like Jesus and playing a significant part in fulfilling the mission He has given to His Church.

Let's turn our attention to some of the pitfalls that await us as we work towards becoming more and more like Jesus and working together in unity with our brothers and sisters in Christ right across the Church.

100% GRACE AND 100% TRUTH

John describes Jesus as "full of grace *and* truth" (John 1:14), which is a very interesting phrase. Fruitful disciples of Jesus who are becoming more and more like Jesus, our teacher, can be expected to grow in both grace and truth.

This is an area where the enemy relentlessly challenges our unity. Depending on our temperament and our background, we all tend naturally to put more emphasis on one rather than the other. And we can easily slip into seeing grace and truth as opposites—as if the more grace we have, the less truth we have and vice versa.

If we are to work in genuine unity, we have to work out how to be like Jesus who was full of grace *and* truth. Let's look at John 8:3-11 to see Him in action:

> *The teachers of the law and the Pharisees brought in a woman caught in adultery. They made her stand before the group and said to Jesus, "Teacher, this woman was caught in the act of adultery. In the Law Moses commanded us to stone such women. Now what do you say?" They were using this question as a trap, in order to have a basis for accusing him.*

The Pharisees had a good theological grasp of truth. Moses did indeed command that adulterers should be put to death. Leviticus 20:10 (ESV) says: "If a man commits adultery with the wife of his neighbor, both the adulterer and the adulteress shall surely be put to death." I'm having trouble working out how you can catch just one person in the act of adultery, so there's a big question as to why they singled out the woman and ignored the man, but nevertheless what they are saying is true. Their doctrine is correct.

> *But Jesus bent down and started to write on the ground with his finger. When they kept on questioning him, he straightened up and said to them, "Let any one of you who is without sin be the first to throw a stone at her." Again he stooped down and wrote on the ground. At this, those who heard*

began to go away one at a time, the older ones first, until only Jesus was left, with the woman still standing there.

Jesus' amazing statement led to them having an uncharacteristic moment of clarity. In their heart of hearts, they all realized that they had sinned too. They were in effect just like the woman. None of them had lived up to the righteous standards of the Law. They may not have committed this particular sin, but all of them were guilty of some sin.

Jesus straightened up and asked her, "Woman, where are they? Has no one condemned you?" "No one, sir," she said. "Then neither do I condemn you," Jesus declared. "Go now and leave your life of sin."

There was only one person there who had never sinned. There was only one person there who truly understood the truth of God's Word. He had every right to stone her to death. Yet He didn't speak a single word of condemnation.

But neither did He condone her sin. He urged her to repent—but only after coming to her in grace. And His gentle words of grace caused God's truth to sear the hearts of hardened hypocrites.

Jesus came to her with both 100% grace and 100% truth— grace that did not compromise truth; and truth that did not compromise grace.

The Pharisees thought that God's primary priority was truth and that people's behavior should be precisely in line with what was right. And they thought their job was to monitor the behavior of others and point out problems with it.

Many of us have been brought up with a similar understanding, made a little more complicated by the fact that our concept of truth has been hijacked by Western rationalism. We have learned to see truth as something that we access primarily via the intellect and that stands on its own, regardless of whether we know it or believe it.

In the Old Testament, the Hebrew word translated "truth" is *emeth* and means "faithful and true." It implies being faithful and true towards somebody else (which is something an objective fact cannot do). It's a relational word.

Similarly, when Jesus promises that we will know the truth and that the truth will set us free, He speaks as the One who also says that He *is* the Truth.

Jesus is 100% truth in that He is a consistent, living demonstration of the nature and character of God. As we put our trust in Him, we discover in experience—not just intellectually—that He is always "faithful and true."

And in being true to the character of the God who is love, Jesus is also 100% grace.

And we are called to be like Him.

FOCUSING ON TRUTH
BUT OVERLOOKING GRACE

When I became a Christian as a teenager, I was really hungry to learn about my new faith in Jesus, and I bought a whole load of Christian books. I wasn't especially discriminating but just picked from the ones that were reduced in price in the bookstore. Well, some of these books were quite complicated—I remember one was a detailed explanation of the book of Revelation! I still have some of them and looking through them, you can see that I made notes in the margin with my pencil. I circled whole paragraphs and wrote "DU" beside them. Now, what do you think that meant? "Don't understand" perhaps? I wish it had, but it actually stood for "Doctrinally unsound!" I was a 13-year-old who had been a Christian about six weeks, but I'd already absorbed the concept that I had to be suspicious of what other Christians were saying. I somehow felt qualified to stamp anything I didn't understand as "DU," doctrinally unsound!

I am still absolutely zealous for the truth of God's Word, though hopefully with a more mature approach, and it still upsets me when God's truth is watered down and those who claim to be God's people do not take His Word seriously.

You too? If a bunch of ordinary people formed a group in your area that was radically committed to the whole of God's truth and to how that truth works out practically in day-to-day life, would you be interested in joining them?

The Pharisees get a lot of bad press. We think of them as shallow hypocrites, but their starting point was exactly that: a group of people who were radically committed to God's Word.

The religious establishment, a group called the Sadducees, had become very liberal. They denied resurrection from the dead, miracles, and the reality of the spiritual world. The Pharisees, on the other hand, gave God's Word a very high place. They were completely committed to living pure and righteous lives untainted by evil. They wanted to handle tempting things like money and sex absolutely properly. They were the sincere, committed people of the day who really wanted to see God's Kingdom established and sin stamped out.

I'm pretty sure that if I'd been there at that time, I'd have been a Pharisee. I'd have been eagerly awaiting the promised Messiah while doing my best to live a righteous life in the meantime.

But when the most pivotal moment in all history came knocking on their door, and the Messiah actually came and stood there talking to them, they completely missed Him! Even worse, Jesus constantly clashed with them and reserved His harshest criticism for them. How on earth could these sincere, committed people who valued truth so highly have messed up so badly?

The Pharisees' problem was that they had a very good grasp of truth, but they didn't have a clue about grace.

Going back to when I first became a Christian, I don't think anyone put it like this, but the impression I distinctly received was that to be a "good" Christian I had to read my Bible every day, give a certain proportion of my income, go to church regularly, not have lustful thoughts, and a load of other things.

If I managed to do the things on the list, I felt pretty good. If I failed, I felt bad. But honestly it was kind of comforting to have a list of dos and don'ts.

The Pharisees loved a good list of rules too. They thought that God gave the Old Testament Law so that people could become righteous before God by obeying it. So they took it very seriously indeed, but in doing so ended up stretching it to the point of absurdity.

For example, God had given a commandment that people were to rest on the Sabbath day. Trying to help people work out what that meant practically, the teachers of the Law had defined 39 types of activity that constituted work including binding sheaves, threshing, kneading, shearing wool, writing two or more letters or erasing two or more letters, making a fire or extinguishing a fire.

Orthodox Jews today still have more or less the same traditions. The discovery of electricity caused a lot of debate for them—when you flick an electric switch to turn on a light, it causes tiny sparks. Does that constitute making a fire? Some teachers say it does; others say it doesn't. If your preferred authority says it does and you would prefer not to sit in darkness on the Sabbath, what can you do about that? Well, most decide to use electric time switches so that they don't actually have to flick the switch themselves on the Sabbath. Very pragmatic!

Do you see how easy it is to shift from the real point of the commandment—to make sure that we have a time to rest and seek God in the midst of the busyness of life—to focusing on the mechanics of turning a light on?

To be fair to the Pharisees, God had given a lot of very specific rules for behavior in the Old Testament, and it's easy to understand why they went down this particular blind alley. Now, the God of the Old Testament is exactly the same as the God of the New Testament. He has not changed, and His eternal purposes have not changed. So let's try to understand why exactly the God of grace gave these rules which are collectively known as "the Law."

In Galatians 3, Paul begins to answer this question. First he makes the point that the Law was not given until hundreds of years after God's original covenant with Abraham. The series of promises that God makes to Abraham in that original covenant are very interesting:

> *"Fear not, Abram, I am your shield; your reward shall be very great." (Genesis 15:1 ESV)*

> *"Look toward heaven, and number the stars, if you are able to number them." Then he said to him, "So shall your offspring be." (Genesis 15:5 ESV)*

There's no, "If you do this, I will do that." God just makes unconditional promises—grace promises. Their outcome does not depend on what Abraham does but purely on God's grace.

> *And he believed the LORD, and he counted it to him as righteousness. (Genesis 15:6 ESV)*

Abraham does just one thing: chooses to believe what God promises. It has always been the case that we enter into God's promises and blessing by faith and faith alone—not by anything we do.

Paul then moves us on a few centuries to the point where God met Moses on Mount Sinai and delivered to him the two tablets containing the Ten Commandments:

> *...the law, which came 430 years afterward, does not annul a covenant previously ratified by God, so as to make the promise void. For if the inheritance comes by the law, it no longer comes by promise; but God gave it to Abraham by a promise. (Galatians 3:17-18 ESV)*

When the Law came, it did not supersede the grace promises God had made. It's not as if the original plan was grace and it somehow went badly wrong and had to be changed to Law.

In Galatians 3:19 (ESV) Paul asks the 64 million dollar question—one that you are probably asking yourself: "Why then the law?" And helpfully goes on to supply the answer to it: "It was added because of transgressions."

What does that actually mean? Let's turn now to Romans 3:

> Now we know that whatever the law says it speaks to those who are under the law, so that every mouth may be stopped, and the whole world may be held accountable to God. For by works of the law no human being will be justified in his sight, since through the law comes knowledge of sin.
> (Romans 3:19-20 ESV)

The Law was given in fact to "stop every mouth," to keep people from saying "Oh I didn't know that was wrong" and to make everybody—the whole world—accountable to God. Its main purpose was to bring knowledge of right and wrong.

The Law was never intended to provide a way to become acceptable to God through our own efforts. It was there to make us aware of the awfulness of sin and its control over us, so that we would realize the complete futility of trying to behave well in order to be acceptable. In other words, it was to show us our need of grace, our need of Christ. The Law itself was actually a means of grace!

The Pharisees had spent years trying to get to the essence of the Law to make sure that they were living in exactly the right way, believing exactly the right things. They did it by expanding on what God had given so they had vast numbers of "helpful" rules and regulations. But these had become a really heavy burden to ordinary people. It's all too easy for our discipleship programs to become something similar and for us in effect to put people back under the Law which, of course, they cannot live up to.

And it's so easy to fall back into a Pharisaic emphasis on truth at the expense of grace, to think that we can boil our Christian life down to a list of dos and don'ts.

Let's look at an example: Is it good to give 10% of our income to the church? Yes. But how much better to get hold of the principle behind giving rather than just follow a rule slavishly. Paul says:

> The point is this: whoever sows sparingly will also reap sparingly, and whoever sows bountifully will also reap bountifully. Each one must give as he has decided in his heart, not reluctantly or under compulsion, for God loves a cheerful giver.
> (2 Corinthians 9:6-7 ESV)

God does not want us to give money because we feel we are "under compulsion." But He does want us to understand that if we give generously, it will bring us a great harvest. He does not mean as some have thought that we will get more money back—giving to get more money back is a worldly principle, not a Biblical one.

> And God is able to make all grace abound to you, so that having all sufficiency in all things at all times, you may abound in every good work.
> (2 Corinthians 9:8 ESV)

When we give generously in love, all grace will abound to us, and we will abound in every good work. What comes back is much more valuable than money. It's an increase in the fruit that we will bear for Him and the good works we'll do.

If we understand this and experience it, it's quite likely that we will end up giving over and above the 10%—and we'll be doing it out of hearts of love rather than with the sense that this is some higher rate of income tax levied by the Church.

Jesus specifically called those who felt weary and burdened by all this in order to offer them His light burden and His easy yoke. Instead of expanding the Law, Jesus reduced the whole thing to just two sentences:

> "You shall love the Lord your God with all your heart and with all your soul and with all your mind. This is the great and first commandment. And a second is

> *like it: You shall love your neighbor as yourself. On these two commandments depend all the Law and the Prophets." (Matthew 22:37-40 ESV)*

He summarized the Law in even fewer words in Matthew 7:

> *"So whatever you wish that others would do to you, do also to them, for this is the Law and the Prophets." (Matthew 7:12 ESV)*

Paul took it one step further:

> *For the commandments, "You shall not commit adultery, You shall not murder, You shall not steal, You shall not covet," and any other commandment, are summed up in this word: "You shall love your neighbor as yourself." (Romans 13:9 ESV)*

If we perfectly fulfilled the Law, what would it look like? We'd be loving God and loving others. And that's the Law that is now written on our hearts. When you truly understand grace, you will also walk in truth.

In Revelation 2:1-7, Jesus commends the church in Ephesus for their hard work, their perseverance, and for identifying and removing leaders who were not true apostles. This is a church with an emphasis on truth. It has correct doctrine. Great teaching. Effective discipline. But Jesus' words to them are devastating: "You have abandoned the love you had at first" (verse 4 ESV). Like the Ephesians, most of us have been taught that truth is the most important aspect of our faith and that we need to uphold it at all costs. This is His instruction to them, "Repent, and do the works you did at first" (verse 5 ESV).

I am just like the Ephesians. I've had to repent of majoring on truth at the expense of grace; I've had to repent of being critical of those who hold different views to my own; I've had to repent of believing that I know best.

APPROACHING THOSE IN
A DIFFERENT PART OF THE CHURCH

Paul tells us to be "eager to maintain the unity of the Spirit in the bond of peace" (Ephesians 4:3 ESV). And when I think that this is what enables us to exercise our spiritual authority to make disciples, I can certainly be eager about that!

That word "maintain" tells us we are already united at one level. But who exactly are we united with?

"If you declare with your mouth, 'Jesus is Lord,' and believe in your heart that God raised him from the dead, you will be saved" (Romans 10:9). Declare, believe. That's it. If you have done that, you're already united with everyone else who has done it too throughout the whole of history—whether you like it or not!

And what does unity look like? Agreement on theology? When churches believed that, what was the outcome? Split after split after painful split.

It's not that good theology isn't important. It most definitely is. But sometimes we can almost end up feeling like we're saved by good theology! Jesus says to the Pharisees, "You study the Scriptures diligently because you think that in them you have eternal life. These are the very Scriptures that testify about me, yet you refuse to come to me to have life" (John 5:39-40). It's entirely possible to have such a focus on the truth of the written Word of God that we miss the One who is the Truth, the Living Word of God.

Do you honestly believe that you or your particular church have 100% correct theology? At the end of the age, there isn't one of us that won't look back at our present beliefs and shake our heads as we realize where we were wrong.

Theology is our human attempt to understand God's truth. In the last 10 years, my theology has changed. What hasn't changed is truth. I don't want to be committed to a particular theology. But I am absolutely committed to the Truth.

What do you think Jesus cares about more: what people believe in their head about the bread and the wine; or whether they love others from the heart? What people believe about just one verse in the New Testament that mentions a thousand year period or whether they are ready to forgive as God has forgiven them?

In the wake of the outbreak of the charismatic movement, there were sharply differing views on the exercise of spiritual gifts. Some churches said that you could not be sure you were a Christian unless there was evidence that you had spoken in tongues. Others said that if you spoke in tongues, it was evidence that you weren't a Christian! What does the Bible say? "Do all speak with tongues?" (1 Corinthians 12:30 ESV) asks Paul, a rhetorical question to which the clear answer is "No." A few paragraphs later he says, "Earnestly desire the spiritual gifts" (1 Corinthians 14:1 ESV), which clearly include tongues. Then in 1 Corinthians 14:39 (ESV), he says, "Earnestly desire to prophesy and do not forbid speaking in tongues."

But above all that he makes clear in 1 Corinthians 13—slap bang in the middle of two chapters about spiritual gifts—that the main thing is love. No matter how much speaking in tongues you do or don't do, no matter how "right" the position you hold on this or any other matter, if you don't have love you gain precisely nothing.

So am I saying that you should condone things that may happen within some parts of the Church that are blatantly not in line with the Bible? No, absolutely not. As we've seen, Jesus did not condemn the woman caught in adultery, but neither did He condone her wrong behavior. He didn't pretend that sin wasn't an issue. He said clearly, "Go and from now on sin no more." However, His heart was not to condemn her but to motivate her to righteous living. And however counter-intuitive it may seem, it's grace that does that.

If you make doctrine the main thing, even if you're right, you're wrong. If you are secure in knowing who you are in Christ, you don't have to be proved right; you don't have to indulge in arguments. You can just keep humbling yourself before others and loving them.

The minute we insist that our current understanding of a non-essential doctrine is better than someone else's, we're no longer walking in love but in pride. We are valuing a difference more than we value our relationship with our brothers and sisters in Christ.

This isn't easy. Every generation faces big, seemingly intractable issues of doctrine that challenge our unity. Let's see how Paul addressed the big unity issue in the Church of his day with 100% grace and 100% truth.

He tells Gentile Christians (in 1 Corinthians 8) that it's perfectly OK to eat meat that's been offered to idols—that's the truth. But, he immediately follows it up with grace and tells them that if they do it in the presence of someone who believes it's not OK, then it becomes sin.

The sin is not the eating of the meat. It's the wounding of the conscience of a brother or sister in Christ who has a different understanding of a non-essential issue. The onus is on the person who thinks they have the correct doctrine—which, of course, we all do!—to act with grace towards those who believe something different.

Which are the parts of the Church that you were taught to be suspicious of? Maybe you even got the impression that if people attend a particular branch of the Church or believe or practice certain things they can't possibly be Christians.

Have you ever checked out for yourself what they believe, and done so in a spirit of humility, "thinking of others as better than yourselves" (Philippians 2:3 NLT)?

FOCUSING ON GRACE
BUT OVERLOOKING TRUTH

Among the seven churches Jesus addresses in Revelation, there is just one, the church in Thyatira (Revelation 2:18-29), that Jesus commends for its love. However, as we read on, we discover that this church has tolerated false teaching along the lines of, "God is love, so He won't mind if we bend the rules." And people had lapsed into idol worship and sexual immorality.

And throughout history there are many such examples of churches who have got hold of the incredible message of God's grace and twisted it to mean essentially that "anything goes."

Tolerating sin, like the church in Thyatira did, is not grace. Neither is sentimental love that demands nothing and does not challenge sin.

Jesus' words about the consequences for the ringleader of what was happening in Thyatira make for hard reading:

> *"Behold, I will throw her onto a sickbed, and those who commit adultery with her I will throw into great tribulation, unless they repent of her works, and I will strike her children dead." (Revelation 2:22-23a ESV)*

Does it shock you that Jesus Himself would say something like this?

If you check your New Testament, you'll see that He spoke time and again about coming judgment and the need to repent. He even called people "hypocrites," "snakes," "blind," "fools," "wicked," "evil," and "cursed."

Jesus' primary focus is never on what people are doing wrong, but neither does He want people to think that wrong choices have no consequences.

The whole point of His harsh words here is to get the ringleader and the church to repent. Jesus' intention is that she will *not* be thrown onto a sickbed and that her children will *not* die. His words of truth are a means of grace.

But this does not give us a license to say nasty things to other Christians. It's easy to deceive ourselves that we are upholding God's truth when actually we're just being arrogant and divisive. When we speak the truth, it must always be genuinely in love. Our intention towards the other person must genuinely be to love them and to seek the best for them, rather than to justify our own prejudices or build up our own ego.

It's also easy to fall into the trap that the church in Thyatira did and think that we're upholding God's love when in fact we are just making excuses for sin. Jesus came with 100% grace, but His desire was that this grace would motivate people to a radical lifestyle of purity, holiness, and love.

He made a statement that would have been absolutely shocking to those who were listening: "I tell you, unless your righteousness exceeds that of the scribes and Pharisees, you will never enter the kingdom of heaven" (Matthew 5:20 ESV).

The scribes and the Pharisees were seen as the most righteous people of their day. But Jesus was saying that not even their standards were high enough to match God's standard of holiness.

He then does an even more astonishing thing. He takes the Law which already seemed an impossible standard and raises the bar even higher. For example:

> *"You have heard that it was said to those of old, 'You shall not murder; and whoever murders will be liable to judgment.' But I say to you that everyone who is angry with his brother will be liable to judgment."*
> *(Matthew 5:21-22a ESV)*

> *"You have heard that it was said, 'You shall not commit adultery.' But I say to you that everyone who looks at a woman with lustful intent has already committed adultery with her in his heart."*
> *(Matthew 5:27-28 ESV)*

Then at the end of that section He hammers the nail into the coffin: "Therefore you are to be perfect, as your heavenly Father is perfect" (Matthew 5:48 NASB).

In a pole vault competition, the competitors keep jumping until the bar is too high for all of them. Even if there is just one person left, the bar keeps being raised. Ultimately, they too will fail.

I guess there was at least a theoretical possibility that someone could fulfill all 613 commandments found in the Old Testament Law. But Jesus raised the bar so high that it became an absolute impossibility.

The true purpose of the Law was to show us that without God's grace, we cannot be pleasing to God. It is meant to take us to the point where we throw ourselves on God's mercy in absolute desperation, realizing the extent of our need of Him. The Pharisees turned that around and used it to raise themselves up, to get respect from others, to convince themselves that they—and only they—were OK. And that's pride.

Each time Jesus raised the bar, He moved it from a law that focused on external behavior to what is inside, the thoughts and intentions of our heart.

At one time, our hearts were "deceitful above all things and beyond cure" (Jeremiah 17:9), but they are no longer.

> *"This is the covenant that I will make with them*
> *after those days, declares the Lord:*
> *I will put my laws on their hearts,*
> *and write them on their minds,"*
> *(Hebrews 10:16 ESV)*

Now that we have become new creations in Christ, we have new hearts and new minds. God's Law is no longer words on a tablet of stone or on a page. It's written inside us.

Jesus has put us back in the place where Adam and Eve were before the Fall, where we can choose to do the right thing. Whereas the Old Covenant gave us ten commandments we couldn't live up to, under the New Covenant, they potentially become ten promises: we will not steal, we will not kill and so on. We obey, not because we have to but because we really want to and because we have the power of the Holy Spirit within us.

So when someone turns to Christ, we don't encourage them to continue living in ways that God warns against. We expect to see dramatic change. Jesus wants the actions of His Church to reflect the purity and holiness that He has given her.

Disciples need to know that, when God tells us not to do something, it's not because He's some kind of killjoy. It's because Jesus came specifically to set us free from slavery to sin and Satan, and we don't need to go back. He's helping us avoid things that will harm us and others.

When we have to bring correction to others, we do it in a spirit of grace, pointing them back to who they are in Christ. For example, notice how James responds when he discerned that some fellow Christians had a problem with the way they spoke:

> *Out of the same mouth come praise and cursing. My brothers and sisters, this should not be. Can both fresh water and salt water flow from the same spring? My brothers and sisters, can a fig tree bear olives, or a grapevine bear figs? Neither can a salt spring produce fresh water. (James 3:10-12)*

He doesn't use harsh words. He just makes the simple point that a freshwater spring doesn't produce salt water—it just doesn't. In the same way, a fig tree doesn't bear olives—of course it doesn't. Deep down inside we are now holy ones. And, if everything is working as it should, we'll do the things that holy ones do. When I lose my temper, grumble, or dwell on a lustful thought, I am acting out of character. It really is as simple as that.

Discipline is done out of love. It's not about punishing people. Godly discipline is about helping them not to make the same mistake again. It's about restoration. It's a means of grace.

Have you ever sent a gift through the mail and never received a thank you? Maybe you worry the gift didn't arrive, but you feel nervous to ask in case the reason they haven't mentioned it is because they didn't like it. Well, in the world of the Biblical writers, if a gift didn't elicit a response, it would imply that it had not been received.

Paul says that God's kindness leads us to repentance (Romans 2:4). God's grace assures us of His love no matter what we do. But if that doesn't move us to respond to Him in repentance, reaffirm our allegiance to Him, and change our behavior, then we have not actually received it.

I've had to repent of thinking that some sins "don't really matter." I've had to repent of thinking I can decide for myself what is right or wrong rather than trusting what God says in His Word.

HEART CHECK-UP

A few years ago, I went through a period of intense conflict in my church. I've since come to understand that conflict is inevitable and is not necessarily a bad thing. It's how you handle it that matters. And God can use conflict to help you become more like Jesus and reinforce unity with the person you're in conflict with.

During this particular time, I was being accused of things that I thought were untrue. Everything within me wanted to prove that I was right, that I knew best. I wanted to get people onto my side. I wanted to focus on truth.

And God was patiently trying to teach me that what really mattered was my character, whether I handled the conflict in a godly way, and how I approached the person who was accusing me. He wanted me to focus on grace.

I developed a sniffle and went through a few nights where I hardly slept because my nose was blocked up. In the end, I decided to go to the doctor and see if I could get something for it. I went to a new doctor whom I hadn't visited before so, before he looked at my nose, he decided to give me a basic medical check-up. He took various measurements and tapped them into his computer. Then he said, "Hmm, let's see if we can get your arms a bit shorter— stretch them out again." So he measured my arms again and said, "No, they're still too long." My retort was, "They've been fine all my life. Is that a problem?" He explained that having overly long arms can be an indicator of a condition called Marfan syndrome which causes muscles to become very flexible. It causes double-jointedness and ultimately the heart muscles become so flexible that they don't really function. It can be fatal. So he said, "Right, I'll book you an appointment at the hospital for a heart check-up." He tapped away at his computer and handed me the appointment form. I said, "But what about my nose?" "Oh it will clear up in a few days," he responded dismissively.

So my sniffle led to a heart check-up at the hospital. They laid me down and did an ultrasound of my heart. The sound of my heart was played loudly through some speakers, which I found alarming. It was wheezing and squeaking and sounded to me like there must be something seriously wrong – I certainly wouldn't want my car sounding like that! But I was reassured that these noises were totally normal.

During this period of conflict, here I was looking at a massive image of my heart on a very large screen in front of me. As I lay there watching it pumping away, with the bizarre sounds it was making filling the room, I felt God say, "In the middle of this conflict situation, all I'm looking at is your heart."

As it turned out, there was no medical issue with my heart—I just have really long arms! But it was a graphic picture to me that I needed to make sure the conflict I was going through did not lead to division. I needed to humble myself before God and before other people and make sure I handled the conflict not just with truth but with grace. God kindly gave me a graphic illustration to encourage me to keep walking in forgiveness and humility and not allow the enemy to bring division despite disagreement.

Because unity in the Body of Christ is so important to fulfilling the mission Jesus has given us, it's the area where Satan wants to attack us the most. If we're not careful, we'll swallow his half-truths and fall for his deception and before we know it, instead of being agents for reconciliation, we will find ourselves doing the enemy's work for him.

APPROACHING THOSE OUTSIDE THE CHURCH

We saw in Chapter 3 how the Church became "judgey," and in many places came to see itself as responsible for the morals of the whole nation. Instead of astonishing people by our acts of love and showing that we are for them, we became known for what we're against.

Instead of being those who preach the good news, we became the bad news.

How does God want us to approach those outside the Church who don't claim to be Christians? What does it mean to come with 100% grace and 100% truth to them?

Paul wrote a letter to the Corinthians in which he told them not to associate with sexually immoral people. And they totally misunderstood what he meant. He had to write them again to explain more fully, and here's what he said:

> I wrote to you in my letter not to associate with sexually immoral people—not at all meaning <u>the people of this world</u> who are immoral, or the greedy and swindlers, or idolaters. In that case you would have to leave this world. But now I am writing to you that you must not associate with anyone who claims to be <u>a brother or sister</u> but is sexually immoral or greedy, an idolater or slanderer, a drunkard or swindler. (1 Corinthians 5:9-11)

They had assumed that Paul meant they should not associate with sexually immoral people *outside* the Church, as if they were the weaker party and would somehow be contaminated by the world.

But Paul clearly says that when it comes to these sin issues, our concern should rather be those *inside* the Church who persistently sin. And let's notice that he doesn't just focus on those who commit sexual sins, but he puts equal weight on those who always want more things, lash out with their tongues, or keep getting drunk.

In the first two chapters of Romans, Paul explains in graphic detail the dire situation that those who don't yet know Jesus are in: their thinking has become futile, their hearts are "darkened" and they indulge in impurity, unnatural sexual passions, murder, deceit, pride, and heartlessness. He affirms that "the judgment of God rightly falls on those who practice such things."

He then gives a stern warning:

> "Do you suppose, O man—you who judge those who practice such things and yet do them yourself— that you will escape the judgment of God? Or do you presume on the riches of his kindness and forbearance and patience, not knowing that God's kindness is meant to lead you to repentance?" (Romans 2:3-4 ESV).

Surprisingly perhaps, this warning is not for the people out in the world who are actually caught in these things. It's for Christians who, despite having experienced God's grace, let their own standards slip—and yet feel free to condemn others. The kindness of God that they have experienced is meant to lead them to repentance, not, as they seem to think, to give them a license to sin with no consequences.

But if we don't point out the sin in the world, doesn't that send a message that what they're doing is OK?

Well, that's not how Jesus worked. We don't see Him pointing out the sin of a tax collector, yet Zaccheus promised to repay everything he'd stolen. A prostitute made an extravagant public display of repentance, and Jesus hadn't even said a word.

God doesn't want us to *judge* people out there for their brokenness. He wants us to show them the way out of it—with kindness. So every single person should know they are welcome in our churches, no matter what kind of darkness they are living with, or in. When they meet people who are experiencing freedom from the power of sin and the fear of death, they're surely going to want to know how they can experience it too!

THE END OF THE STORY

The New Testament writers use many images and metaphors to try to convey the wonder, grandeur and breadth of our identity as the Church. But they save the best one till last.

In Ephesians 5, Paul starts by giving advice to married couples but ends up lost in wonder about Christ and His Bride. He says, "Christ loved the church and gave himself up for her to make her holy, cleansing her by the washing with water through the word, and to present her to himself as a radiant church, without stain or wrinkle or any other blemish, but holy and blameless" (Ephesians 5:25-27).

The marriage relationship, when two people fully and wholeheartedly give themselves in love to one other and become "one flesh," is held up as a picture of the relationship between Jesus and His Church. If you think about it, that's a shocking statement. Outrageous even. If it wasn't the words of Paul the Apostle himself written in Holy Scripture, we might be tempted to write it off as blasphemous. No wonder Paul describes it as a mystery. But it's profound.

Revelation 19 describes the moment in the future when this will be fulfilled: "Then I heard what seemed to be the voice of a great multitude, like the roar of many waters and like the sound of mighty peals of thunder, crying out, 'Hallelujah! For the Lord our God the Almighty reigns. Let us rejoice and exult and give him the glory, for the marriage of the Lamb has come, and his Bride has made herself ready'" (Revelation 19:6-7 ESV).

Our bridegroom has paid the Bride price. Right now, we are betrothed to Him and are waiting for Him to come for us and take us to His Father's house, where there will be a celebration, and the marriage will be consummated.

As *individual* Christians, we stand with our sandals, our ring, and our robe. But *together* as the Bride of Christ, we, the Church, will be unimaginably glorious.

In the meantime, we are to prepare ourselves. We have a mission from Jesus Himself to disciple nations. He's given us everything we need to fulfill it together. As we walk in grace and love each other, we can expect to see His blessing.

"His Bride has made herself ready." God has such confidence that we will respond to His love and walk in our identity together as His Body that He has stated it in the past tense. It is going to happen. We are going to be at that celebration, ready for the Bridegroom, our mission fulfilled!

And standing before the Lamb will be "a great multitude that no one could number, from every nation, from all tribes and peoples and languages" (Revelation 7:9 ESV).

PEACEMAKER?

"Blessed are the peacemakers, for they will be called children of God" (Matthew 5:9).

Are you up for living out of your identity as a child of God and being a peacemaker within the Church? So that the blessing of God is released to those outside as we love one another?

And are you ready to reach out to those who do not yet know Jesus so that together we will disciple the nations?

There is much more I could say but the Apostle Paul says it far better:

> *Make every effort to keep the unity of the Spirit through the bond of peace. There is one body and one Spirit, just as you were called to one hope when*

you were called; one Lord, one faith, one baptism;
one God and Father of all, who is over all and
through all and in all. (Ephesians 4:3-6)

I invite you to pray the following prayer along with me:

Lord Jesus,

We join You in Your prayer to the Father that Your children would be one—because, like You, we want the world to believe that the Father sent You. You have said in Your Word that where there is unity You command a blessing, and we want to see that blessing come in full force. Just as You—the great King of Kings—humbled Yourself by taking the form of a servant, even to the point of choosing to die a humiliating and agonizing death on a Cross, we choose to give up our pretensions of being in any way righteous or right in our own strength and we humble ourselves before You.

It's all about You and Your Kingdom, Lord, and not about us. We choose also to humble ourselves before each other in Christ and to come not just with truth but with grace—just as You come to us. We choose to consider others more important than ourselves and to put their interests above our own. We recognize that without genuine love, anything we do is no more than a noisy gong or clanging cymbal.

Even if our Christian doctrine and tradition are one hundred percent right, without love they are worth nothing.

Lord, we are eager to maintain the unity of the Spirit in the bond of peace. We therefore ask You to fill us afresh with the Holy Spirit and to lead us in love.

We choose to be peacemakers not nitpickers.

We choose relationship above rules.

We choose love above law.

We choose to be real rather than right.

We pray all this in the Name of the humble Jesus, the One who has now been lifted up to the very highest place and who has the Name that is above every other name. Amen.

(Based on Psalm 133, John 1:14–17, John 17:20–23, 1 Corinthians 13, Ephesians 4:1–7, Philippians 2:1–11)

MAKING THE GRACE CONNECTION

In this chapter and the previous two, we've seen how the false motivator of pride prevents us from walking in grace in a variety of different ways.

If we are to be peacemakers, if we are to be effective, fruitful disciples, it's imperative that we lay down pride. You are invited to take some time now to ask the Holy Spirit to show you where there are areas of pride in your life and to turn away from each one.

Start this time by asking the Holy Spirit to speak to you as you read the following verses slowly:

> *Therefore if you have any encouragement from being united with Christ, if any comfort from his love, if any common sharing in the Spirit, if any tenderness and compassion, then make my joy complete by being like-minded, having the same love, being one in spirit and of one mind. Do nothing out of selfish ambition or vain conceit. Rather, in humility value others above yourselves, not looking to your own interests but each of you to the interests of the others.*

*In your relationships with one another, have the
same mindset as Christ Jesus:*

*Who, being in very nature God,
 did not consider equality with God something to be
used to his own advantage;
rather, he made himself nothing
by taking the very nature of a servant,
being made in human likeness.
And being found in appearance as a man,
he humbled himself
by becoming obedient to death—
even death on a cross!*

*Therefore God exalted him to the highest place
and gave him the name that is above every name,
that at the name of Jesus every knee should bow,
in heaven and on earth and under the earth,
and every tongue acknowledge that Jesus Christ is
Lord, to the glory of God the Father.
(Philippians 2:1-11)*

Dear Lord,

I confess that I have believed that my ways and my preferences are better than those of other people. I ask You to reveal to me now the ways in which this sin of pride has been an issue in my life so that I might turn away from it.

In Jesus' name. Amen.

Write down areas of your life where you now realize that you have been proud. Consider, for example, your attitude towards:

- Family members
- Church leaders
- Christians from other parts of the Church
- Work colleagues

Consider too if you have been proud of:

- Your understanding of Christian doctrine
- Your worldly achievements
- The things you have done for God

In what other ways have you been proud?

For each area that the Holy Spirit has brought to mind, pray this prayer:

Lord Jesus,

I confess and renounce that I was proud by/towards_____ _____(say what you did and to whom). I now choose to have the same attitude You had. I humble myself before You and before other people. I declare the truth that I am in no way better than they are and I choose from now on to consider them more significant than myself. Thank You that, because I know I am Your child, I no longer have to lift myself up but can rely on You to lift me up at the right time.

In Your name. Amen.

CHAPTER 9

THE STEPS TO EXPERIENCING GOD'S GRACE

TRUTH, TURNING, AND TRANSFORMATION

In the last chapter, we defined a disciple as, "Someone who is learning to become more and more like Jesus in character; and to do the works that God has prepared for them in the strength that He supplies."

Freedom In Christ is a discipleship ministry and for nearly 40 years, we've been equipping churches to help Christians cultivate a lifestyle of unstoppable spiritual growth.

We've concluded that, for a church to equip its people to walk in freedom and keep growing, it needs three elements in its culture of discipleship: "Truth, Turning and Transformation."

Truth is about getting God's Word from our head to our heart, so that we really know the incredible love of God in our heart; know just who we now are in Christ; understand the nature of the spiritual battle and the resources we have in Christ to stand firm. It's about understanding what's right with us (rather than focusing on what's wrong with us) now that we are in Christ.

We may have come to believe that we are useless or dirty or don't match up to expectations. The truth is that in Christ we are holy. We are loved and accepted by God Himself. And we have a crucial role in His family with specific things God has prepared in advance for us to do.

The preceding chapters are full of the truth from God's Word that we need to know (in our heart, not just our head) in order to cultivate a lifestyle of unstoppable spiritual growth. But just knowing the truth is not enough.

Turning is seeing reality as the Bible tells us it us. It's about understanding the reality of the spiritual world and how to take back any ground we have previously given to the enemy. It's about understanding and practicing repentance, so that we ruthlessly close any doors we've opened to the enemy through past sin and don't open any more.

It's about helping us draw a line and no longer following the ways of the world which views sex as an appetite to be fulfilled, drugs as recreation, gambling as entertainment, or astrology as harmless fun. It's about renouncing other allegiances just as those in Acts burned their astrology scrolls.

The main tool we have to help people to do this is *The Steps To Freedom In Christ*, and I strongly recommend that to you—I go through it myself once a year as a kind of spiritual check-up.

In this chapter, you are invited to go through *The Steps To Experiencing God's Grace*, which is a similar process that specifically focuses on the issues that stop us from making a real heart-connection with God's grace. Setting aside half a day to carefully and prayerfully go through this process is an appropriate response to the preceding chapters. It's where you will be able to deal with the "false motivators" of shame, guilt, fear, anxiety, and pride and other issues such as compulsive sin.

Transformation is about the renewal of the mind. We all have the world's values ingrained in our thinking, and we have to make a conscious effort if we want to replace those old faulty beliefs with what is actually true according to God's Word.

Romans 12:2 tells us clearly that it is only by renewing our minds that we will experience genuine transformation. In the next (and final) chapter, I will introduce you to "stronghold-busting," a highly practical way of replacing faulty beliefs with the truth that many refer to as "life-changing."

I am absolutely passionate about seeing every Christian—no matter what they have experienced in life—living as a genuinely fruitful disciple of Jesus. I am convinced that, if enough Christians are continuing to walk according to these Biblical principles, we will see whole communities transformed and in due course have an impact on nations.

As you come to *The Steps To Experiencing God's Grace*, I'm excited for you! Please take your time and ensure you "do business" with God! I know that He is so eager to help you become an even more fruitful disciple as you take hold of His grace in your heart, not just your head, and ensure that it is love for Him—and only love for Him—that drives you from this point onwards.

INTRODUCTION TO THE STEPS

This kind, gentle process of prayer and repentance is for every Christian who wants to grow in Christ, learn to live the "grace-rest" life, and bear fruit that will last for eternity. God the Father offers you an invitation to come "home," just as the father in the story of the prodigal son did. *The Steps To Experiencing God's Grace* will enable you to affirm your love for God, and allow Him to point out areas in your life that need some attention. If you feel distant from God, if your Christian walk has become a heavy, dull, lifeless burden, or if you are losing hope that you will ever break free from slavery to sin or fear, these Steps will be especially helpful. They will help you take hold of who you are and what you have in Christ to live in God's grace where there is genuine "rest for your soul"—a different way to live!

The "grace-rest life" could look like this:

- You live for God and show love to others because of the love you yourself have received from Him and not for any other reason.

- You experience daily victory over temptation as a consequence of the power of the Holy Spirit within you, rather than any power or effort you have to exert.

- You find yourself becoming abundantly fruitful, bringing God much glory, by staying in a dependent relationship of rest in Him.

When we begin to see our lives from His perspective, it can be painful to realize just how far we may have wandered away from Father God. Remember, as we return to that place of experiencing grace, God does not require us to try harder to please Him. Quite the opposite, for it was this "slaving away" that kept the elder son at a distance from the father.

Returning to our Father begins with having a change of mind (what the Bible calls "repentance"), committing ourselves to confessing and rejecting lies we have believed, and choosing instead to believe what is really true (as revealed in His Word, the Bible) about who He is, who we now are in Christ, and the circumstances of our lives.

We encourage you to allow the Holy Spirit to reveal not only actions, but also attitudes and false beliefs that have kept you from living in the daily reality of God's grace and producing fruit that will last forever. We recommend that you make a note of any false beliefs and lies that you become aware of during the process in the Lies List at the end of this book. We will explain how to replace these with truth using "stronghold-busting" so that you can renew your mind and be transformed (Romans 12:2).

Striving for acceptance from God or others through performing well can look very spiritual on the outside. But it reveals beliefs that misrepresent who God is and who we are. It may not be obvious to others from your actions that there is anything amiss, because your external behavior itself may not look that different from that of those who are living in the experience of grace. But *inside* there is all the difference in the world. Remember, God looks inside at the heart. Thankfully, in Christ we have all been given a brand-new heart!

Throughout this process we will depend completely on the Holy Spirit, whose role is to lead us into all truth, so that we can take hold of the freedom God has given us as His precious children and offer our whole selves back to Him in love and gratitude, knowing that He "is able to do far more abundantly than all that we ask or think, according to the power at work within us" (Ephesians 3:20 ESV).

To begin, take a moment to remind yourself of who God is and what He has done and praise Him.

Then, when you are ready, say the prayer and declaration on the next pages aloud.

OPENING PRAYER

Dear Heavenly Father,

I thank You that You love me and that Your Son died and rose again so that I could have an intimate relationship with You. I want to live my life on the basis of Your acceptance of me and relate to You not only through head knowledge, but also through true heart experience. Your Word says it was "for freedom Christ has set us free" (Galatians 5:1 ESV), and I ask You to help me take hold of that freedom today. There are many ways in which I have not stood firm in Your new covenant of grace, but instead have allowed a yoke of slavery to weigh me down and wear me out. Please help me take hold of my freedom from all slavery to sin, fear, or performance. Please bring to my mind all the attitudes and actions that have kept me from receiving and giving away Your love. Help me to know the truth so that I will be set free to love You and others in the way that You love me. In Jesus' name I pray. Amen.

(Prayer 1.A)

OPENING DECLARATION

In the name and authority of the Lord Jesus Christ, I command Satan and all evil spirits to release me, in order that I can be free to know and choose to do the will of God. As a child of God seated with Christ in the heavenly places, I agree that every enemy of the Lord Jesus Christ be bound to silence. I say to Satan and all your evil workers that you cannot inflict any pain or in any way prevent God's will from being accomplished in my life. I belong to God and the evil one cannot touch me. I refuse all fear, anxiety, doubt, confusion, deception, distraction, and any other interference that comes from the enemies of the Lord Jesus Christ. I choose to take my place in Christ, and I declare that all His enemies have been disarmed, and that Jesus Himself came to destroy the devil's work in my life. I declare that the chains of bondage have already been broken by Christ and that I am in Him. Therefore His victory is my victory.

(Declaration 1.B)

STEP ONE: CHOOSING TO BELIEVE THE TRUTH

In this first Step we will affirm some key truths from the Bible. It is important to reject all the lies you have become aware of during *The Grace Course* and instead choose to declare and believe what is actually true according to God's Word. God may also use the affirmations to reveal more faulty thinking to you.

Start by praying the following prayer aloud:

> Dear Heavenly Father,
>
> Your Word is truth and Jesus Himself is the Truth. The Holy Spirit is the Spirit of truth and it is knowing the truth that will set me free. I want to know the truth, believe the truth, and live in accordance with the truth. Please reveal to my mind all the lies I have believed about You, my Father God, and about myself, Your beloved child. I want to renounce those lies and walk in the truth of Your grace and Your acceptance of me in Christ. In Jesus' name I pray. Amen.
>
> *(Prayer 1.C)*

THE TRUTH ABOUT OUR FATHER GOD

Having a wrong view of God's character and His expectations of us will hinder the development of a close intimate relationship with Him. These declarations about your Father God will give you an opportunity to renounce out loud the lies you have believed about God, and to affirm the truth about His character. We encourage you to do this boldly, especially for those truths that seem hard to receive for you today. Meditating on the truth of who God is can be one of the most important aspects of your freedom and healing in Christ.

Declare out loud all of the statements on the next two pages.

I reject the lie that You, Father God, are distant and uninterested in me.

I choose to believe the truth that You, Father God, are always personally present with me, have plans to give me a hope and a future, and have prepared works in advance specifically for me to do. (PSALM 139:1–18; MATTHEW 28:20; JEREMIAH 29:11; EPHESIANS 2:10)

I reject the lie that You, Father God, are insensitive and don't know me or care for me.

I choose to believe the truth that You, Father God, are kind and compassionate and know every single thing about me. (PSALM 103:8–14; 1 JOHN 3:1–3; HEBREWS 4:12–13)

I reject the lie that You, Father God, are stern and have placed unrealistic expectations on me.

I choose to believe the truth that You, Father God, have accepted me and are joyfully supportive of me. (ROMANS 15:7; ZEPHANIAH 3:17)

I reject the lie that You, Father God, are passive and cold toward me.

I choose to believe the truth that You, Father God, are warm and affectionate toward me. (ISAIAH 40:11; HOSEA 11:3–4)

I choose to believe the truth that You, Father God, are always present and eager to be with me and enable me to be all that You created me to be. (PHILIPPIANS 1:6; HEBREWS 13:5)

I reject the lie that You, Father God, are absent or too busy for me.

I reject the lie that You, Father God, are impatient or angry with me, or have rejected me.

I choose to believe the truth that You, Father God, are patient and slow to anger, and that when You discipline me, it is a proof of Your love, and not rejection. (EXODUS 34:6; ROMANS 2:4; HEBREWS 12:5–11)

I reject the lie that You, Father God, have been mean, cruel, or abusive to me.

I choose to believe the truth that Satan is mean, cruel, and abusive, but You, Father God, are loving, gentle, and protective. (PSALM 18:2; MATTHEW 11:28–30; EPHESIANS 6:10–18)

I reject the lie that You, Father God, are denying me the pleasures of life.

I choose to believe the truth that You, Father God, are the author of life and will lead me into love, joy, and peace when I choose to be filled with Your Spirit. (LAMENTATIONS 3:22–23; GALATIANS 5:22–24)

I reject the lie that You, Father God, are trying to control and manipulate me.

I choose to believe the truth that You, Father God, have set me free, and give me the freedom to make choices and grow in Your grace. (GALATIANS 5:1; HEBREWS 4:15–16)

I reject the lie that You, Father God, have condemned me, and no longer forgive me.

I choose to believe the truth that You, Father God, have forgiven all my sins and will never use them against me in the future. (JEREMIAH 31:31–34; ROMANS 8:1)

I reject the lie that You, Father God, reject me when I fail to live a perfect or sinless life.

I choose to believe the truth that You, Father God, are patient toward me and cleanse me when I fail. (PROVERBS 24:16; 1 JOHN 1:7–2:2)

I AM THE APPLE OF YOUR EYE!

(DEUTERONOMY 32:9–10)

(Declaration 1.D)

Now look back over the list and mark any truths that you find difficult to believe. You can use the "Stronghold-Busting" process outlined at the end of *The Steps* to ensure that you replace lies with truth. But for now, use the following prayer to affirm those truths about your Father God that you have marked.

> Dear Heavenly Father,
>
> I thank You for Your grace and forgiveness. I choose to believe the truth(s) that You are _____ _____ (list the truths). Please change the way I worship, pray, live, and serve in the light of those truths and fill me with your Holy Spirit. In Jesus' name. Amen.
>
> *(Prayer 1.E)*

THE TRUTH ABOUT WHO WE ARE IN CHRIST

The term the Bible most often uses for those who are now in Christ is "holy ones." But we often have the impression that God sees us as "sinners," which is the term most often used in the Bible for those who do not yet know Jesus as their Savior. Because we behave according to how we see ourselves, it is of crucial importance that we understand who God says we are. Remember, we have not earned any of this—our new identity is a pure grace gift from Him. But it is nevertheless true!

Declare out loud the statements below.

I joyfully announce the truth that I am safe and secure in Christ:

I am loved by God as much as He loves Jesus (JOHN 17:23)

I have been purchased by the blood of His Son
(1 CORINTHIANS 6:20)

I am connected to Jesus like a branch to the vine (JOHN 15:5)

I am protected and held in Jesus' and the Father's hands
(JOHN 10:27-30)

I am the righteousness of God in Christ, therefore in Him I
do measure up! (2 CORINTHIANS 5:21)

I died with Christ to the rule of sin and have been raised
up to live a new life (ROMANS 6:3-4)

I died to the law through the body of Christ (ROMANS 7:4)

I will never be deserted or abandoned by Christ
(HEBREWS 13:5)

I am my Father's workmanship, His "poem" (EPHESIANS 2:10)

**I joyfully announce the truth that the Holy Spirit lives in me and
He is my strength:**

I am the Temple of the Holy Spirit, who was given to me
by my Father (1 CORINTHIANS 6:19)

I am sealed by the Spirit, who was given to me as a pledge
of my full inheritance in Christ (EPHESIANS 1:13)

I am led by the Spirit of adoption and am no longer a slave
to fear; He enables me to cry out "Abba! Father!"
(ROMANS 8:14-15)

I have been baptized by the Holy Spirit and placed into the
body of Christ as a full member (1 CORINTHIANS 12:13)

I have been given spiritual gifts by the Holy Spirit (1
CORINTHIANS 12:7, 11)

I can walk by the Holy Spirit instead of giving in to the
lusts of my flesh (GALATIANS 5:16-18, 25)

I am the apple of His eye! (DEUTERONOMY 32:9-10)

(Declaration 1.F)

Now look back over the list and mark any truths that you find difficult to believe. You can use the "Stronghold-Busting" process outlined at the end of *The Steps* to ensure that you replace lies with truth. But for now, use the following prayer to affirm those truths about yourself that you have marked.

> Dear Heavenly Father,
>
> I thank You for Your grace and forgiveness. I choose to believe the truth(s) that I am _____ _____ (list the truths). Please change the way I worship, pray, live, and serve in the light of those truths and fill me with your Holy Spirit. In Jesus' name. Amen.
>
> *(Prayer 1.G)*

RECEIVING YOUR NEW NAME

In Chapter 1 (and in Session 2 of *The Grace Course*) we saw that God has cleansed us from shame, and that He has given us a new name. In fact, there are many names God gives us in the Bible. Here are some of them:

- Beloved (Colossians 3:12)
- Chosen (Ephesians 1:4)
- Precious (Isaiah 43:4)
- Loved (1 John 4:10)
- Clean (John 15:3)
- Presentable (Luke 17:14)
- Protected (Psalm 91:14; John 17:15)
- Welcomed (Ephesians 3:12)
- Heir (Romans 8:17; Galatians 3:29)
- Complete (Colossians 2:10)
- Holy (Hebrews 10:10; Ephesians 1:4)
- Forgiven (Psalm 103:3; Colossians 2:13)
- Adopted (Ephesians 1:5)
- Delight (Psalm 147:11)
- Unashamed (Romans 10:11)
- Known (Psalm 139:1)
- Planned (Ephesians 1:11–12)
- Gifted (2 Timothy 1:6; 1 Corinthians 12:11)
- Enriched (2 Corinthians 8:9)
- Provided For (1 Timothy 6:17)
- Treasured (Deuteronomy 7:6)
- Pure (1 Corinthians 6:11)
- Established (Romans 16:25)
- God's Work of Art (Ephesians 2:10)
- Helped (Hebrews 13:5)
- Free from Condemnation (Romans 8:1)
- God's Child (Romans 8:15)
- Christ's Friend (John 15:15)
- Christ's Precious Bride (Isaiah 54:5; Song of Songs 7:10)

Pray the following prayer:

Dear Heavenly Father,

Thank You that You have given me a new name! Please show me which of these names you particularly want me to take hold of now. In Jesus' name. Amen.

(Prayer 1.H)

For each new name that God is impressing upon you say:

Thank You, Father God, that my new name is

_____.

(Prayer 1.I)

We strongly encourage you to continue declaring your new name(s) every morning for at least the next 40 days and at other times throughout the day whenever you feel attacked in your mind by the lies of the enemy.

STEP TWO: WALKING BY THE SPIRIT RATHER THAN THE FLESH

Even though we are now new creations in Christ at the deepest level of our beings, we still have a tendency toward sin that the Bible calls "the flesh." Every day we can choose either to walk by the Spirit or by the flesh. In this Step we will invite our Father to show us where we have believed the lies that the flesh feeds us and allowed ourselves to return to slavery to sin.

To begin this Step, say this prayer aloud:

Dear Heavenly Father,

You have told me in Your Word to "put on the Lord Jesus Christ, and make no provision for the flesh in regard to its lusts" (Romans 13:14 NASB). Thank You that Jesus has not only forgiven my sins but given me the power to overcome sin in my life. I acknowledge, however, that by giving in to temptation, I have given sin the opportunity to reign in my body (Romans 6:12). Please reveal to my mind all the sins of the flesh I have committed so that I may now take hold of my freedom from sin. In Jesus' name. Amen.

(Prayer 2.A)

The following list of sins of the flesh is based on Galatians 5:19–21. Mark any that you need to confess:

- ☐ Sexual sins

- ☐ Drunkenness

- ☐ Other forms of impurity

- ☐ Worship of something other than God

- ☐ Engaging in occult activities

- ☐ Hatred

- ☐ Anger

- ☐ Divisiveness

- ☐ Envy and jealousy

- ☐ Selfish ambition

- ☐ Other sins of the flesh: _____

Dear Heavenly Father,

I confess that I have given in to the flesh and sinned against You in the following ways: _____
_____.

Thank You for Your forgiveness and for Your complete cleansing of me through the blood of Jesus. Thank You that You have made me pure and holy.

I choose no longer to present the parts of my body to sin but instead to present them to You to be used for righteousness.

Thank You that, because I have died with Christ, I have been set free from sin and that, because I have risen with Him, I need never return to being a slave to sin. I declare that I am dead to sin and alive to God in Christ Jesus.

Thank You that You have promised always to provide a way out of temptation—please help me to recognize it and take it. (See 1 Corinthians 10:13.)

I ask You to fill me afresh with Your Holy Spirit and I choose to allow You to develop the fruit of the Spirit in my life, which is "love, joy, peace, patience, kindness, goodness, gentleness, faithfulness and self-control."

In Jesus' name I pray. Amen.
(See Galatians 5:22–23.)

(Prayer 2.B)

STEP THREE: PRIDE, PERFORMANCE, AND PERFECTIONISM

The elder brother mistakenly believed that he had to earn anything that would come from his father, but the truth was that he could have been enjoying everything the father had all along. We're going to begin this Step by asking God to reveal to us the expectations, standards, and demands of others that we have felt we need to live up to in order to feel good about ourselves, to measure up, or to be acceptable. Pray the following prayer:

Loving Father,

I thank You that in Christ all of Your expectations of me have been fully met (Romans 8:4), and that You have forgiven me all my sins and canceled out my certificate of debt by nailing it to the cross (Colossians 2:13–14). I confess that I have believed the lie that I have needed something more than Christ in order to gain or maintain acceptance from You and others.

Please would You reveal to me now all the expectations, standards, and demands that I have been living under, by which I have sought to become more acceptable and feel less guilty, so that I can return in simple faith and rely only on what Jesus has done on my behalf. I ask this in the name of Jesus Christ, who died for me. Amen.

(Prayer 3.A)

Now spend time evaluating where you have lived under false expectations and write the false expectations, standards, and demands you have lived under on a separate sheet of paper:

- Expectations you wrongly believed were from God
- Expectations from parents and family
- Expectations from teachers
- Expectations from churches and church leaders
- Expectations from employers
- Other expectations, standards, and demands:
  _____

Then use the following prayer to reject every false expectation:

> I reject the lie that I have to live up to the expectations, standards, and demands of others in order to feel good enough, valued, or accepted. I specifically reject these false expectations: _____.
>
> Thank You, Lord Jesus, that in You I meet all of God's expectations and that nothing I could do could make You love me more or love me less. Amen.
>
> *(Prayer 3.B)*

You may like to rip up your piece of paper in order to symbolize that you choose from now on to trust in Jesus alone to make you right with God. Then move on in freedom and confidence! Before you do so, make a note of any persistent lies you have believed so that you can address them later with a stronghold-buster.

We will now consider other areas where we have lived our lives in our own strength instead of from a place of rest in what God has done. Say the following prayer aloud:

Dear Lord,

I ask You to reveal to me now the ways in which the sins of performance, perfectionism, pride, power, and pleasureless living have been issues in my life so that I can turn away from them. I want to confess those times that I have lived my life in my own strength rather than resting in You, when I have believed that my ways are better than Your ways or that my preferences are better than those of other people. In Jesus' name. Amen.

(Prayer 3.C)

Consider these potential areas of weakness and mark any actions and attitudes that the Holy Spirit shows you:

Performance

- ☐ Centering my life around keeping laws and rules rather than knowing God

- ☐ Trying to keep God's commands in order to gain His acceptance or favor

- ☐ Trying to keep God's commands in my own strength

- ☐ Being driven to work harder and harder in order to achieve

- ☐ Believing achievement is the means of gaining personal happiness and a sense of worth

Perfectionism

- ☐ Living in the fear of failure

- ☐ Being afraid of going to hell because I have not kept God's laws perfectly

- ☐ Being unable to accept God's grace because I think I need to be "punished" even though Jesus paid for all my sins in full on the cross

- ☐ Being obsessed with keeping things in exact order, and being unable to experience joy and satisfaction when life is not perfect

- ☐ Being overly concerned or punishing others with minor flaws and/or having unreasonable expectations of perfection

- ☐ Being angry at others when they disrupt my neatly controlled world and/or resisting new ideas

Pride and Judgmentalism

- ☐ Thinking I am more spiritual, devoted, humble, or devout than others

- ☐ Thinking that my church, denomination, or group is better than others

- ☐ Not being willing to associate with others who are different (having an independent spirit)

- ☐ Not being willing to tolerate different religious opinions on nonessentials (e.g., baptism, communion, end times theology, etc.) in order to promote love, peace, and unity among true brothers and sisters in Christ

- ☐ Finding it hard to admit that I am wrong, or wanting to prove that I am right

☐ Criticizing Christian ministers and leaders

☐ Judging others' motives and character
or labeling others

Power and Control

☐ Experiencing anxiety when I am not able to
be in control

☐ Finding security in rules, regulations, and standards
rather than in the Lord

☐ Being more concerned about controlling others
(by means of strong personality, overbearing
persuasion, fear, or intimidation) than developing
self-control

☐ Being driven to attain positions of power or
accomplish my own agenda

☐ Feeling unhealthy responsibility for the lives
and well-being of others

☐ Using guilt and shame tactics to get others to do
what I want or think is best

Pleasureless Living

☐ Living a joyless life of duty and obligation

☐ Feeling guilty for experiencing pleasure or being
secretive in pursuing it

☐ Being unable to relax and rest

☐ Being strongly attracted to (or giving in to) illegal
substances, illicit sex, pornography, etc., in order to
escape or to find some gratification

Use the prayer below to confess and renounce aloud those things the Holy Spirit has revealed to you:

Dear Heavenly Father,

I confess that I have _____
(name the items you marked).

I agree that these attitudes and actions do not reflect who I truly am in Christ and I renounce them all. I turn away from living in my own strength according to my own ideas and choose now to adopt the same attitude You had and humble myself before You and before other people. I declare the truth that Your ways are higher than my ways. I declare that I am in no way better than other people, and I choose to consider others as more significant than myself.

Thank You for Your forgiveness. Thank You that, because I know I am Your child, I no longer have to lift myself up but can rely on You to lift me up in due course. In Jesus' holy name I pray. Amen.

(Prayer 3.D)

In order to make a permanent change to your thinking, you will need to renew your mind. You will find stronghold-busting helpful for this.

STEP FOUR: FORGIVING OTHERS

Experiencing God's forgiveness in your own life frees you to forgive others.

The pain we feel in our lives because of the physical, verbal, emotional, sexual, or spiritual abuse we have suffered can be devastating. It is a very human thing to experience anger toward those who have hurt or offended us; Jesus Christ can enter into those wounded places and begin to heal the damage done to our souls and free us from the hold they have over us. The healing begins when we make a choice to forgive from our hearts.

We may also need to forgive ourselves for wrong choices we have made, as well as surrender our false beliefs about God's character.

To forgive means:

- Choosing not to hold someone's sin against them anymore.

- Canceling their debt and letting them off our hook, knowing that they are not off God's hook and that He will make everything right in the end.

- Releasing the person and what they did into God's hands and resolving not to bring the offense up in conversation anymore.

- Trusting Him to deal with that person justly—something we are not able to do.

- Letting go of the right to seek revenge.

Holding on to your anger hurts you more than it hurts them. If you want to be free, you need to forgive them from your heart. Forgiving someone from the heart simply means being honest both with God and yourself about how what was done to you made you feel. Allow Jesus to bring to the surface the feelings that you have held inside for so long, so that He can begin to heal those emotional hurts and pain.

Begin by saying the following prayer aloud:

Dear Heavenly Father,

Thank You for the riches of Your grace, kindness, and patience toward me, knowing that Your kindness has led me to repentance. Please show me all the people I need to forgive, including myself. Show me too where in my suffering I have believed lies about You. In Jesus' name I pray. Amen. (See Romans 2:4.)

(Prayer 4.A)

Make a list (by name if possible) of all those the Holy Spirit brings to your mind, which could include

- *Anyone* who was used by the enemy to rob me of freedom and joy, including any perpetrators of abuse or neglect, or who caused me to believe I was worthless, unlovable, or valuable only when I "performed well."

- *Anyone* who stifled the free expression of grace or spiritual liberty in my life and who forced me to conform to unattainable standards.

- *Parents, church leaders, school teachers, or officials* who were harsh, critical, or judgmental and who fostered a performance-based rather than a grace-based environment.

- *Myself* for imposing on myself heavy burdens and thus robbing myself of freedom and joy.

- *God Himself*—It is vital for our freedom that we acknowledge and turn away from any false beliefs we have developed about God's character because of what He has allowed in our lives, even though we may not understand why He allowed it. The truth is He has done no wrong, and has never left us or abandoned us. He promises to work all things together for our good (Hebrews 13:5; Romans 8:28). We can receive His grace afresh and put our trust in Him again.

When you are ready, start wherever you want on your list, and begin to forgive from your heart those people who have hurt you, whether they did it deliberately or not. Take your time and be sure to be honest with God by telling Him every painful memory and how they made you feel.

Dear Heavenly Father,

I choose to forgive _____
(the name of the person or group) for _____
_____ (be specific in what they did or
failed to do), which made me feel _____
(be honest in expressing how you felt or still feel.)

(Prayer 4.B)

Once you have forgiven all those on your list, pray a blessing on each of them (including yourself):

Dear Heavenly Father,

I choose no longer to seek revenge or to hold on to my bitterness toward _____ (name). Thank You for setting me free from the bondage of my bitterness. I now ask You to bless _____ _____ (name). In Jesus' name. Amen.

(Prayer 4.C)

A PRAYER TO RELEASE GOD FROM UNFULFILLED EXPECTATIONS

If you realize that you have had angry thoughts toward God, say this prayer aloud:

> Dear Heavenly Father, I release You from my unfulfilled expectations and the secret anger and bitterness I have held against You. I reject the lie that You are like those who have failed me, and I declare the truth that You love me with an everlasting love. I now bless You. Amen.
>
> *(Prayer 4.D)*

We recommend that you consider taking another look at what you said after "which made me feel" in Prayer 4.B above. If you find the same word or expression repeated two or three times, it may indicate a false belief that you hold that you can deal with using the "stronghold-busting" process.

STEP FIVE: FREEDOM FROM FEAR

In this Step we will be asking God to reveal any unhealthy fears. An unhealthy fear is something that we wrongly believe is both present and powerful.

Begin by saying the following prayer out loud:

Dear Heavenly Father,

I come to You as Your child and acknowledge that You are the only legitimate fear object in my life. I confess that I have been fearful and anxious because of my lack of trust and unbelief in Your protective care. I have not always lived by faith in You and too often I have relied on my own strength and resources. I thank You that I am forgiven in Christ. I choose to believe the truth that You have not given me a spirit of fear, but of power, love, and a sound mind (2 Timothy 1:7). Therefore, I reject any spirit of fear. I ask You to reveal to my mind all the unhealthy fears that have been controlling me. Show me how I have become fearful and the lies I have believed. Open the eyes of my heart to Your wonderful truths. I desire to live a responsible life in the power of Your Holy Spirit. Show me how these fears have kept me from doing that. I ask this so that I can confess, reject, and overcome every fear by faith in You. In Jesus' name. Amen.

(Prayer 5.A)

The following list may help you recognize some of the unhealthy fears that have been hindering your walk of faith. Mark the ones that apply to you, as well as any others not on the list that the Spirit of God has revealed to you.

- ☐ Fear of Satan
- ☐ Fear of death or the death of a loved one
- ☐ Fear of not being loved by God
- ☐ Fear of the future
- ☐ Fear of financial problems
- ☐ Fear of losing my mind or of being a hopeless case
- ☐ Fear of never getting married
- ☐ Fear of never having children
- ☐ Fear of not being able to love others
- ☐ Fear of rejection/disapproval/embarrassment
- ☐ Fear of marriage or divorce
- ☐ Fear of failure
- ☐ Fear of confrontation
- ☐ Fear of being a victim of crime
- ☐ Fear of having committed the unpardonable sin
- ☐ Fear of specific animals or objects
- ☐ Other unhealthy fears _____

Remember, behind every unhealthy fear is a lie. It will help you hugely if you are able to identify these lies, because renouncing them and choosing the truth is a critical step toward gaining and maintaining your freedom in Christ. You have to **know** and choose to **believe** the truth in order for it to set you free.

When you are ready, use the following table (or a separate piece of paper) to write down the unhealthy fear. Then work out the lie behind the fear and the corresponding truths from the Word of God. This is not easy because the lies seem true and have probably been with you a long time. If you can, get some help from a mature Christian friend.

Fear	Lie	Truth
Example: Failure	If I fail it will make me worthless	"I am precious in His sight and He loves me" (see Isaiah 43:4).

Express the following prayer for each of the controlling fears that you have identified:

Dear Father,

I confess and repent of the fear of _____.
I have believed _____ (state the lie). I
reject that lie and I choose to believe the truth
_____ (state the truth). I also confess
any and all ways this fear has resulted in living
irresponsibly, or compromising my witness for
Christ. I now choose to believe Your promise that
You will protect me and meet all my needs as I
live by faith in You (Psalm 23:1; 27:1; Matthew
6:33–34). In Jesus' trustworthy name. Amen.

(Prayer 5.B)

FEAR OF PEOPLE

Proverbs 29:25 says, "Fear of man will prove to be a snare, but whoever trusts in the Lord is kept safe". Fearing people ultimately leads to pleasing people—and that indeed is bondage. People-pleasers find themselves more and more concerned about what others around them think, because they wrongly believe that their personal worth and happiness are dependent upon the acceptance or approval of others.

When we make it our goal to keep people happy, we end up becoming enslaved to them and we remove ourselves from the safety and security of serving Christ alone (Galatians 1:10). To allow the Holy Spirit to examine your heart in this area, begin by praying:

Dear Heavenly Father,

I know that I have not always walked by faith but have allowed the fear of people to control me. I have been too concerned about gaining approval from others, and I have been led astray from a simple, pure devotion to Christ. I want to walk in a healthy fear and awe of You and not of people. Thank You for Your forgiveness. I now ask You to bring to my mind the specific ways that I have allowed the fear of other people to control me. In Jesus' name I pray. Amen.

(Prayer 5.C)

Now mark on the following list areas that the Holy Spirit is revealing to you:

- ☐ I constantly need the affirmation of other people in order to feel happy, significant, or worthwhile and can easily become depressed and discouraged and give up.

- ☐ I have been afraid to say what I really think or feel for fear of being reprimanded, ridiculed, or rejected.

- ☐ I am afraid to say no when asked to do something for fear of experiencing disapproval or anger, and I am often tired, on the verge of burn-out, or feeling used.

- ☐ I can't seem to bring myself to set healthy boundaries in my life.

- ☐ I find myself easily intimidated by strong personalities.

- ☐ I don't handle criticism well; it is painful because it makes me feel like a failure.

☐ I make sure that others know about the "good" things I have done.

☐ I have found myself lying in order to cover things up in my life that might result in disapproval from others.

☐ I have been more concerned with following human traditions in our church than with obeying God's Word.

☐ Other ways I have allowed the fear of others to control me _____.

Now use this prayer to confess your fear of people:

Dear Heavenly Father,

Thank You for showing me how my life has been influenced by the fear of people, and how I have tried to please them rather than You. I specifically confess _____ (list the areas that the Holy Spirit revealed to you).

Thank You for Your gracious forgiveness and that You already love, accept, and approve of me, so I don't have to go looking for those things in other people. You are indeed trustworthy, so I choose to believe You, even when my feelings and circumstances tell me to fear. You are always with me and You will strengthen me, help me, and uphold me with Your righteous right hand.

Teach me what pleases You, regardless of others' opinions. I trust in Your power within me to walk in awe of You alone. In Jesus' mighty name. Amen. (See Isaiah 41:10.)

(Prayer 5.C)

STEP SIX: EXCHANGING ANXIETY FOR GOD'S PEACE

Paul said, "Do not be anxious about anything, but in everything by prayer and supplication with thanksgiving let your requests be made known to God" (Philippians 4:6 ESV). He also told us to cast our anxiety onto Christ, who cares for us (1 Peter 5:7). In this Step we will put into practice the principles we learned about casting our anxiety onto Christ in Chapter 6.

Prayer is the first step in casting all your anxiety on Christ. Ask God to guide you by saying the following prayer aloud:

> Dear Heavenly Father,
>
> As Your child I declare my dependence upon You, and I acknowledge my need for You. I know that apart from Christ I can do nothing.
>
> You know the thoughts and intentions of my heart, and You know the situation I am in from the beginning to the end. I do not want to be double-minded and need Your peace to guard my heart and my mind.
>
> I place my trust in You to supply all my needs according to Your riches in glory and to guide me into all truth. I ask for Your guidance so that I may fulfill my calling to live a responsible life by faith in the power of Your Holy Spirit.
>
> Search me, O God, and know my heart. Test me and know my anxious thoughts. Point out anything in me that offends You, and lead me along the path of everlasting life. In Jesus' precious name. Amen. (See Psalm 139:23–24.)
>
> *(Prayer 6.A)*

You are responsible only for that which you have the right and ability to control. You are not responsible for that which you don't. Your sense of worth should be tied only to that for which you are responsible.

If you aren't living a responsible life, you should feel anxious! Don't try to cast your responsibility onto Christ—He will throw it back to you. But do cast your anxiety onto Him because His integrity is at stake in meeting your needs if you are living a responsible and righteous life. State the problem—what is making you anxious?

Use this table prayerfully to examine what you are anxious about:

State the Problem	What are the facts of the situation?	What assumptions am I making?	What can I control and what is my responsibility?
Example: I've discovered a growth on my arm.	The growth is getting larger.	It's going to be cancerous and my arm will be amputated.	To take my thoughts captive. To pray and seek wise medical help.

The rest is God's responsibility. Your only remaining responsibility is to continue to pray and focus on the truth according to Philippians 4:6–8. Any residual anxiety is due to your assuming responsibilities that God never intended you to have.

Assume responsibility for what is yours to do by praying the following:

> Dear Heavenly Father,
>
> Thank You for helping me bring the situations that make me anxious into the light. I turn away from making assumptions and from now on choose to fix my mind on what I know to be the facts of the situation. I turn away from trying to deal with things that are not my responsibility but commit myself to doing the things that are my responsibility. On that basis I cast my anxiety onto You, confident that You will deal with these situations in Your infinite love and wisdom. I leave them with You. In Jesus' mighty name. Amen.
>
> *(Prayer 6.B)*

A FIVE-DAY WORKOUT TO COMBAT ANXIETY

You may find this exercise helpful in the following days.

DAY 1
Practice appreciation for what God has done for you, His child. Look up and read the Bible verses for some of the statements of *The Truth About Who We Are In Christ* in Step One above. Take one and spend time thanking Him for what it means to you.

DAY 2

Practice appreciation for who God is using *The Truth About Our Father God* list in Step One. Pick one truth and ask God to remind you of how He has shown Himself to be true to this character quality. Write a prayer to thank Him. Share it with someone else.

DAY 3

Think back through each season of your life. Thank God for His grace gifts. Thank Him too for an unanswered prayer—can you now see how He has used it for good? Share one grace gift and a thanksgiving for an unanswered prayer with someone else.

DAY 4

Dwell in stories of people in the Bible who overcame fear and anxiety. Read one of the stories below. Where do you see similarities to your story? How did God come through? What characteristics of your Heavenly Father do you see in the outcome?

- Moses (Exodus 3:1–9)
- Elijah—when the evil Jezebel desired to pursue and kill him (1 Kings 19)
- Joseph—His brothers plotted to kill him but instead sold him into slavery. Isn't this the enemy's plan for all of us? Read the outcome in Genesis 39:2–4, 21–23, and 50:19–21.
- Paul (2 Corinthians 4:7–11)

DAY 5

Read the Bible verse(s) for some of the new names that you have because of being "in Christ," from Session 2 of *The Grace Course*. How is God working out one today in your life? What would life look like if you really took hold of your new name? Thank God that He has given you a future and a hope. Journal and share with another.

STEP SEVEN: SURRENDERING AS A LIVING SACRIFICE

Are you now ready to make a commitment to God to love Him with an undivided heart, not because you are in any way compelled to, but simply out of love? It is a scary thing to think about surrendering ourselves as a living sacrifice and putting ourselves unreservedly into the hands of another—even if it is God. But remember that He has already shown the depth of His commitment to us by dying for us. In fact, when we surrender ourselves fully into the hands of our loving Father, we are putting ourselves in the only place where we are completely secure.

As children of God, we have the promises that "To all who did receive him, who believed in his name, he gave the right to become children of God" (John 1:12 ESV) and "All things belong to you, and you belong to Christ, and Christ belongs to God" (1 Corinthians 3:22–23 NASB). When we lose (surrender) who we are naturally, we discover who we really are in Christ.

To begin this Step, say the following prayer:

> Dear Heavenly Father,
>
> I acknowledge that You are the God who is love and that You have always been faithful to me and will continue to be true to who You are, regardless of my circumstances or how I feel (Lamentations 3:22–23).
>
> I confess that I have not always trusted that You have my best interests at heart, or that You can be relied upon to come through on Your promises. I repent of any doubts I may have had concerning Your character and all the ways I have tried to take my life into my own hands.

Please show me all the areas where I have held my life back from You. I now ask You to help me take a step of greater trust and dependence on You by surrendering all I am and all I have to You. In Jesus' name. Amen.

(Prayer 7.A)

What do you specifically need to surrender to God now?

- [ ] Living my life in my own strength and resources
- [ ] Saying what I want to say when I want to say it
- [ ] Going where I want to go whenever I please
- [ ] Living wherever I want to live
- [ ] Having the kind of job or house I want
- [ ] Having the kind of financial security I desire
- [ ] Being single or married
- [ ] Having the number (and gender) of children I want to have
- [ ] Having all of my children grow up to love and walk with the Lord
- [ ] Being in control or right all the time
- [ ] Always being loved, accepted, and understood and having a good reputation
- [ ] Having the friends I want
- [ ] Being used by God in specific ways

- ☐ Knowing the will of God all the time
- ☐ Being able to "fix" people or circumstances around me
- ☐ Having good health and being free from pain or suffering
- ☐ Having a specific idea of what a "successful" Christian ministry looks like
- ☐ Receiving forgiveness from those that I have hurt
- ☐ Being spared heartache, crisis, and tragedy
- ☐ Acting in anger toward, or in rebellion against, those who have hurt me
- ☐ Other things the Holy Spirit is laying on my heart:
  _____

Now pray the following prayer of surrender:

Dear Heavenly Father,

I choose to surrender myself unreservedly to You just as Jesus surrendered Himself for me. I specifically surrender the things you have shown me: _____. I take my hands off them.

I give You permission to do in me and through me whatever You desire, and whatever will glorify You. Place me wherever You want to place me. Use me however You choose to use me. May Your will be done in me.

I joyfully accept my responsibility to follow Your good, pleasing, and perfect will for me by the power of the Holy Spirit. In Jesus' name I pray. Amen.

(Prayer 7.B)

CONCLUDING PRAYER

In this final prayer of surrender, we invite you to offer yourself to God as a living and holy sacrifice. You will also complete the process of submitting to God and resisting the devil by commanding every enemy to leave your presence.

> Dear Heavenly Father,
>
> As Your redeemed child, I have been bought out of slavery to sin, guilt, shame, and obeying rules. Thank You that because of Christ, the law of God has been written on my heart and mind. I now submit myself to You as an instrument of righteousness, a living and holy sacrifice who will glorify You.
>
> Having submitted to You, I resist the devil, and I command every spiritual enemy of the Lord Jesus Christ to leave my presence.
>
> Father, please fill me with Your Holy Spirit. I commit myself daily to taking every thought captive and renewing my mind. I choose to be motivated by love and nothing else. Thank You that I now live in the grace, forgiveness, acceptance, peace, and rest that are mine in the Lord Jesus Christ. Amen.
>
> *(Prayer 7.C)*

FINAL AFFIRMATIONS

As a final act of faith, make these declarations out loud to affirm some astonishing biblical truths concerning God's truly amazing grace:

I affirm that God's Word to me is, "Grace to you and peace from God our Father and the Lord Jesus Christ." (GALATIANS 1:3)

I affirm that it was for freedom that Christ has set me free. I therefore choose to keep standing firm and no longer be subject to the yoke of slavery. (GALATIANS 5:1)

I affirm that the purpose of the Law was to show me my need for Christ, but now that faith has come I am no longer under the Law. (GALATIANS 3:24-25)

I affirm that I am now an unconditionally loved, accepted, and secure child of God in Christ. (GALATIANS 3:26; EPHESIANS 1:5-6)

I affirm that I am now dead to the Law through the body of Christ and that I have been joined to the risen Christ in order to bear much fruit for God. (ROMANS 7:4)

I affirm that I am a living sacrifice through Jesus Christ and that my life's purpose is to please Him, not others. (GALATIANS 1:10)

I affirm that God's strength is now made perfect in my weakness and that His grace is sufficient for me. (2 CORINTHIANS 12:9)

I affirm that, having begun by the Spirit, I am not going to finish through the flesh, but through the transforming power of the Spirit of freedom. (GALATIANS 3:3; 2 CORINTHIANS 3:17-18)

Therefore I affirm that by the grace of God I am what I am and that by His grace I stand. (1 CORINTHIANS 15:10; ROMANS 5:2)

All to the praise of His glorious grace, which He freely bestowed on me in Christ. (EPHESIANS 1:6)

(Final Affirmations 7.D)

CHAPTER 10

TRANSFORMED!

RESPONDING TO GOD'S GRACE

You've invested quite a lot of time reading this book. I trust that the God of all grace has spoken to you through it. But how much lasting difference do you think it will make in your life?

> *Do not merely listen to the word and so deceive yourselves. Do what it says. Anyone who listens to the word but does not do what it says is like someone who looks at his face in a mirror and, after looking at himself, goes away and immediately forgets what he looks like. But whoever looks intently into the perfect law that gives freedom, and continues in it— not forgetting what they have heard, but doing it— they will be blessed in what they do. (James 1:22-25)*

James says it would be ridiculous for someone to look intently at themselves in a mirror and then go away and forget what they look like.

But it is all too easy to look at God's Word, agree with it mentally, but then carry on our lives without it having any real effect on us. How many Christian books have you read or conferences attended where you've thought, "That's fantastic. It will revolutionize me," but the effect has lasted just a couple of days or weeks?

This final chapter is all about our response to God's grace. It's about making sure that whatever God has said to you as you have been reading this book works its way into your life for the long term.

The prize is that living out of God's grace becomes a way of life. You are no longer driven by guilt or shame or fear or anxiety or pride; instead, you work for Him because you want to, not because you feel you have to, and you do it from a position of genuine internal rest.

Romans 12 starts like this: "I urge you, brothers and sisters, in view of God's mercy...." Paul then gives us two specific ways to respond to God's mercy.

The first is "to offer our bodies as a living sacrifice, holy and pleasing to God." We will conclude this chapter and indeed the whole *Grace Connection* book with an invitation to do just that.

The other response Paul invites us to make is this:

> Do not conform to the pattern of this world, but be transformed by the renewing of your mind. Then you will be able to test and approve what God's will is— his good, pleasing and perfect will. (Romans 12:2)

This is the only place in the New Testament that tells us explicitly how we can be transformed. It is by the renewing of our mind.

WHAT ARE STRONGHOLDS?

Why do our minds need to be renewed? Ephesians 2:1-3 says we all used to follow the "ways of this world and the ruler of the kingdom of the air, the spirit who is now at work in those who are disobedient...All of us lived among them...following its...

thoughts." Colossians 2:8 adds, "See to it that no one takes you captive through hollow and deceptive philosophy, which depends on human tradition and the elemental spiritual forces of this world rather than on Christ."

Since our earliest years, the world and the devil have teamed up to confuse our thinking and make us believe things that are not true. There is a battle going on for our minds. A battle between the Spirit of Truth and the Father of Lies.

We all have a different family background, different past experiences, and differing worldviews. We have all unconsciously developed a set of beliefs and ways of thinking and reacting to life's circumstances. These are our "default" beliefs, if you like, and they work out into "default" behavior.

We may not be fully aware of them, but trust me, they are there. Many of the beliefs we've developed are not based on what God says in His Word. In fact most are contrary to His Word. I have come to realize that, for me, the ongoing process of maturing as a Christian is all about uncovering my faulty beliefs and replacing them with what is really true so that I can go on to make good choices based on a solid foundation.

Perhaps it started out back in childhood when a little thought was planted in your mind by something that happened to you—maybe you were bullied, or someone said something negative about you: "You're useless", "You're a failure", "You're ugly", or "It's all your fault."

Later on, the enemy lined up someone else who said or did the same thing. Since he knows your particular vulnerabilities, he ruthlessly exploits them by lining up people or circumstances one after the other to give you the same wrong message.

The world then adds insult to injury with its constant bombardment of lies about what it means to be successful or happy or loved.

As it gets stronger and stronger, it becomes part of our default thinking and works itself into our behavior. Then, whenever someone suggests we could go for a particular job or lead a small group at church, a voice plays in our mind, "I couldn't do that. I'm useless at that." We've believed it for so long that it has become part of our lives, and we can't imagine it being any different.

The Bible calls these ingrained beliefs "strongholds." The literal meaning of the word is a fortress, a strong defensive building. Paul says:

> For though we live in the world we do not wage war as the world does. The weapons we fight with are not the weapons of the world. On the contrary, they have divine power to demolish strongholds. We demolish arguments and every pretension that sets itself up against the knowledge of God, and we take every thought captive to make it obedient to Christ. (2 Corinthians 10:3-5)

Paul mentions *arguments* and *pretensions* that set themselves up against the true *knowledge* of God. He talks about taking every *thought* captive to make it obedient to Christ. The context is clearly our mind, our thinking. And the word "stronghold" refers to a faulty belief that is deeply ingrained. It's been reinforced many times throughout your life, and it's sitting there in your mind strong and impenetrable—like a thick castle wall.

A good definition of a stronghold is, "a belief or habitual pattern of thinking that is not consistent with what God tells us is true."

Feelings of inferiority, insecurity and inadequacy are all strongholds. Because no child of God is inferior, insecure or inadequate.

Strongholds can show up in things we know we should do but don't seem able to. And also when know we should not do something but don't seem able to stop.

A stronghold is a lie that's been reinforced so many times, that it gets a strong hold on you and causes you to think and act in ways that contradict God's Word.

It's like a truck that drives through a muddy road the same way every day. It makes deep ruts that are then baked in the sun.

Eventually you could take your hands off the steering wheel, and the truck would follow the ruts.

Ingrained habitual ways of thinking—strongholds—are like deep ruts in our minds.

During *The Steps To Experiencing God's Grace*, you resolved the spiritual issues that the Holy Spirit revealed to you. You removed those invisible dogs hanging off you and closed the door to other dogs by submitting to God through confession and repentance and resisting the enemy so that he has had to flee from you (James 4:7). Once you have dealt with any footholds of the enemy, a mental stronghold is simply a habitual way of thinking. Can you break a habit? Of course—but it takes some effort over a period of time.

Steering out of these ruts is possible, but it requires intentional effort. I want to introduce you to "stronghold-busting," a very practical way to renew your mind that will help you experience the life transformation that God wants for you and make living out of God's grace a way of life.

DEMOLISHING STRONGHOLDS

They may have a strong hold on us but God's clear promise is that we can demolish strongholds. Not just cope with them, work around them, or do them a bit of damage. Demolish them!

Before we look at stronghold-busting itself, I'd like to share a story with you from someone who was surprised at her own power to demolish a deeply ingrained stronghold and see her life totally transformed:

> I was brought up in a Christian home. I became a Christian at the age of seven, and went to church every Sunday, but behind the scenes I was being sexually abused by an extended family member. So from an early age, I learned to do the talk, the walk, the look, the kind of "fit in Christian thing."

But inside I was screaming at God saying, "Where are You? Why didn't You protect me?"

And all that turmoil led to me having an eating disorder for over 15 years. It was my escape. If I had emotions coming up that I couldn't deal with and I didn't know what to do with them, then I would just binge and I would eat, and stuff them all down. I call it "the dark thinking." It would just come over me.

I began to realize that I had to do something. I'd been to counselors—Christian counselors, non-Christian counselors—but I didn't get to the root of it. Nothing changed. My addiction was still there.

I was trying, and trying, and trying, and then giving up. And then trying, and trying, and giving up. And it's exhausting to try and do it in your own strength.

I recognized that I had an issue with eating, but I didn't associate it with a "stronghold." I went through *The Steps To Freedom In Christ* but I honestly didn't think that anything could really get rid of it. I thought it's a habit now. It's so ingrained in me. I'm always going to have an issue with it. It's never really going to go away. I just have to handle it the best I can.

A couple of months later she was at the point of desperation, and she went back to her notes from the *Freedom In Christ Course* and created a "stronghold-buster."

I was like, I cannot live the rest of my life like this. I am going to speak aloud and declare these over my life as long as it takes until something happens, because something has got to happen. So every morning and every night, I would read it out over my life.

About six weeks later I remember waking up one day and the "dark thinking" had gone. I thought, "OK, maybe I'm just having a really good mood day." But inside I knew something had changed. And then when I went through an emotional time, I didn't go to food, and I was like, oh my goodness, it's gone! It's broken!

I didn't expect it to happen. I thought I would always have an issue with eating. Always. I never believed it would be completely gone, broken just like that.

That was about two years ago. If I'd known, I'd have done it earlier!

STRONGHOLD-BUSTING

As we look at "stronghold-busting," let me give you a health warning.

We see tremendous change in people's lives as they respond to God through our teaching. And it's amazing! But we also see people who seem to enjoy our courses for eight or ten weeks and learn some great stuff, but the impact gradually fades away because they don't make the effort required to change their thinking longer-term.

There are three factors to take into account:

First, this is your responsibility. Nobody else can renew your mind for you. And God won't do it either—in His wisdom and grace, it's something that He gives you the responsibility *and* ability to do. So, if you don't do it, it's not going to get done. And there'll be no lasting transformation.

Second, removing the footholds of the enemy that we've given him through sin can be done in a day by going through *The Steps To Freedom In Christ* or *The Steps To Experiencing God's Grace*. But busting a stronghold takes time, several weeks in fact. You will need to persevere—but it will be more than worth it.

Thirdly, by definition, the lies you believe *feel* absolutely true to you. They're not easy to recognize. It requires humility and intentionality to really bring your thoughts into the light of God's truth.

Because they have been part of our thinking for such a long time, we think deep down that they can never be changed. And if you recognize that way of thinking in yourself, congratulations, you've just identified a stronghold that can be torn down!

So, how do you create and use a stronghold-buster?

1. Identify The Faulty Belief You Want to Change

First, identify the faulty belief you want to change, the lie that you now realize is contrary to God's Word. This is what it means to "take captive every thought to make it obedient to Christ" (2 Corinthians 10:5). It means noticing what we are thinking, and evaluating whether or not it is in line with what God tells us is true in the Bible.

2. Consider What Effect Believing That Lie Is Having in Your Life

Next, think about what effect believing that lie is having in your life. Realizing the negative effects will spur us on to tear the stronghold down. Think about how different your life would be if you were not held back by that false belief.

Your past experiences may, for example, have left you with a sense that you are helpless and that it would be hopeless to try to change. This has become a belief in your heart. If someone tries to tell you it's a lie, you respond by thinking, "No, it's true." Imagine if, deep down inside, you knew that you were not helpless, that you could change. What opportunities would open up for you?

3. Make A List of Key Bible Verses That Counteract The Lie

Third, find the truth from God's Word that counteracts the lie. You can use a concordance, a Bible app, or a wise friend to help you find verses that speak truth to oppose the lie you believe. Some people are tempted to find many verses. But often it's more effective to keep it simple and focus on just a couple of verses that plainly put forward God's truth.

If you identify with that sense that you are helpless and that it would be hopeless to try to change, for example, turn to your Bible. What does it say?

Hebrews 13:5 says God will never leave you or forsake you. Philippians 4:13 tells you that you can do all things through Him who gives you strength. Romans 8:37 assures you that you are more than victorious through Jesus who loves you. Or take 2 Peter 1:3, which makes the astonishing statement that God's divine power has already given you everything you need for life and godliness. It may feel true to you but it is not in line with the Bible.

4. Write A Declaration Based on The Verses

Use the following pattern:

> **I refuse to believe the lie that...**
> [e.g., I am hopeless and will never change.]
>
> **Believing this lie has...**
> [e.g., caused me to feel defeated and stopped me from overcoming sin in my life.]
>
> **I embrace the truth that...**
> [e.g., God's divine power has given me everything I need to live a godly life (2 Peter 1:3); that I can do all things through Him who gives me strength (Philippians 4:13); and that in Christ who loves me, I am more than victorious (Romans 8:37).]

There are three sample stronghold-busters at the end of this chapter. Do not be tempted to use one of them "as is" even if you have the same issue but write your own. There's something about going through the process of creating a stronghold-buster for yourself that is powerful.

5. Read The Declaration Out Loud Every Day For 40 Days

Then read the declaration out loud every day for 40 days, all the time reminding yourself that, if God has said it, it really is true. The more you do it, the better. You could do it both morning and evening and also "in the moment"—when you realize you're thinking or acting on that lie.

The Bible says that, "The tongue has the power of life and death" (Proverbs 18:21) and speaking out loud seems to help our minds take hold of the truth more effectively than simply reading silently.

This is not as easy as it may sound because the lie behind the stronghold *feels* true to you and making your declaration day after day will soon *feel* like a complete waste of time. Many give up, and that's a tragedy.

This analogy may help. Imagine a demolition ball swinging against a strong concrete wall. It withstands 10, 20, or 30 blows with no visible sign that anything is happening at all. That's exactly how it can feel as you work through a stronghold-buster day after day. In reality, tiny cracks are forming which are weakening the wall.

After 37 swings there are still no signs of damage to the wall.

On the 38th swing—sooner or later—cracks become visible.

On the 39th swing, the cracks get bigger until finally the wall completely collapses. Your stronghold is broken down. Your mind—in that particular area—has been renewed.

Even though only the final three swings appear to have had an effect, without the previous 37, the wall would not have fallen.

I encourage you to persevere until you have completed at least 40 days (or maybe even more) even though throughout most of that time it will feel like a complete waste of time. I promise you that if you persevere you will tear the stronghold down. And you will be transformed.

Don't do more than one stronghold-buster at a time. The process of renewing your mind is a long-distance race not a sprint. What is the most significant lie that you have become aware of during the course? Start with that one. When you have seen that torn down, do another one. And so on.

People who really get hold of this can do six, seven, or eight stronghold-busters a year, each of which can make a huge difference. They transform before your eyes as they take hold of the truth of God's Word in their hearts not just their heads.

Although I have emphasized the need for perseverance and made clear that nobody can renew your mind for you, please don't think that it is by your own efforts that you will be transformed and grow to serve God more faithfully.

1 Peter 1:13 (NASB) says, "Prepare your minds for action." By renewing your mind, bringing it into alignment with God's truth—what He says about Himself and what He says about you—you will be much better equipped to serve God in this world, and bear abundant fruit for His kingdom.

But the verse continues, "...set your hope fully on the grace to be given you when Jesus Christ is revealed." The grace God showed us when Jesus went to the cross and the grace He will show us when Jesus returns is the same grace He shows us day by day to help us renew our minds and walk with Him.

This is all about resting in His grace and taking God at His word. Don't lapse into legalism—if you miss a day or two, God is not upset with you! Just pick up where you left off and keep going.

I was amused by what Josh Shaarda, one of the presenters on *The Grace Course*, shared:

> For my first eight years of involvement with Freedom in Christ teaching, I failed to do even a single stronghold-buster. I didn't think I believed

any lies! But three years ago, I made my first stronghold-buster. Do you want to hear it?

"I reject the lie that I do not believe any lies. This lie stops me from growing closer to God. I accept the truth that my love for temporary worldly things shows that I do not yet love my Heavenly Father as I should. I invite the Spirit of Truth to guide me into all truth and show me the lies I believe."

As I declared that daily for 40 days, the Holy Spirit gently revealed to me no fewer than seven lies that I believed. And that was just the beginning! Yes, it was humbling. He showed me these lies in three ways.

One was as I argued against God's truth. As we were reading the new names in Christ, I got to the statement that said "my new name is pure" and I thought very sincerely "I want to be pure someday"—as if me being pure TODAY depended on my actions, not on what Christ had done for me... stronghold!

Reading through lists like "Who I am in Christ"— when you want to argue against one of them, thinking that it may be true of others but not of you; or even, you hope that can be true of you someday, but it's not today—this reveals a stronghold in your thinking.

Emotionally overreacting to simple situations also revealed to me that I had lies I believed about myself. Something that started as a small, insignificant issue brought out intense emotion and defensiveness on my part. Later I thought, "Why did I get so upset?" I realized I had a stronghold in there somewhere.

The third way God spoke into my life was through mature, grace-filled Christian friends. Friends pointed out strongholds to me. When they heard a lie revealed in my speech, they brought it to my attention. It's often easier to see the lie in someone else than to see it in yourself. After all, the lie you believe feels true to you.

BECOME A LIVING SACRIFICE

As we approach the end of *The Grace Connection*, let's come back to the first thing Paul invites us to do as a response to God's grace:

> *I urge you, brothers and sisters, in view of God's mercy, to offer your bodies as a living sacrifice, holy and pleasing to God (Romans 12:1).*

Earlier this year, I had the privilege of attending church in a thatched building with walls of mud in rural Uganda. It was a wonderful experience.

Just after the offering had been taken, I was surprised to see a chicken wandering around the church. It seemed to be having difficulty walking, and I noticed that there was some string around one of its legs that was restricting its movement. A woman reached down and picked the chicken up, and I assumed she was going to remove the string so that the chicken could walk freely. Instead, she tied the string around the other leg too and made it tighter so that the chicken couldn't walk at all. Then she laid the chicken next to the offering bowl at the front of the church. The chicken was someone's offering but had been attempting to make its escape!

The idea of a live animal being placed on an altar as a *living* sacrifice is amusing—because it can jump up and run away!

But in urging you to become a living sacrifice, God does not tie your legs up or in any way force you to live for Him. You are totally free. The idea here is that when you know Him and His grace, you will freely make a choice to place yourself on the altar day-by-day as a living sacrifice. And you will choose of your own free will to remain there.

Think about the hours that Jesus hung on the cross in incredible agony, every breath a massive, painful effort, until His heart burst from the strain. He was a literal living sacrifice. He could have left at any moment—He was God after all. But He chose not to. And I am eternally thankful He made that choice.

Why on earth would we choose to become a living sacrifice? "In view of God's great mercy." Because of His grace.

Let's remind ourselves of some of the things we now know about God's grace in all its wonder:

Jesus became a sacrifice for you, paying an unimaginable price so that you are now declared completely innocent.

Jesus *became* sin on your behalf, and you *became* the righteousness of God, a holy one.

You are genuinely free. Free from the power of sin, the power of Satan and the power of death. Free to make good choices.

You are now safe and secure. No one can take you out of His hands. And His love can drive out every unhealthy fear.

You can cast *all* your anxiety on Him and walk in peace because He cares for you.

You need only to focus on remaining in Him in order to bear lots of fruit. And He will use every breaking experience in your life to make you even more fruitful.

You are now secure enough in who you are in Christ to humble yourself before God and before others—with no need to try to control events or people.

You know that you can do absolutely nothing in your own strength but that He can do absolutely anything through you.

You are part of the Body of Christ, the most dynamic organization that has ever existed, and part of the Bride of Christ, who is making herself ready for Jesus to return.

So here you are, a son or daughter of the King of Kings, dressed in your rich robe, your ring of authority and your sandals.

And God Himself is looking at you with eyes of pure love and delight.

You might say, "God, thank You so much. I really do want to be even more fruitful. What do you want me to do for you?" I suspect His response might be, "There are things for you to do. But what I really want is you. All of you."

Can I join Paul and urge you to climb onto that altar as a living sacrifice? To lay down everything at His feet? To make Jesus your King—and your very Life?

It's OK to come like the younger son, in complete weakness and brokenness. God will run to you and embrace you. He'll never abandon you. He'll never take you beyond what you can bear as He gives you strength.

I invite you right now to make a radical commitment to God. To lay down absolutely everything at His feet—your health, your future, your money and property, your family, your ministry. To reaffirm that you are His bondslave. I invite you to make Jesus your Lord (boss of your life) and recognize that, in fact, He is your very life.

Not because in any way you feel you *have* to. But because you *want* to.

Thankfully you don't have to do this in your own strength but can come to Him and collapse into His arms. This is the place you were always meant to be. He'll always be there. He'll never leave you. He'll never take you beyond what you can bear in Him. If you let

Him, He will fill your life with wonderful exploits and fruit that will last for eternity. Whatever time you have left in this life, you can use it to make a real difference.

He is the God of all grace. And He extends all of that grace to you. All of the time. What a great God!

Loving Father God,

Thank You for sending Jesus, Who, being in very nature God, did not consider equality with God something to be used to His own advantage but made Himself nothing and humbled Himself by becoming obedient to death—even death on a cross.

I choose right now to trust in You with all my heart. I deliberately turn away from relying on my own understanding. I submit to You in all my ways, in every part of my life. Thank You that You will make my paths straight.

Thank You for the Bible, Your clear Word to us. I pray that You will help me understand it in all of its wonderful fullness as I come with an open heart ready to hear Your instructions, encouragement and correction. I refuse to water Your Word down, gloss over it, or try to make it say what I think it should say. Thank You that your Holy Spirit will lead me into all truth.

Please help me root out the deeply ingrained lies I have believed and replace them with truth so that I may truly be transformed by the renewing of my mind.

As a response to Your grace, I choose here and now to offer You my body and all that I am as a living sacrifice, holy and pleasing to You. This is my true and proper worship.

And I worship You now.

Amen.

MAKING THE GRACE CONNECTION

As you think back through the book you have just finished, what is the most significant faulty belief that God has highlighted to you?

If you're not sure, pause to ask Him.

Seize the moment and write a stronghold-buster to help you replace that lie with truth and so be transformed.

1. **Identify The Faulty Belief You Want To Change**

2. **Consider What Effect Believing That Lie Is Having In Your Life**

3. **Make A List Of Key Bible Verses That Counteract The Lie**

4. **Write A Declaration Based On The Verses**

   Use the following pattern:

   I refuse to believe the lie that...
   [e.g., I am hopeless and will never change.]

   Believing this lie has...
   [e.g., caused me to feel defeated and stopped me from overcoming sin in my life.]

   I embrace the truth that...
   [e.g., God's divine power has given me everything I need to live a godly life (2 Peter 1:3); that I can do all things through Him who gives me strength (Philippians 4:13); and that in Christ who loves me, I am more than victorious (Romans 8:37).]

5. **Read The Declaration Out Loud Every Day For 40 Days**

   Write the numbers 1 through to 40 and check a number off every day.

There are three sample stronghold-busters below to give you the idea.

Remember: it will feel like a complete waste of time because the lie is so deeply entrenched. But if you persevere, the stronghold will collapse and you will be transformed.

I'm rooting for you!

STRONGHOLD-BUSTER EXAMPLE 1

Fear Of Disapproval

THE LIE: that I am unacceptable or just not good enough.

EFFECTS IN MY LIFE: feeling intimidated; fearing people; compromising my convictions; changing my appearance; anxious about saying and doing the "right thing."

THE TRUTH:

- You did not choose me, but I chose you...
  (John 15:16)
- [He] has put his seal on us and given us his Spirit in our hearts as a guarantee. (2 Corinthians 1:22 ESV)
- He will rejoice over you with gladness; he will quiet you by his love; he will exult over you with loud singing. (Zephaniah 3:17 ESV)
- Man looks on the outward appearance, but the Lord looks on the heart. (1 Samuel 16:7 ESV)
- The Lord is on my side; I will not fear. What can man do to me? (Psalm 118:6 ESV)
- We have been approved by God to be entrusted with the gospel, so we speak, not to please man, but to please God who tests our hearts. (1 Thessalonians 2:4 ESV)

Dear Father God,

I refuse to believe the lie that I am not good enough or unacceptable.

Believing this lie has caused me to feel intimidated, to fear people, to compromise my convictions, to change my appearance, and to be over-anxious about saying and doing the "right thing."

I embrace the truth that You chose me and that I have received a new heart and therefore I have Your seal of approval. Even when others are not pleased with me, You take great delight in me and Your opinion matters much more.

I now choose to please You rather than other people, and rely on Your promise to be with me wherever I go as I share the good news with others.

Amen.

1	2	3	4	5	6	7	8	9	10
11	12	13	14	15	16	17	18	19	20
21	22	23	24	25	26	27	28	29	30
31	32	33	34	35	36	37	38	39	40

STRONGHOLD-BUSTER EXAMPLE 2

Fear Of Failure

THE LIE: when I fail I am worthless (or worth less than I was before).

EFFECTS IN MY LIFE: unwilling to attempt new challenges that are outside my comfort zone; being task-focused rather than people-focused; anger; competitiveness; striving for perfection

THE TRUTH:

- You are precious in my eyes and I love you. (Isaiah 43:4 ESV)
- In [Christ] you have been made complete. (Colossians 2:10 NASB)
- We are his workmanship, created in Christ Jesus for good works, which God prepared beforehand. (Ephesians 2:10 ESV)
- [God] is able to do far more abundantly than all that we ask or think, according to the power at work within us. (Ephesians 3:20 ESV)
- It is God who works in you, both to will and to work for his good pleasure. (Philippians 2:13 ESV)

Dear Heavenly Father,

I refuse to believe the lie that when I fail I am worth less than before.

Believing this lie has caused me not to attempt new things, to focus on tasks rather than people, to strive for perfection, and to feel angry and competitive.

I embrace the truth that I have been handcrafted by You and am precious, honored and loved by You regardless of the success or failure of what I do. I declare that I am already fully complete in Christ and that You are working in me for Your good pleasure and to do far more abundantly than all I could ask or think.

In Jesus' name. Amen.

1	2	3	4	5	6	7	8	9	10
11	12	13	14	15	16	17	18	19	20
21	22	23	24	25	26	27	28	29	30
31	32	33	34	35	36	37	38	39	40

STRONGHOLD-BUSTER EXAMPLE 3

Feeling Irresistibly Drawn To Porn

THE LIE: that I cannot resist the temptation to look at porn.

EFFECTS IN MY LIFE: deep sense of shame; warped sexual feelings; unable to relate to other people as God intended; harmful to my marriage.

THE TRUTH:

- In the same way, count yourselves dead to sin but alive to God in Christ Jesus. Therefore do not let sin reign in your mortal body so that you obey its evil desires. Do not offer any part of yourself to sin as an instrument of wickedness, but rather offer yourselves to God as those who have been brought from death to life; and offer every part of yourself to him as an instrument of righteousness. For sin shall no longer be your master, because you are not under the law, but under grace. (Romans 6:11–14)

- Do you not know that your body is a temple of the Holy Spirit? (1 Corinthians 6:19)

- No temptation has overtaken you except what is common to mankind. And God is faithful; he will not let you be tempted beyond what you can bear. But when you are tempted, he will also provide a way out so that you can endure it. (1 Corinthians 10:13)

- So I say, live by the Spirit, and you will not gratify the desires of the flesh. (Galatians 5:16)

- But the fruit of the Spirit is love, joy, peace, patience, kindness, goodness, faithfulness, gentleness, and self-control. (Galatians 5:22–23)

I refuse to believe the lie that I cannot resist the temptation to look at porn.

Believing this lie has given me a deep sense of shame, warped my sexual desires, prevented me from relating to other people as God intended, and harmed my relationship with my spouse.

I embrace the truth that God will always provide a way out when I am tempted and I will choose to take it. I announce the truth that if I live by the Spirit—and I choose to do that— I will not gratify the desires of the flesh and the fruit of the Spirit, including self-control, will grow in me. I count myself dead to sin and refuse to let sin reign in my body or be my master. Today and every day I give my body to God as a temple of the Holy Spirit to be used only for what honors Him.

I declare that the power of sin is broken in me. I choose to submit completely to God and resist the devil who must flee from me now.

1	2	3	4	5	6	7	8	9	10
11	12	13	14	15	16	17	18	19	20
21	22	23	24	25	26	27	28	29	30
31	32	33	34	35	36	37	38	39	40

WHAT NEXT?

A 40-DAY ADVENTURE INTO GOD'S GRACE

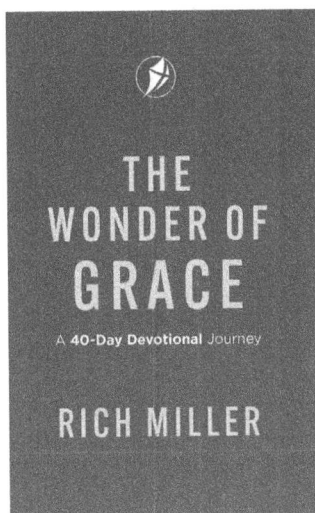

This book has been written specifically for people who have just completed *The Grace Course* or read *The Grace Connection*.

Rich Miller invites you to engage afresh with the Father who loves people, runs to meet a wayward son, and throws an excellent party. Here are 40 days of easy-to-read, entertaining reflections that are full of wisdom and will help you explore more searchingly than a course can offer just what it means to enter into the "grace-rest life". Each reflection is followed by helpful prompts and a prayer so that you can apply the truth in your own life.

As you wrap your *heart* around God's grace, you will be forever changed.

OTHER BOOKS BY STEVE GOSS

Free To Be Yourself
Enjoy Your True Nature In Christ

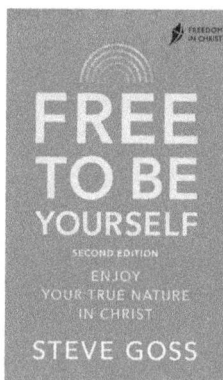

Many Christians end up acting as they think a Christian should act and finding that they simply can't keep it up. They either drop out or burn out.

True fruitfulness comes from realizing that we became someone completely new the moment we became Christians.

Living out the truth of who we now are makes all the difference.

Win The Daily Battle
Resist And Stand Firm In God's Strength

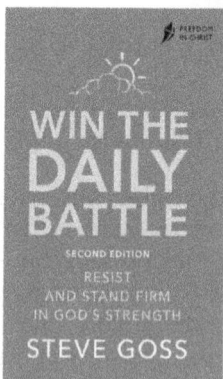

Christians are in a raging battle, whether we like it or not. Our only choice is to stand and fight or to become a casualty.

Arrayed against us are the world, the devil, and the flesh. They seem formidable. However, once you understand just who you are in Christ and how your enemies work, you can expect to emerge victorious from every skirmish with them.

This practical and straightforward book demystifies the spiritual battle so that you can live as the conqueror you now are in Christ.

Break Free, Stay Free
Don't Let The Past Hold You Back

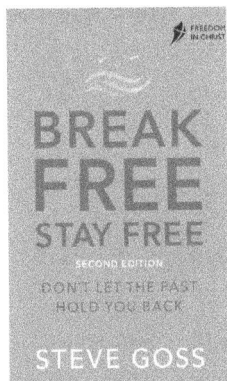

Every Christian has a past. It can hold us back big-time. Those of us carrying a lot of "stuff" know that only too well. But even those who have had a relatively trouble-free existence thus far will benefit from understanding how to identify and resolve past sin and negative influences that stop us moving on.

The great news is that Jesus came specifically to resolve past issues. He does not offer to change our past but He does allow us to walk completely free of it, no matter what it is, as we play our part.

The You God Planned
Don't Let Anything Or Anyone Hold You Back

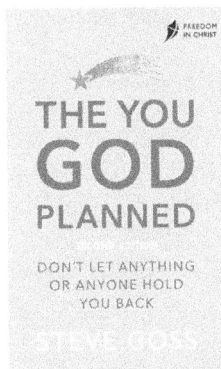

Once we have claimed our freedom in Christ,how do we remain in it to ensure that we become the people God is calling us to be?

How do we know what God is calling us to be anyway? Are the goals we have for our lives in line with His goals? How on earth do we stop other people getting in the way of our growth to fruitfulness? And how do we avoid getting in their way?

The You God Planned answers these questions and shows how we can play our part in the Church, the Bride of Christ, as she prepares herself for His return.

FREEDOM IN CHRIST IN YOUR CHURCH

Freedom In Christ's discipleship resources give church leaders and their churches a proven road map to spiritual maturity that makes discipleship a joy, not a burden, and empowers people to disciple others.

As a result, leaders gain renewed energy in their calling as they grow flourishing communities of lifelong disciples, fulfill God's purposes, and make a difference in the world.

"Men, women, and middle and high school students have been radically transformed."
Bob Huisman, Pastor, Immanuel Christian Reformed Church, Hudsonville, MI, USA

"I recommend it highly to anyone serious about discipleship."
Chuah Seong Peng, Senior Pastor, Holy Light Presbyterian Church, Johor Baru, Malaysia

"The Freedom In Christ Course changed me and put me in a position to minister to people in a much more effective way."
Frikkie Elstadt, Every Nation Patria, Mossel Bay, South Africa

"Our church has changed as a result of this course. Those who come to Christ and who do the course end up with a rock-solid start to their faith."
Pastor Sam Scott, Eltham Baptist Church, Australia

We eschew "try harder" or "behave better" messages and replace them with simple, powerful, biblical principles for life that anyone, anywhere, anytime can use and pass on to others.

To find out more, please contact your national office. Details at:

FreedomInChrist.org/Leaders

BECOME A FRIEND OF FREEDOM IN CHRIST

Freedom In Christ Ministries was founded over 30 years ago by Dr. Neil T. Anderson. We offer a unique approach to discipleship based on our three core principles of Truth, Turning, and Transformation.

Now based in 40 countries with translations in over 40 languages, Freedom In Christ has equipped millions of Christians worldwide to cultivate a lifestyle of unstoppable spiritual growth.

Will You Stand With Us?

Have you seen people's lives transformed through FIC? Would you like to be involved in making the impact even greater? If you are excited about the effect this teaching can have on individuals, churches, and communities, we'd love to have you on the team!

Join Our Team Of International Supporters

Freedom In Christ exists to equip the Church worldwide to make fruitful disciples. We rely heavily for financial support on people who have understood how important it is to give leaders the tools that will enable them to help people become fruitful disciples, not just converts, especially when we are opening up an office in a new country.

Typically your support will be used to:

- help us equip church leaders around the world
- open Freedom In Christ offices in new countries
- translate our discipleship resources into other languages
- develop new discipleship resources

To find out more about partnering with us please go to:

FreedomInChrist.org/Friends

ABOUT THE AUTHOR

Steve Goss has been married to Zoë for 40 years and they live in Berkshire in the South of England. They have two grown-up daughters, three granddaughters, and one pug (also female).

Having embarked upon a career in marketing and eventually starting his own mail order business, Steve has no idea how he ended up working full-time for Freedom In Christ Ministries, writing books, presenting video courses, and speaking at conferences around the world.

He started Freedom In Christ's UK office in 1999 thinking he would "give it Friday afternoons" and it all went from there.

His passions are discipleship and unity. He wrote (with Dr. Neil T. Anderson) *The Freedom In Christ Course* which quickly became a best-seller. It has now been used by millions of people and has been translated into around 40 languages.

He became Freedom In Christ's International President in 2012 and now spearheads its work around the world (it operates in around 40 countries). Weirdly, he maintains a list of the countries he has visited as part of his role:

Albania	India	Portugal
Australia	Ireland	Romania
Brazil	Italy	Singapore
Canada	Jamaica	South Africa
Curaçao	Kenya	Spain
Czech Republic	Korea	Sri Lanka
Ecuador	Latvia	Switzerland
France	Malaysia	Trinidad & Tobago
Germany	Netherlands	Uganda
Great Britain	New Zealand	UK
Hungary	Norway	USA

www.ingramcontent.com/pod-product-compliance
Lightning Source LLC
Chambersburg PA
CBHW060003100426
42740CB00010B/1382